INDIANA CARS

A History of the Automobile in Indiana

By Dennis E. Horvath
and Terri Horvath

First Edition
Published by Hoosier Auto Show & Swap Meet, Inc.

Printed by Jackson Press
Indianapolis, Indiana

Edited by Kendra Eldridge and Mary Beatley
Cover jacket design by John Glowacki

© Copyright 2002
ISBN: 0-9644364-5-0

Dedication

The authors would like to dedicate this book
to our parents, Val and Marjorie Horvath
and Norman and Lorraine Vernon.

Table of Contents

Author's Acknowledgements

We wish to thank the directors of the Hoosier Auto Show & Swap Meet, Inc., for their support in our desire to share Indiana's automotive heritage with future generations. Their vision and assistance enabled us to fulfill a dream we've had for several years.

Thanks also to the research libraries at the Auburn Cord Duesenberg Museum, the Henry Ford Museum, and the National Automotive History Collection at the Detroit Public Library. The research staff at these institutions provided us with valuable assistance in our research for this book.

Our thanks to a group of individuals and members of Indiana marque-specific car clubs who supplied resource material and photographs not available elsewhere: Leroy D. Cole of the Cole Motor Car Club of America; William J. Greer of The Stutz Club; George and Stacey Hanley, authors of *The Marmon Heritage;* William S. Locke, author of *Elcar and Pratt Automobiles;* Henry Blommel, automotive historian from Connersville; Jay D. Wolf of the Elgin Motorcar Owners Registry; and Lisa Bayne with the Eli Lilly and Company archives department.

Thanks to another group of individuals who encouraged our efforts of spreading the word about Indiana's automotive history: Bob Barnard, past president of the Hoosier Heritage Chapter of the Society of Automotive Historians, and Gregg Buttermore, publicist, and Jon M. Bill, archivist, at the Auburn Cord Duesenberg Museum.

From the Hoosier Auto Show & Swap Meet

The Hoosier Auto Show & Swap Meet was incorporated in January 1968, under the laws of the State of Indiana, as a not-for-profit entity. The organization is dedicated to the preservation, restoration and public display of historic motor vehicles, particularly those manufactured in Indiana. Another purpose of the corporation is to educate the public on the historical significance of the role that Indiana has played in the automobile industry.

The start of the Hoosier Auto Show & Swap Meet can be credited to several people with an interest in the "old-cars" hobby. They include Paul Griner, Frank Litherland, James Silvey, Anthony L. (Tony) Miles, C. McCord Purdy, Jerry W. Jones, William O. Burns, and William A. Dyer, Jr. Two of the founders continued through the years on the board: Miles now is executive director and treasurer, and Jones serves as legal counsel. Other current board members are Charles Crafton, president; James Hoggatt, secretary; and Walter Reynolds.

Prior to 1967, many of the founding members had been active in promoting small, local antique car shows and swap meets. The founders decided to approach Indianapolis Motor Speedway owner, Anton (Tony) Hulman, for his permission to use the facility for an annual car show and swap meet. He and the track superintendent, Clarence Cagle, approved.

Four local auto clubs gave $100 each in support: the Indianapolis Model A Ford Club; Classic Car Club of America, Indiana Region; the Hoosier Model T Club; and the Hudson-Essex-Terraplane Club. The groups were repaid after the initial meet.

The first event in September 1967 was small in participation. The annual show and swap meet however, has grown each year to become one of the premier events of its kind in the country. Currently the event is held at the Marion County Fairgrounds in Indianapolis to accommodate the growth.

Another event sponsored by the group is the indoor automotive literature and small collectibles show held every January to continue public interest in the hobby during the winter. This event has been ongoing since January 1968. Plus, the board sponsors a swap meet every May at the fairgrounds.

The board members want to thank all the volunteers and the hobbyists who participated in the events. Their support and participation have caused the events to flourish and provide the board the means to publish this book, which has been a long-time goal.

The board members hope that this book will further educate the populace, especially the youth, regarding Indiana's major contribution to a national industry that has greatly affected the people of the United States and the world.

Photo Credits

ACDM	Auburn Cord Duesenberg Museum
AMG	Photo courtesy of AM General Corporation
DCHC	DaimlerChrysler Historical Collection
DOCC	Photo courtesy of *The Diesel Odyssey of Clessie Cummins,* Carnot Press, 1998
EHM	Photo courtesy of Elwood Haynes Museum
ELCA	Photo courtesy of Eli Lilly and Company Archives
FMCA	Photo courtesy of Ford Motor Company Archives
GMTG	Photo courtesy of GM Truck Group
HAS&SM	Photo courtesy of Hoosier Auto Show & Swap Meet
IMAI	Photo courtesy of Isuzu Motors America, Inc.
IMS	Photo courtesy of Indianapolis Motor Speedway
LDC	Photo courtesy of Leroy D. Cole
MEK	Michael E. Keller
NAHC	National Automotive History Collection, Detroit Public Library
OMV	Photo courtesy of Marjorie Teetor Meyer, author of *One Man's Vision: The Life of Automotive Pioneer Ralph R. Teetor*
SNM	Studebaker National Museum
SOAI	Photo courtesy of Subaru of America, Inc.
TAC	The Author's Collection
TMH	Photo courtesy of George & Stacey Hanley, authors of *The Marmon Heritage*
TMMI	Photo courtesy of Toyota Motor Manufacturing, Indiana
TSC	Photo courtesy of The Stutz Club
UCBC	Photo courtesy of Union City Body Company
WSL	Photo courtesy of William S. Locke

Introduction
Indiana Cars: A History of the Automobile in Indiana

Indiana once vied for Michigan's title as the automotive titan of the United States. It was a time when the names of automobiles like Haynes, Auburn, Studebaker, Duesenberg, Stutz, and Cord brought worldwide acclaim to the Hoosier state. Innovation and activity were particularly rich in Indiana during the early 1900s, and the state's contributions to automotive history throughout the decades have been numerous. Tilt steering, cruise control, and hydraulic brakes are just three examples of the innovations introduced by Indiana automotive pioneers. Yet the innovators themselves have become nearly forgotten—overlooked as we take their inventions increasingly for granted as part of the standard equipment on today's models.

Innovators like Fred and August Duesenberg, Elwood Haynes, and Howard C. Marmon worked during a time that Indiana dared to rival Michigan. They were among the pioneering Hoosiers found in more than 40 Indiana cities and towns in which automobiles were manufactured or assembled.

More than 400 automobiles, trucks, and cyclecars with various names can claim Indiana production or assemblage, which accounts for more than 8 percent of the approximate 5,000 vehicle names produced in the United States. In 1909, Indiana was the second largest producer (13.1 percent) of the nation's automobiles after Michigan (51.1 percent). David L. Lewis notes in *The Automobile in American Culture* that until 1905, Indianapolis contained more auto plants than any city in Michigan.

"In light of history, it now seems possible that Indianapolis missed passing Detroit and becoming the world's automotive center merely because it failed to advance the spark at the correct moment," writes Carl B. Glasscock in *Motor History of America: The story of the men who made it*. Many believe that under different circumstances, Indiana would have risen to prominence as America's automotive capital.

Historians record that the automobile industry in the late 1800s and early 1900s was the natural offspring of carriage and bicycle manufacturers.

These companies could provide both the needed parts and skilled labor. Indiana had a good share of these manufacturers who made the transition.

A growth spurt between 1910 and 1920 separated the nation's automakers into two groups —the auto giants with mass-production and the craftsmen. Most of Indiana's automakers chose to remain craftsmen, purchased automotive parts, and assembled them by hand. As a result, these companies were small, and many became known for producing high-class and high-priced cars. Nearly every one of the Indiana cars that became well-known was in this category—including Duesenberg, Cord, Stutz, and Cole—and they appealed to the upper-end of the consumer market.

Until about 1920, there seemed to be enough demand for both the mass-produced and the high-quality cars. However, a series of economic factors at this time helped contribute to the decline of Hoosier automaking. For example, the economic recession in the early 1920s added more financial burdens on the population, which became increasingly interested in the less-expensive autos that were mass-produced. Hoosier manufacturers were ill-prepared for this kind of competition. Most wanted to remain craftsmen choosing to concentrate on medium- and high-priced vehicles instead of diversifying. Plus, the Hoosier financial community generally proved of little assistance to its local automobile industry.

The Great Depression of the 1930s finished off many manufacturers. A notable exception was Studebaker in South Bend. The company continued Indiana production until December 1963.

The 1980s and 1990s saw a revival in Indiana auto production with the introduction of the autos and sport utility vehicles at Subaru Isuzu Automotive, Inc. in Lafayette; sport utility vehicles and full-size pickups at GM Truck Group in Fort Wayne; and off-road and military vehicles at AM General Corporation in Mishawaka. Toyota's North American Truck Plant in Princeton also ramped up to produce full-size pickups and sport utility vehicles.

That is only part of the equation of Indiana's impact on the automotive industry. Indiana is a leading producer of automotive components, electronics, and parts. If you drive an American-produced automobile, there is an excellent chance that a good part of it is made in Indiana. For instance, all Chrysler auto transmissions are made in Kokomo.

Indiana employment accounts for a large share of the American auto parts workers. U.S. Census Bureau statistics rank Indiana third in the number of employees in its transportation-equipment industry. Only Michigan and Ohio employ more. Indiana also ranks number one in the production of truck and bus bodies, and second in making carburetors, pistons, piston rings, and valves. Manufacturers include Bosch Braking Systems, Cummins Engine Company, Delphi Automotive, and New Venture Gear. The "Big Three"—GM, Ford, and DaimlerChrysler—also continue to invest in Indiana.

Indiana's automotive history is indeed rich and extensive. The authors of this book, however, have chosen to dedicate it particularly to those early pioneers of Indiana's automotive history. Throughout the following pages, you will find stories of innovation and perseverance as you review the events that shaped the state's automotive history.

An Auto Prayer from the 1912 Wisconsin Motorist

Teach us to drive through life without skidding into other people's business.
Preserve our brake linings that we may stop before we are ditched.
Help us to find the knocks in our own motors and
harken not so much to clashing of other men's gears.

This Cole model provided plenty of space for the family. (c. 1912)
LDC

A General Overview by Decades

1890-1899

The sparks that ignited the American automotive industry were just starting to glow by the end of the 19th Century, and Indiana helped add to the effect.

In the late 1800s, steam propulsion powered some of the first self-propelled vehicles developed. For example, in 1880, William Siefker of Seymour, Indiana, built a steam automobile, featuring a 14-inch fire-tube boiler and two separate engines— one for each set of wheels. The Siefker automobile used coal for fuel and was reported to reach a speed of 10-12 m.p.h. The steam car was his only manufactured automobile.

Suitable gasoline-fueled, internal-combustion engines were not available in the United States until the late 1880s or early 1890s. The gasoline-powered automobile was the likely result of a number of individuals working independently on their dream of a "horseless carriage." In fact, most of these pioneering individuals were unaware of other automotive developments in this early age. A handful of people were actively pursuing their goal at the same time in the early 1890s.

Who developed the first automobile in America? Although a group of native and long-time Indiana residents lay claim to that title, most historians agree that a number of individuals working independently developed the auto concurrently. The general agreement is that the auto in America emerged naturally as the needed technology developed.

When historians must name a titleholder, generally they point to J. Frank and Charles E. Duryea. By Frank's account, they produced their first operable machine in Springfield, Massachusetts. A contemporary story in the town's newspaper *The Republican* on September 22, 1893, confirms the initial, rather disappointing test run. In 1896, the Duryea brothers used the same design for manufacturing. This is accepted as the start of the commercial auto industry in America. The Duryea Motor Wagon Company, however, failed in 1898.

Claiming the title of the country's "first automotive manufacturer" was Elwood Haynes of Kokomo. Prior to setting up shop as a manufacturer, he successfully demonstrated his Pioneer automobile along Pumpkinvine Pike on July 4, 1894. This run preceded commercial production of Haynes-Apperson automobiles by four years. With the failure of the Duryea firm, Haynes was recognized as the proprietor and inventive genius behind the oldest automobile company in America.

Another Hoosier claim for first was made by Charles H. Black, who drove a German-made Benz around Indianapolis in 1891. This was probably one of the first automobiles driven in the country. His construction of a Black automobile at any time predating the Duryea and Haynes vehicles has not been established. No contemporary newspaper accounts have been found to corroborate Black's claim.

Then there was John W. Lambert of Ohio City, Ohio, a town just across the state line near Decatur. A 1960 article in *Antique Automobile* and an entry in the *Encyclopedia Britannica* credited John W. Lambert with building America's first successful automobile in 1891. This predated both the Duryea and Haynes claims of the first American auto. Lambert may not have pressed his claim because he felt that, although the car was extremely successful on a mechanical basis, the

Elwood Haynes, pictured above with the "Pioneer," advertised his vehicle as "America's First Car." He based his claim on the grounds that the 1893 Duryea was only a motorized buggy.
EHM

business was a financial failure. He had not been able to generate sufficient sales to build it. Other notable contemporaries were Alexander Winton from Ohio, and Ransom E. Olds, Charles B. King, and Henry Ford from Michigan.

More on Indiana's early contributions

Indiana's documented automotive innovation began with Elwood Haynes' thoughts of developing a mechanical vehicle to replace his overworked horse. He developed the idea while he was a field superintendent for a natural gas pipeline construction company in 1890.

He reported, "One afternoon, or night, rather, while driving home after a hard day's work, I thought to myself that it would be a fine thing if I didn't have to depend on the horse for locomotion. From then on my mind dwelt a great deal upon the subject of a self-propelled vehicle, that could be used on any country road or city street." (Additional information on Haynes is in the section on automobile makes.)

Haynes formed a partnership with the Apperson brothers to build his vehicle. The first sales for The Haynes-Apperson Automobile Company occurred in 1896. Thus, commercial automobile production was on its way across America.

By 1900 The Haynes-Apperson Automobile Company was one of the few car manufacturers in the country with annual production exceeding 100 units. Others—both large and small—were soon to follow.

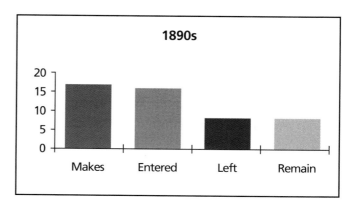

10

1900-1909

In the early 20th Century, auto manufacturing in Indiana, as well as across the country, was a highly skilled, non-automated and expensive process. A small number of workers assembled autos by hand on a unit-by-unit basis. This type of manufacturing yielded a high number of manpower hours per vehicle, which was produced, therefore, at a relatively high cost.

Other factors that most successful auto manufacturers had in common were:

- Nearness to materials, such as lumber and steel.

- Nearness to markets. Indiana lies in the middle of the country and is within a few hours of major cities, such as Chicago.

- Waterpower. A steady stream of rivers flows through the state.

- Favorable climate. Indiana only has a couple of months of severely cold weather.

- Supply of labor. Industrial centers throughout the state had already been established.

However, Indiana was missing two important factors:

- Available capital. Capitalization was not one of Indiana's strongest areas. The state's financial community was not overly willing to invest in the automobile industry. Michigan, however, had an advantage because its financiers had prospered during the lumber boom of the late 1800s and were willing to invest in new industries.

- Momentum of an early start. Michigan, again, had an advantage over Indiana because two of its large manufacturers—Olds Motor Vehicle Company and the Ford Motor Company—embraced the low-priced, mass-produced automobile. This trend would prove to be the future of the automotive industry. By 1904, Olds was recognized as America's first quantity-produced car with 5,508 autos. Ford produced 1,745 cars for 1904. These two companies controlled over 29 percent of the nation's total output of automobiles for the year.

Because of—or in spite of—these factors, Indiana began to make its mark on automotive history. Several prominent automakers started

between 1900 and 1909 within the state's borders. In 1900 for example, the Auburn Automobile Company was founded. This company soon gained recognition for the high-quality cars it produced. Another newcomer to auto manufacturing was the Studebaker Brothers Manufacturing Company.

After producing wagons and carriages for 50 years, Studebaker entered the automotive market with 20 cars in 1902. Studebaker would go on to become the longest-producing Indiana automaker.

Howard C. Marmon's Nordyke & Marmon Company entered auto production in 1902. This company made its mark with its innovative uses of aluminum in automotive applications. In 1909, Cole Motor Company introduced the Cole 30. In the next decade, Cole ranked second only to Cadillac in sales among America's high-priced automobiles. Also in 1909, the Overland Auto Company produced 4,907 automobiles making it one of the largest producers in Indiana.

By the end of the decade, 67 Indiana concerns were engaged in the production of automobiles and automobile bodies and parts. The 1910 census showed that 6,797 wage earners were employed by these 67 companies. The largest was Overland Auto Company with more than 1,000 workers. A further breakdown in size indicated that:

- 22 of the firms employed 1-5 workers each
- 13 employed 6-20
- 11 employed 21-50
- 4 employed 51-101
- 10 employed 101-250 workers
- 4 employed 251-500 workers
- 2 employed 501-1,000 workers.

Total production for the state was 17,253 cars in 1909, placing Indiana second after Michigan among the states.

The cars produced by these Indiana companies, like most of the nation's auto manufacturers, were marketed in the 1900s for the well-to-do who looked upon the horseless carriage as a sporting venture. Indiana producers were small, but their product was becoming known as one of quality. Many of them did a great deal of custom work.

The quality and intensive labor requirement were reflected in the relatively high initial price of the automobile. For example, the factory price for a 1903 Haynes-Apperson, four-passenger phaeton was $1,500 with annual production of 237 cars. Across America, the majority of autos produced were over $1,000. These prices limited auto sales to the wealthy.

The limitation on pricing, however, did not stop Indiana's entrepreneurial spirit. During this decade, Indiana manufacturers introduced 167 makes of automobiles. Models ranged from A to Z, with names like American, Great Western, Inter-State, Marion, McIntyre, Mohawk, National, Premier, Waverley, and Zimmerman. Although the promise of this new industry seemed to be taking root, evidence of its fragility was also present. Fifteen of the 16 manufacturers that were started in the 1890s were gone from the scene. The decade's tally shows that 149 companies entered production. By the end of the decade, 112 companies had left the business.

To A.R.Erskine   Thos A Edison.

Renowned inventor Thomas Edison (pictured at left in this early Studebaker electric car) also contributed to Indiana's mark on automotive history. In 1904, he introduced the Edison battery, which was used by Studebaker in its electric cars, as well as by other manufacturers.
SNM

By 1909 the remaining companies started considering members of the middle-class as prospective customers. The automobile was no longer just a device for leisurely Sunday drives. It was rapidly becoming a dependable means of transportation. There were still a number of obstacles in the path of the automobile, but the frontiers had been pushed back. Automakers still faced such challenges as:

- dependability in engineering
- seasonal aspects that made driving hazardous
- bad roads
- high upkeep for automobiles
- difficulty in operating the automobile
- cash transactions instead of credit plans, making the purchase out of reach for the majority of people.

Even with these challenges, automakers had laid a solid foundation for building a promising future.

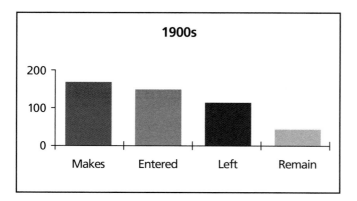

1900s

Makes	Entered	Left	Remain

In 1909, there were 2.2 million miles of road in the United States. Only about 190,000 miles were surfaced. Most travel was in urban areas, with travel into the country being attempted in fair weather. Rain quickly turned country roads into thigh-deep mud ruts, making travel extremely difficult. Many travelers had to enlist the aid of a nearby horse team to extract them from the quagmire. Good roads came as automotive transportation and commerce expanded across the nation.
NAHC

Early Indiana Automotive Statistics

- The 1900 census ranked Indiana seventh in the number of automobile manufacturers and wage earners, and ninth in value of product.

- The 1905 census showed Indiana contributed 6 percent of the industry's total national value of product.

- Until 1905, Indianapolis contained more auto plants than did any city in Michigan.

- In 1909, Indiana was the second largest producer (13.1 percent) of the nation's automobiles after Michigan (51.1 percent).

1910-1919

During these years, a shift to production with lower- or low-skilled workers and automated processes yielded reasonably priced automobiles for a growing market. Henry Ford is credited with a major role in lowering prices. By 1913, Ford revolutionized manufacturing with the introduction of the automotive assembly line at his Highland Park plant in Michigan. Ford's idea was to transfer

Significant historical events from 1910 to 1919

- The Titanic sinks in 1912.

- World War I begins in 1914 with the United States entering in 1917. An armistice signed in 1918 ends the war.

- The Panama Canal opens in 1914.

- Albert Einstein introduces his Theory of Relativity to the world in 1915.

work from people to machines. Many parts of Ford automobiles were put together mechanically, and the number of jobs that still required worker input was severely reduced.

As a result, he lowered the cost of production dramatically. Plus, the average time to complete an automobile dropped from 12.5 hours to 1.5 hours. The savings in production costs were then passed on to the consumer.

This innovation, however, was not beneficial to most of Indiana's carmakers. Now the mass-producer with a low number of manpower hours per vehicle had the advantage in the marketplace. Most of

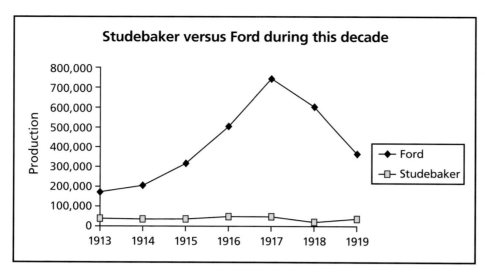

Studebaker versus Ford during this decade

Indiana's manufacturers, however, continued to make assembled automobiles. This meant that their designs used standard components from outside manufacturers. They had to assemble their vehicles by hand. Many of Indiana's automakers continued manufacturing highly crafted and high-priced products.

Unfortunately, the market for high-priced cars underwent a decline between 1913 and 1916. At the same time, popularity of the low-priced car was making rapid advances. In 1910, automobiles costing less than $1,000 comprised 30 percent of the market. By 1916, the number rose to 82 percent. The majority of Indiana producers, however, were in the 18 percent of those making vehicles costing above $1,000.

Plus, the market for new cars was even spreading to the lower-income groups. Henry Ford was one of those helping to make ownership of a car more affordable. In addition to creating less expensive cars, he also ensured his workers earned enough to afford a car. In January 1914, Henry Ford instituted the $5 day wage (which was twice the previous basic pay rate) for his workers. This pay scale meant that his workers could afford to buy a Ford product.

The good news in Indiana

The 1914 Census of Manufacturers ranked Indiana third in the production of automobiles with 3 percent of the market, after Michigan with 78 percent, and Ohio at 12 percent respectively.

Some Indiana companies were also considering how to make their product more affordable for the common man. For example, in 1916 the Studebaker Corporation introduced its Twelve Equal Monthly Payment Plan. Under this plan, a purchaser paid an initial 25 percent down payment. The 75 percent balance was spaced out over 12 equal monthly payments. Within 10 years, 75 percent of all cars sold in America—both new and used—were bought on the installment plan.

Other prominent news occurring this decade:

- The Stutz Motor Car Company was founded in 1912. The Stutz Bearcat model is probably one of the most easily recognizable automobiles from this decade.

- The Lexington Motor Company moved to Connersville, Indiana, in 1910. By the mid-twenties, Lexington was acquired by the Cord Corporation to form a base for its southern Indiana operations.

- McFarlan Motor Car Corporation of Connersville opened in 1910. McFarlan became known for building custom autos. An example is the 1923 gold-plated Knickerbocker Cabriolet priced at $25,000.

- ReVere, another high-end Indiana automobile, debuted in 1918. The company is particularly known for its 1926 model that may have served as the forerunner of power steering with dual steering wheels—one for normal driving and one for parking.

The famous Stutz Bearcat sports car appeared in 1912 for a run of 10 years.
TSC

The Pratt-Elkhart Model 40 pictured above sold for approximately $1,600 in 1911. Within a couple of years, company executives realized that the public wanted lower-priced cars. The company responded by offering the 1916 Elcar for $795. Many other companies across the country followed suit.

By mid-decade, in 1914, 54.3 percent of autos produced were in the $675 to $875 range; 27 percent of autos produced were in the $875 to $1,375 range; 15.3 percent of autos produced were in the $1,375 to $2,775 range; and 18.7 percent of autos produced were above $2,775.
WSL

One hundred thirty-four new makes of Indiana automobiles entered the market between 1910 and 1919. Among them were Amplex, Comet, De Soto, Elcar, Empire, Henderson, Hercules, Howard, Madison, McFarlan, Merz, Monroe, Nyberg, Ohio Falls, and Pathfinder. The tally shows that 103 companies entered production during the decade, with 122 companies leaving the business and 27 remaining in production. Thirty-five manufacturers from the previous two decades exited the industry.

For the first time in two decades, the number of companies leaving the market exceeded the number of companies entering production. This marked the beginning of a decades-long trend for Indiana's automotive industry.

The start of Indiana's decline in auto manufacturing was also evident in figures from the Census of Manufacturers. The census showed that Indiana dropped from its third place position in 1914 to fifth place in 1919, with 4 percent of the country's automobiles. Michigan led the count with 40.2 percent, followed by Ohio at 12.6 percent, New York at 6.3 percent, and Wisconsin with 4.3 percent.

Early Indiana automotive statistics

- In 1914 Indiana produced 5.7 percent of the nation's automotive parts. The census showed 38 automotive manufacturers and 48 body and parts manufacturers.

- In 1919 the number of Indiana auto manufacturers fell to 27. In 1921, the number dwindled to 10.

- Between 1910 and 1920 in the United States, the number of automobiles produced per year by each autoworker rose from 1.7 to 5.5. (National's productivity figures were the best with four cars per worker, Premier produced three cars per worker, and Marmon was slightly over one car per worker.)

- In 1910 automobiles costing less than $1,000 composed 30 percent of the market. By 1916, the number rose to 82 percent. Unfortunately the majority of Indiana producers were in the 18 percent above $1,000.

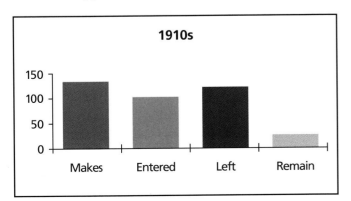

1910s

1920-1929

Significant historical events from 1920 to 1929

- The use of alcoholic beverages is banned in the United States in 1920.

- The Union of Soviet Socialist Republics is established in 1922.

- *Ulysses*, which has been acclaimed as the greatest novel by many critics, is published in 1922.

- Alexander Fleming discovers penicillin in 1928.

- The U.S. stock market crash in 1929 triggers The Great Depression.

Celebrities, such as the Marx Brothers, helped spread the popularity of automobiles. They are pictured here in a 1930 Cord L-29 Phaeton. ACDM

A series of factors in the 1920s further contributed to the decline of numbers in Indiana auto manufacturing. First, an economic recession in the early 1920s added financial concerns. Second, larger manufacturers began to offer value-added features as options to their standard cars.

Prices reached their peak in May 1920 then decreased, and business activity fell off. At first the business decline seemed gradual. As the year moved on, however, the decline gained momentum. The market for many manufactured goods, including medium- and high-priced automobiles, dropped.

Yet, even with the decrease in the consumer's purchasing power, 1920 proved to be the largest production year in the country's short history of the automobile industry. The U.S. production of passenger cars totaled 1,905,560, which was a 15 percent increase over 1919. Ford produced 806,040 autos, which amounted to 42.3 percent of the industry's total. The 1921 auto production showed 1,468,067 units for a decline of 23 percent.

For the first time in the industry, the production capacity exceeded the country's need for automobiles.

The assemblers found they were unable to compete on a price basis. The automobile industry, therefore, continued to witness the demise of the assembled car manufacturer.

The large integrated companies were able to mass-produce in a very economical manner. Since they manufactured the vast majority of their own parts, they could stop and start the flow of parts as they saw fit. Thus, they could carry the major portion of their inventory in the form of raw material.

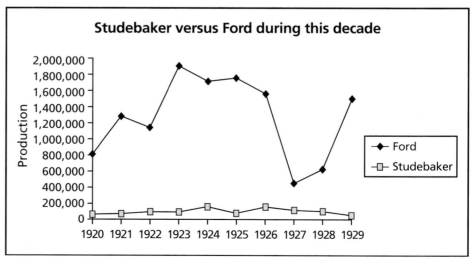

Studebaker versus Ford during this decade

16

In contrast the assemblers carried an inventory in the form of finished components purchased through firm contracts. Their inventory was subject to obsolescence and vulnerable to price fluctuations. Once the assembler was committed, he was not in a position to lower his contracted amount without severe monetary penalties.

As a result, the low-price automobiles made great strides in absorbing an increasingly large share of the market. Between 1921 and 1924, the production of automobiles selling for less than $1,375 more than doubled. The production of cars selling from $1,376 to $2,775 remained relatively constant, while the market for cars selling for more than $2,775 declined approximately 50 percent.

The majority of Indiana producers did not offer a product selling in the low-price market.

Another perceived problem was the used-car evil, which was receiving widespread discussion by mid-decade. The industry considered it a major problem. Manufacturers now had to contend with people who would buy a used car instead of a new one. Plus, car dealers were struggling with newfound problems. One survey revealed that the greatest cause of dealer failures was giving too much of an allowance for used cars. The survey further showed that lack of capital was listed as the second reason for failure. These problems further added to the burden on the automobile industry.

Even with the problems, the public's fascination with the automobile was growing tremendously. In 1926, the automobile industry produced 4.2 million cars, making it the largest industry in the nation. A 1926 survey showed that one in six Americans owned an automobile. By 1927, Americans owned 39 percent of all automobiles around the globe.

Although the future of auto manufacturing was steadily declining in Indiana, the state continued to make its contributions.

News during this decade included:

- Duesenberg, one of America's most prestigious automobiles, debuted at the end of 1920. The Duesenberg Model A pioneered the use of the straight-eight engines and four-wheel hydraulic brakes.

Introduced in 1929, the Marmon Roosevelt was the first eight-cylinder car in the world to sell for less than $1,000. TMH

- The Cord Model L-29 introduced in 1929 was the first production automobile with front-wheel drive. It was designed to fill the corporation's gap between the low-price Auburn and the top-of-the-mark Duesenberg.

- Marmon's 1929 Roosevelt model had the distinction of being the first eight-cylinder car in the world to sell for less than $1,000.

- The year 1929 also saw the introduction of Stutz Motor Car Company's Blackhawk. This Stutz model offered a 30 percent savings. (Unfortunately for the Marmon and Stutz 1929 offerings, the market for more price-sensitive offerings found few purchasers. These models only lasted two years under these nameplates.)

The era of assembled automobile was rapidly drawing to a close. During the decade, 37 makes of automobiles emerged in Indiana, with names like Durant, Elgin, Erskine, Frontenac, Graham-Paige, H.C.S., Lafayette, and Sheridan. The number of new makes introduced was 28 percent of the rate from the 1910s. The tally shows that 31 companies entered production and 13 remained in production

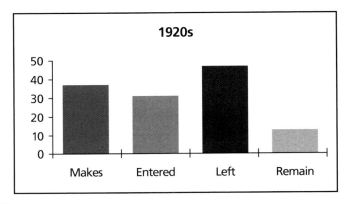

Studebaker introduced the Rockne for the 1932 model year at prices starting around $600.
SNM

during the decade. Of the 47 companies leaving the business, 20 manufacturers from the previous three decades exited the industry. The ratio of the number of manufacturers leaving the business versus the companies entering production was almost 30 percent higher than the preceding decade.

1930-1939

The demand for assembled and higher-priced cars was falling significantly by 1930. The decade also brought another concern that began to eat away at the market of smaller manufacturers: General Motors Corporation began focusing its corporate energy on new sales techniques. GM's goal was to achieve a growing share of total auto sales and more satisfactory profits from each car sold.

GM President Alfred P. Sloan's philosophy dealt with mass-producing a full line of cars graded in quality and price. This meant that the automobiles should change each year, and, correspondingly, become more expensive.

In the early 1930s, GM turned to producing three standard types of auto bodies offered in a wide diversity of auto models. With this strategy, the company continued to make profits even while demand was slowly growing. GM's new policies were soon successful. In 1935, the company made

more after-tax profit per vehicle than it had made in the record-producing year 1929.

Offering annual model changes and highly styled autos became the rule across the industry. Trying to meet this challenge greatly strapped those manufacturers who didn't have the financial resources needed to continually change their offerings. Outside of the Big Three—GM, Ford, and Chrysler—the resources of most auto manufacturers were severely tested during the 1930s. Many went through corporate reorganizations where possible, or simply closed their doors.

Significant historical events from 1930 to 1939

- The jet engine is invented in 1930.

- Astronomers discover Pluto in 1930.

- Adolf Hitler is named chancellor of Germany in 1933. Germany invades Poland in 1939, triggering the start of World War II.

- The age of Prohibition in the United States ends in 1933.

- The Spanish Civil War from 1936 to 1939 brings Franco to power.

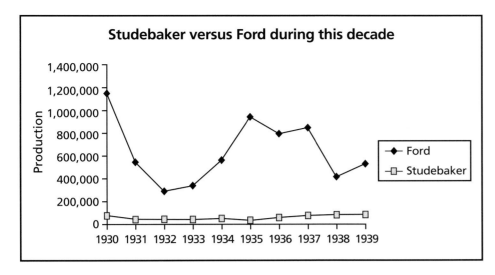

Studebaker versus Ford during this decade

Together these seven companies had 97.3 percent of all production. That's a significant jump from 1925 when the Big Three accounted for 62.6 percent and the total for the top seven producers was only 77.4 percent.

A look at Indiana

Ten of the 13 makes launched in Indiana during the decade were not around by 1940. The number of new makes introduced was a 35 percent decrease compared with the previous decade. Names like Auburn-Cummins, Lever, Mercer, and Rockne enjoyed a short run in Indiana. El-Fay, Allied, Super Allied, and Prosperity were various taxicab offerings from two Elkhart companies that lasted from one to five years in the early 1930s.

The tally shows that eight companies entered production during the decade, and four remained in production. The ratio of the number of manufacturers leaving the business versus the companies entering production is 212 percent higher than the 1920s. Seventeen companies left the business, with 12 of these dropouts coming from the first four decades of auto making in Indiana.

The four remaining Indiana-built makes included Crosley, Chrysler Corporation's Plymouth, Pak-Age-Car, and Studebaker.

As the era of assembled automobile drew to a close, a significant part of the industry's output was being furnished by large manufacturers. By 1935, the Big Three sold 90 percent of all passenger cars while Hudson, Nash, Packard, and Studebaker produced an additional 7.3 percent of the total.

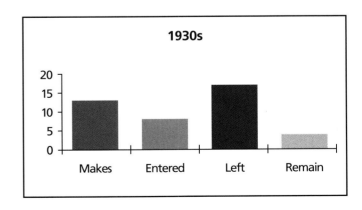

1930s

1940-1949

General Motors rose to manufacturing dominance as American auto manufacturing entered the 1940s. GM's ability to bracket the market from the popular price level through the luxury level enabled the company to offer a broader range at increasing levels of profitability.

World War II, however, affected all U.S. manufacturing. In 1940, the American industry began supplying large quantities of equipment to the U.S. War Department and to England's War Ministry. The American auto industry also did its part and, as a result, was called "the arsenal of democracy." Then the United States entered World War II on December 7, 1941. During the summer of 1941, the American government began restricting materials and devoted them for military use. On January 1, 1942, civilian sales of passenger cars were halted.

As a result, the U.S. automotive industry— including the four remaining manufacturers in Indiana—retooled plants to produce military vehicles and material. Richmond-based Crosley produced the popular "CoBra" (copper-brazed) sheet steel engine under contract for naval applications as generator sets and refrigeration units. Plymouth's Evansville Ordinance Plant produced over three billion rounds of small arms ammunition, 1,660 reconditioned Sherman tanks, 4,000 rebuilt Army trucks, 800,000 tank grousers and 100,000 incendiary bombs. Studebaker in South Bend

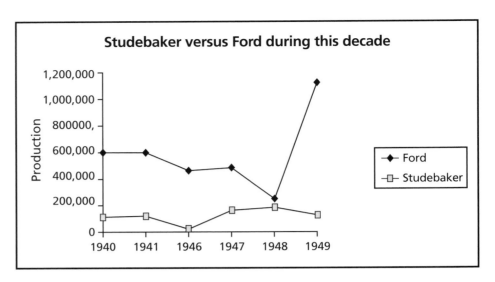

made 64,000 Cyclone aircraft engines, 15,000 M-29 amphibious cargo carriers known as the "Weasel," and 197,000 2½-ton 6x6 trucks. Auburn-Central, which was the non-automotive stamping business of the remains of Cord Corporation in Connersville, built 445,000 Jeep bodies over a 45-month period for Willys-Overland and Ford.

By the war's end, the average car was nine years old. Plus, for the first time in 15 years, Americans had the money for new cars. Most of the tooling for prewar cars was still available, so new autos finally rolled off the lines. Material shortages and labor strikes slowed everyone's plans, but the seller's market was there. In the first few years after World War II, manufacturers sold every car and truck they could make.

Indiana's auto manufacturers also aided the W.W. II effort. For example, the Plymouth plant in Evansville, pictured here, converted its auto lines to produce war materials.
DCHC

Studebaker in South Bend exuberantly entered this post-war market with its late-Spring 1946 introduction of the newly styled 1947 lineup. Its advertising proudly proclaimed, "Studebaker—First by far with a postwar car." The company provided the first all-new postwar body designs from any American manufacturer. Production models were divided into two series—the Champion starting at $1,446 and the Commander starting at $1,661. The five-passenger coupes, with their wrap-around rear windows, grabbed popular attention as few automotive designs had in recent past.

With this early introduction, Studebaker beat its competition by 18 months. An impressive 161,498 cars were built during the 1947 model run. Studebaker's market share rose to slightly over 4 percent and remained there for almost five years. Plus, it surpassed its prewar production levels about two years ahead of other American producers.

Consumer demand for postwar cars also encouraged Plymouth to turn out as many as 400 cars per day from its Evansville plant.

The 1940s and 1950s provided more challenges for Indiana's two other remaining independent producers—Crosley and Pak-Age-Car.

For Crosley, prewar production from 1939 to 1942 totaled 5,757 units, with manufacturing conducted at the Richmond plant. In the postwar boom, its production peaked at almost 28,000 cars in 1948. Crosley's Marion plant assembled postwar production from 1946 to 1952. The American public, however, wanted large, powerful cars, which the Crosley was not. This consumer preference eventually led to Crosley's downfall.

The end of the Pak-Age-Car was swifter. Auburn Automobile Company had purchased all the tooling and machinery for the production of the Pak-Age-Car in 1938 from the Stutz Motor Car Company of America. Auburn continued production as a subsidiary in Connersville. Then, Diamond T Truck assumed Pak-Age-Car sales and service operations in 1939. In March 1941, Auburn ceased Pak-Age-Car production to concentrate on defense work at its Connersville plants. Postwar auto production never returned to these plants.

The decade did see the introduction of one new Hoosier make—the Packard Darrin, which enjoyed a two-year production run in Connersville from 1940 through 1941.

As America closed out the decade of the 1940s, only Studebaker, Plymouth, and Crosley were present for a roll call of Indiana auto makers.

By 1949, car sales finally passed their 1929 peaks. This decade led to a new record in 1950. Manufacturers were able to reach this only once again later on in the 1950s.

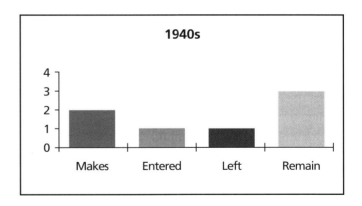

1950s and 1960s

In the 1950s, engineering and styling features pushed automotive advances. Overhead valve (OHV) V-8 engines became available in low- and mid-priced cars. This innovation added more horsepower to any kind of car. But it also meant less fuel efficiency.

Advances continued rapidly. For example, by 1954 almost all new cars had 12-volt electrical systems. In 1955, 70 percent had an automatic

Two Indiana companies contributed to the life of the Pak-Age-Car: the Stutz Motor Co. and the Auburn Automobile Company. TAC

transmission. By 1956, 80 percent of all American cars were sold with OHV V-8 engines. Plus, designs included longer, lower, and wider body styles. This meant that autos rode lower to the ground for a whole new look and feel.

Quickly following the 1950 production peak, however, was the first of the many recessions that were to shape the automotive economy ever since.

Never again could auto corporations rely upon the nearly uninterrupted market growth of the pre-1930s. Plus, although American manufacturers were still the heavy hitters, imports were also coming to bat. By 1959, the market share for imports reached 10 percent of all new car sales.

The U.S. auto market moved toward saturation in the ratio of people to automobiles in the early 1950s. With one car for nearly every four Americans, there were more passenger cars in America than there were households. From 1950 to 1970, the companies were able to increase the passenger-car population of America significantly compared with previous rates.

The news in Indiana

The 1950 model year proved to be the high watermark for Studebaker as an auto producer. A remarkable total of 343,164 cars and trucks rolled off the lines.

By 1952, Crosley was still toeing the line on prices at $925 for a pickup, but production halted in July after 1,522 cars were built. Since 1949,

Powell Crosley had lost more than $3 million in his battle as an auto manufacturer.

The one millionth Plymouth came off Evansville's assembly line in 1953. During the next few years, production rates varied from 500 to 800 cars per day. Plymouth's Evansville operation shut down in 1959.

Significant historical events from 1950 to 1959

- U.S. Senator McCarthy begins inquiry into "un-American activities" in 1950.

- The Korean War begins in 1950 and ends in 1953.

- India elects its first prime minister, Jawaharlal Nehru, in 1952.

- Scientists discover DNA in 1953.

- The oral contraceptive is developed in 1955.

- Russia launches the first artificial satellite, Sputnik I, in 1957. The United States follows with the Explorer I launched in 1958.

Significant historical events from 1960 to 1969

- Russian Yuri Gargarin is the first man in space in 1961.

- Communists erect the Berlin Wall in 1961.

- The United States sends thousands of advisors to Vietnam in 1961. Fighting continues until the communists seize control of Saigon in 1975.

- U.S. President John Kennedy is assassinated in 1963.

- The 1964 U.S. Civil Rights Bill is enacted.

- The Six-Day War is fought between Israel and Arabs in 1967.

- American astronauts Neil Armstrong and Buzz Aldrin land on the moon in 1969.

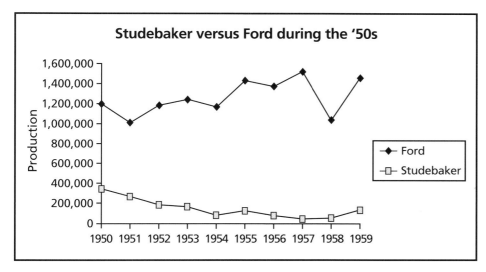

Studebaker versus Ford during the '50s

As the 1950s wore on, America's independent auto manufacturers were locked in a mortal battle with the "Big Three." Studebaker, Indiana's last automaker, was scrapping along at the end of the decade.

Studebaker's big news for 1951 was the introduction of a 232 c.i.d., overhead valve, V-8 engine. The 1953 Studebaker coupes became known for their sleek low profile and wrap-around windows at the front and rear. Introduction of the economical Lark in 1958 and the Avanti personal luxury car in 1962 did little to stave off Studebaker's losses.

Automobile production in 1963 totaled 83,845 cars, which was barely half of what was considered a reasonable break-even point.

Studebaker's Indiana auto production ended in December 1963. The writing had been on the wall for over a decade, with many years of labor strife and corporate restructuring. Yet the cessation of auto production in South Bend was met with much anger and disbelief. Luckily, the city has weathered the storm and has a vibrant community today.

Consolidation of the auto industry finally became a reality with the demise of Studebaker, the last independent automaker in Indiana, as well as America.

The 1963 Lark was one of the last models ever produced by Studebaker in South Bend.
SNM

In early 1961, Studebaker tried to improve its image with a new car. Designer Raymond Loewy was hired for the task. He developed the Avanti (pictured above). This was one of the first American passenger cars to use caliper-type brakes. Plus, its safety theme was prominent throughout with a recessed and padded instrument panel with red lights for night vision, built-in roll bar, and safety-cone door locks. Unfortunately, the new car could not save the company. Studebaker halted production in South Bend in December 1963 and moved to Canada. All operations closed in March 1966.
TAC

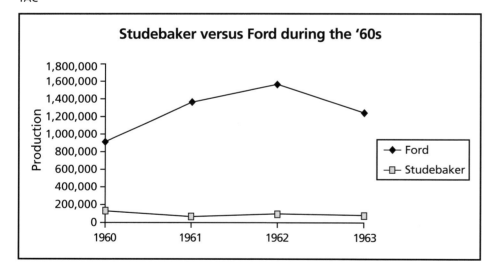

1970s to Today

Today Indiana continues to play an important, yet supporting, role in the automotive industry. The focus in Indiana in recent decades has been primarily on supplying parts. The state has become a leading producer of automotive components, electronics and parts. In fact, if you drive an American automobile, there is an excellent chance that a good part of it was made in Indiana.

Automotive manufacturing never entirely left, even though by the 1970s there was only one company that assembled an entire vehicle—AM General in Mishawaka. At the time, it answered to an out-of-state headquarters. The company continues to produce vehicles today. Its consumer product, the HUMMER, is a version of its military vehicle.

Within the past couple of decades, AM General got some company in Indiana. Three other auto manufacturers have joined the ranks: GM Truck and Bus Group in Fort Wayne, Subaru-Isuzu Automotive in Lafayette, and Toyota Motor Manufacturing in Princeton.

So in both parts and automobile manufacturing, Indiana's interests have always had a tie to the automotive industry. Therefore, any issues affecting the nation's auto manufacturers also has influenced work in Indiana.

Important issues in the 1970s dealt with such concerns as heightened safety and emission regulations, a recession, and gas shortages that helped popularize the more fuel-efficient imports that increasingly appeared on the American landscape. The Clean Air Act of 1970 forced the industry to reduce exhaust emissions for the first time in automotive history.

The Arab oil embargo of 1973 also influenced design and engineering changes. Prior to that, Americans were accustomed to big cars with fuel-inefficient engines. The oil embargo hit, and the country reconsidered. During the mid-decade, import cars offering fuel efficiency sold as fast as they came into the country. In 1977, America's first "downsized" cars were introduced. These offerings did little to stem the loss of market share to imports.

The introduction of safety interlocks added more complexity to the American automobile. Plus, the Corporate Average Fuel Economy (CAFE) standards took effect in 1978. (The initial CAFE standard was 18 m.p.g.)

Imports were still making inroads, and by 1979, these cars attained a 27 percent market share. Plus, European manufacturers were building auto plants in the United States and developing joint ventures with American manufacturers.

By the 1980s, American auto manufacturers finally got the idea that consumers wanted cars with better gas mileage and turned their attention toward that arena. They worked to improve designs and change outdated production techniques.

Yet American automakers continued to face fierce competition from abroad. By 1987, imports had 31 percent of the market, according to *Motor Age*. American manufacturers breathed a little easier when pressure to limit Japanese imports finally had an effect. By then, however, major Japanese manufacturers had made plans to build cars in the United States instead of importing. This decision proved to benefit Indiana's economy.

Significant historical events from 1970 to 2001

- The Watergate scandal ends President Richard Nixon's term as president in 1974. Presidents Gerald Ford and Jimmy Carter also serve during the '70s.

- Mars Space probes, Viking 1 and 2, are launched by NASA in 1976.

- A method for developing test-tube babies is introduced in 1978.

- Israel and Egypt sign a peace treaty in 1979.

- Ayatollah Khomeini leads revolution against Shah of Iran and overthrows the government in 1979.

- Ronald Reagan is elected U.S. president in 1980.

- The space shuttle Columbia marks the beginning of the U.S. space shuttle program in 1981.

- George Bush becomes U.S. president in 1988.

- The Berlin Wall falls in 1989, and East and West Germany reunite in 1990.

- Yugoslavia breaks apart along ethnic and religious lines in 1991.

- South Africa abolishes Apartheid laws in 1990 and 1991.

- Bill Clinton is elected U.S. president in 1992.

- The federal building in Oklahoma City, Oklahoma, is bombed in 1995.

- Control of Hong Kong reverts to China in 1997.

- The first successful cloning of a mammal is announced in 1997.

- George W. Bush becomes president in 2000.

- Terrorists attack the World Trade Towers in New York and the Pentagon in Washington, D.C. in 2001.

Toyota Manufacturing is one of the newest members to Indiana's automotive family. Pictured above is the Tundra. Below is the Sequoia. Both were made at the Princeton plant. TMMI

Japanese-owned Fuji Heavy Industries and Isuzu Motors Unlimited decided to plant their first joint venture in Lafayette, Indiana. This venture was christened Subaru-Isuzu Automotive, Inc. The first vehicles—a Subaru Legacy sedan and an Isuzu pickup truck—rolled out of the plant in September 1989. (Unfortunately, during production of this book, Isuzu announced that it would sell its stake in the Lafayette facility to Fuji.)

By the early 1990s, the U.S. car companies devised and concentrated on niche markets that they innovated: minivans, sport utility vehicles, and light trucks. SUVs, in particular, have captured the hearts of Americans for the vehicles' versatility and handling. By mid-decade, Japanese automakers also saw the opportunities and began offering vehicles in each of these markets. By the end of the '90s, the Japanese makes were the vehicles of choice in many surveys regarding minivans and SUVs.

Japanese entrepreneurship in these niches also benefited Indiana. For example, in 1998 Toyota Motor Corporation produced its first vehicles from its Indiana plant— a Tundra pickup truck and Sequoia full-size sport utility vehicle.

The changes in the automotive industry in Indiana and the country have led to many options for consumers. In fact, after more than 100 years of automotive innovation, they can buy a car to fit any kind of lifestyle. Cars are available with any level of horsepower, style, efficiency, on- or off-road capability, and an ever-increasing level of automatic features. The public should also see increased availability of alternative-power or hybrid-power source cars as America makes the transition to zero-emissions and high-efficiency automobiles. Whatever the changes and advances in the automotive industry, Indiana will continue to play an important role.

The Subaru Legacy GT Sedan, pictured above, is one of the vehicles produced by the Subaru-Isuzu facility located in Lafayette. Another example is the Isuzu Rodeo, pictured below.
SOAI and IMAI

Several of Indiana's first automotive executives are pictured above.
TAC

INCREASED BUSINESS THROUGH BOWSER

The Prestige and Patronage

OF

BOWSER
ESTABLISHED 1885

Piston Type Measuring Pumps
Will Build a Profitable Business

The prestige of Bowser piston type pumps for serving gasoline is built on their consistent record of ACCURACY — RELIABILITY — SAFETY — SPEED — ECONOMY and PURIFICATION of GASOLINE.

ACCURACY—determined by positive mechanical means—and indicated on a scale at eye level.

RELIABILITY—hand power always available—easy operation prevents fatigue.

SAFETY—no danger of breakage and spilling gasoline to endanger lives and property.

SPEED—the fastest service pump on the market—more than 20 gallons per minute.

ECONOMY—the least cost per gallon in time and pump depreciation.

PURIFICATION—Bowser centrifugal filter positively separates all impurities—all the pep, but no water, reaches the car.

S. F. BOWSER & COMPANY, Inc.

Fort Wayne, Indiana   U. S. A.

S. F. Bowser & Co. of Texas.
Dallas.

S. F. Bowser Co., Ltd.
Toronto.

This ad taken from the November 25, 1920 issue of *Motor Age* illustrates one of the country's first gas pumps, which were made in Fort Wayne. In fact, Sylvanus F. Bowser of Fort Wayne invented the world's first gas pump in 1885. Today the city is headquarters for Tokheim Corporation, one of the world's largest producers of gasoline pumps and service station dispensing equipment. HAS&SM

Significant Automobiles
Made in Indiana

American Underslung, 1906-1914

The American Motor Car Company is most noted for an innovative design referred to as the underslung. While most car frames of the period were mounted on top of the axles, the American built the chassis of its sports roadsters under the axles. This created a vehicle that was lower to the ground.

Yet designers took about one year after the company's establishment to invent the American Underslung, which underwent a series of name changes at first, including American Tourist, American Roadster, American Traveler, and American Scout.

American's genesis was at 910 State Life Building, Indianapolis, in 1905. Founders V.A. Longaker and D.S. Menasco invested in the company after making a fortune in the lumber business in the Northwest. Soon they hired Harry C. Stutz to design the first American cars, which premiered in 1906.[1]

The first American cars, which were conventional chassis touring cars, hit the road under the slogan "No Noise But The Wind." Early on, American offerings were assembled cars like many other automobiles at the time. The company had no facilities for manufacturing component units. So instead American purchased completed engines, transmissions, drive lines, axles, and steering gears for assembly. Shortly after building the prototype touring car, American learned that Continental—its engine supplier—did not have sufficient capacity to furnish complete engines.

Longaker then asked Charles and John Teetor, who managed the Light Inspection Car Company in Hagerstown, to build a suitable engine. The Teetor's machine shop was small, employing no more than 25 people, and knew nothing about building four-cylinder engines. After considerable discussion and upon learning that American would only need 25 or 30 engines in the first year, the Teetor brothers agreed to tackle the job. The Teetor engines were known later as Teetor-Hartley.[2]

By early 1906, the ambitious and restless Harry Stutz transferred his energies to the Marion Motor Car Company, where he remained for the next four years as chief engineer and factory manager. *(See Stutz, H.C.S, and the Stutz Fire Engine Company for the continuation of the Harry C. Stutz story.)* He literally changed places with Fred I. Tone, former chief engineer at Marion. Tone's first assignment as chief engineer and designer for American was to design a completely "All-American car from American-made materials."

Interestingly, the inspiration for this low sports roadster design came serendipitously. One day in 1906, when the frames were delivered to American, they were unloaded upside down. Tone seized upon the idea to mount the frame under the axles. The "underslung" was born. From that day on, American built all roadsters underslung, while continuing to make touring cars and sedans on conventionally overslung chassis. Tone and the entire staff worked non-stop to bring the American Roadster to market.

When the 1907 Roadster and the conventional Tourist—both selling for $3,250—were announced in November 1906, American stated that output would be limited to 150 cars for the year. The American Roadsters that garnered numerous headlines in races during the summer of 1907 inspired building a more powerful roadster.[3]

American offered four models for 1908: the Model 40 Tourist and Roadster priced at $3,250, and the Model 50 Tourist and Roadster selling at $3,750. Soon, American cars were becoming well-known for attention to detail. The magnificent marquee of an eagle on top of the world adorned the radiator face. Plus, copious amounts of highly polished brass and nickel were used throughout.[4]

In the summer of 1908, Tone added the American Speedster to the line-up. By 1909, American offered seven models. Four were mounted on a similar chassis—the five- and seven-passenger Tourist; five-passenger Gadabout toy tonneau; and the Wayfarer close-coupled, five-passenger touring car with removable rumble seat. The model year also introduced American's first closed car, the luxurious Limousine with folding seats and leather or broadcloth upholstery priced at $5,000. The Roadster and Speedster rounded out the line-up. In the summer of 1909, Tone designed a modified four-passenger roadster with a divided rear seat. The roadster was called the Traveler, which remained in the company's line until its demise.

For 1910 the Gadabout and Wayfarer models dropped from the line-up leaving the Tourist and the Limousine being built on similar-sized chassis. These, along with the Roadster and the Traveler, were equipped with the 50 h.p. engine and sold for $4,000. For an additional $1,000, the customer had his choice of a 60 h.p. Roadster or Traveler Special model.

Under American's 1910 slogan "A Car For The Discriminating Few," the company produced 300 units for the year.[5]

American's line-up for 1911 saw few changes. Its nine models were sold as "America's Greatest Car." The Roadster, Roadster Coupe, Roadster Special, and Speedster were on the 112-inch wheelbase. The Traveler, Traveler Coupe, Traveler Special, Tourist, and Limousine all had the 124-inch wheelbase. The reliable 50 h.p. and 60 h.p. engines carried over with prices ranging from $4,250 to $5,250 depending on the chassis and engine combination. Steering moved to the left-side with the shift lever mounted in the center and the emergency brake remaining outside.

After the 1911 models were introduced, Fred I. Tone left American over a disagreement about his bonus arrangement. In January 1911, J.I. Handley, a prominent figure in the automobile industry, purchased shares in American and helped organize the new American Motors Company. (In June 1912, Handley also became president of the Marion Motor Car Company of Indianapolis.) He assumed the presidency with Longaker remaining as chairman of the board and general manager.

Menasco, known as the "Selling Trouble Shooter," stayed on as vice president.[6]

The American Underslung was named after the unusual method of mounting the frame under the axles.
NAHC

This new regime immediately set out to reconfigure the American line-up to compete in the medium price market for 1912. The first offering, The American Scout, debuted in May 1911 as a 1912 model at the company's lowest price ever of $1,250. The mid-line offering was the Tourist in roadster and touring car versions with a 34 h.p. engine on a 118-inch wheelbase priced at $2,250. The Traveler still occupied the prestige position in the line with a four- and six-passenger touring car priced at $4,250 and $4,500, respectively.

All of these models rode on the underslung chassis, and the company adopted "American Underslung" as the car's name. The closed models dropped from the line-up after one year. Model year 1912 became American's biggest sales year, with an estimated 1,000 units produced. This was a 183 percent increase over the preceding year.[7]

American announced its 1913 line in September 1912. The Scout was priced at $1,475 and sported a new 105-inch wheelbase. Prices on the Tourist rose to $2,350. Closed models returned in 1913 after a one-year hiatus. The Scout three-passenger coupe sold for $2,000. The Tourist Limousine, priced at $3,500, was finished in black leather on a 124-inch chassis. The luxurious Traveler Limousine came equipped with quality goatskin and taffeta on a stretched 140-inch chassis, with every accessory possible—all for $6,000. All models included electric starting and lighting systems.[8]

The company announced the 1914 American Underslung Six on April 12, 1913 in the *Saturday Evening Post.* Yet, this proved to be an inopportune time for new automobiles because the country was trying to shake off the effects of the disastrous floods in late March and early April. This natural phenomenon virtually wiped out the anticipated spring business boom. Cash flow at American was severely strained due to a heavy debt incurred through past plant expansions. Furthermore, many American dealers had previously invested in four-cylinder Traveler models, with the assurance that they would be continued along with the new six-cylinder models. For 1914, the four-cylinder Traveler model was discontinued, thus enraging dealers who had an inventory in these older models. American recruited Frank E. Smith, a reputed efficiency expert, as assistant general manager to help solve problems.

In November, however, the Federal Court adjudged American bankrupt and appointed Smith as receiver. By the spring of 1914, Smith deemed it advisable to suspend operations.[9]

Supplier Ralph R. Teetor of the Teetor-Hartley Motor Company, purchased the last American Underslung built in 1914. The car was a magnificent, 75 h.p., six-cylinder, seven-passenger touring car painted a brilliant lavender. Perhaps Teetor has provided the best epitaph for this Indiana-built car: "I do believe that the American Underslung cars had the most dramatic appeal of any cars that were ever built, and ever since that company failed, have wished that it could have survived."[10]

NOTE OF INTEREST

The Pathfinder 40, a car built in Indianapolis, was selected in 1913 by the U.S. government and the American Automobile Association to cross the continent three times in one season. It was a remarkable feat at the time. The Pathfinder was chosen because of its record for economical upkeep and freedom from mechanical trouble.

Endnotes

1. Seeley, Walter, *The American Underslung: A Car For The Discriminating Few,* Hershey PA, Antique Automobile, vol. 36, no. 4, Jul/Aug 1972, p 6.
2. Meyer, Marjorie Teetor, *One Man's Vision: The Life of Automotive Pioneer Ralph R. Teetor,* Indianapolis, Guild Press of Indiana, © 1995, p 46.
3. Seeley, p 7.
4. Seeley, p 10.
5. Seeley, p 12.
6. Seeley, p 13.
7. Seeley, p 15.
8. Seeley, p 16.
9. Seeley, p 19.
10. Meyer, p 47.

Additional specifications on selected models

The first American five-passenger touring car featured a side-entrance tonneau and a divided front seat with a 327 c.i.d., 35-40 h.p., Teetor engine, built on a 111-inch wheelbase. Prices began at $3,000, with standard equipment including Prest-O-Lite acetylene headlights, two oil side lights, one oil tail light, air horn, and a complete set of tools and jack carried in a box on the running board.

The 1907 two-passenger roadster had a new 393 c.i.d., 40-50 h.p., four-cylinder engine, on a 106-inch wheelbase. The underslung suspension with the engine and transmission mounted on a sub-frame allowed a straight drive shaft direct to the patented full floating rear end.

A more powerful Roadster, called the Model 50, was designed in 1907 with a 476 c.i.d., 50 h.p., four-cylinder engine, on a 110-inch wheelbase with electric side lights.

The 1908 American Speedster was a 571 c.i.d., 70 h.p., highly-modified lowered roadster, on a 110-inch wheelbase. Price was $5,000.

The 1909 line-up had four models using the 124-inch chassis and a new 499 c.i.d., 50 h.p., engine. They were the five- and seven-passenger Tourist, five-passenger Gadabout toy tonneau, and the Wayfarer close-coupled five-passenger touring car with removable rumble seat. These all sold for $3,750 except for the seven-passenger Tourist at $4,000.

1910 improvements included a gear-driven oil pump with a sight-gauge on the dash, a positive-displacement air pump, spiral gear transmission, and a Bosch high tension ignition system.

The 1912 Scout available as a roadster or five-passenger touring car had a new 318 c.i.d., 22 h.p. 4-cylinder engine on a 102-inch wheelbase.

The 1913 American Underslung had a 456 c.i.d. 6-cylinder T-head engine that produced 60 h.p. and rode on a 132-inch chassis. Both a two-passenger roadster and a four-passenger touring car were available for $2,750. A six-passenger touring car with a new 573 c.i.d., 75 h.p., 6-cylinder engine on a 140-inch wheelbase at $4,500 topped off the line. The power rating on the four-cylinder Scout roadster was increased to 39 h.p. and the price was reduced to $1,550.

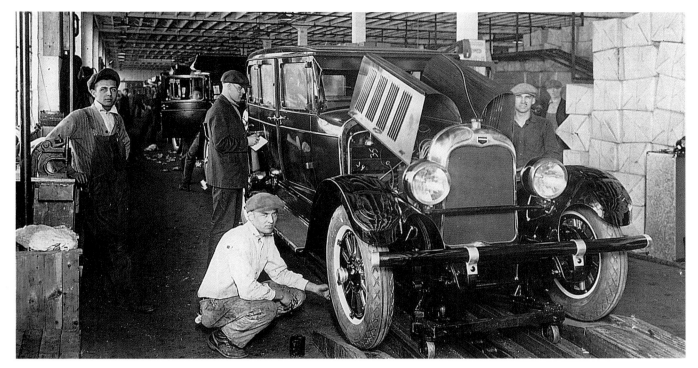

Auburn was reborn when E.L. Cord took over in 1924. Production at the Auburn factory in 1925 is pictured above.
ACDM

Auburn, 1900-1936

The Auburn Automobile Company made its mark on Indiana with style. The company's most notable model—the Auburn boattail speedster designed by Gordon Buehrig in 1934—had the look that would be remembered for many years to come. Today the speedster is still regarded by enthusiasts as one of the most stylish cars ever made.

The boattail speedster came late in Auburn's life, which sprung from the foundation of the Eckhart Carriage Company in 1874.

Charles Eckhart worked as a wheelwright for the Studebaker Brothers Manufacturing Company in South Bend before moving to Auburn and founding the carriage company.[1] In 1896, Eckhart turned control of the carriage company over to his sons Frank and Morris. Although it is difficult to establish a date for their first automobile, the Auburn Automobile Company extensively indicated that it was established in 1900.[2]

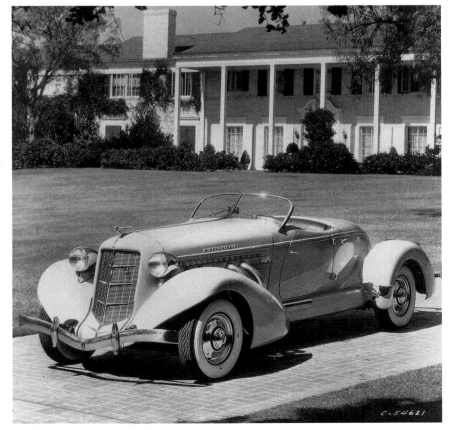

The 1936 Auburn Speedster was photographed on the front lawn of CordHaven, the estate of E.L. Cord in Beverly Hills, California.
ACDM

The Auburn Automobile Company was incorporated August 22, 1903 with Charles, Frank, and Morris Eckhart listed as directors and officers. Capital was set at $7,500. By 1903, the Auburns were more substantial and were offered with pneumatic tires. Multi-cylinder offerings came in shortly afterward—two-cylinders with 18 h.p. in 1905, four-cylinders with 30 h.p. in 1909, and six-cylinders with 50 h.p. in 1912.[3]

In 1906, the company leased the former Model Gas Engine Works buildings at the end of Main Street just south of the Vandalia Railroad from the Auburn Commercial Club. (In 2002, the main building housed the Auburn Street Department.)

In the 1910s, Auburns were known as good solid cars and competed fairly well in the marketplace. With increased competition late in the decade, Auburn's sales began to falter. The Eckharts sold the company in 1919 to a group of Chicago investors headed by William Wrigley, Jr., the chewing gum magnate and the owner of the *Chicago Tribune* and the Chicago Cubs. Introduction of the Auburn Beauty-Six in 1919 briefly gave sales a short-lived boost. In 1924, Auburn was producing only six units per day. Over 700 unsold touring cars filled the storage lot.[4]

Auburn took a dramatic turn when the Chicago investors installed Errett Lobban Cord as general manager in 1924. Cord had garnered the investors' attention while he was the enterprising sales manager of the Moon Automobile Agency in Chicago. Cord agreed to work without a salary with the understanding that, if he turned the company around, he could acquire a controlling interest.

Upon arriving in Auburn, Cord ordered the sluggish inventory repainted in snappy colors and had trim and accessories added for a more engaging look. The inventory was soon sold. In 1925, he updated the Auburns with the addition of Lycoming straight-eight engines to the line-up. He then paid a reputed $50 for a flashy new design in time to put it on the floor of the 1925 New York Auto Show—all without getting the company one cent in debt. This new styling theme was used for nine years and featured a graceful beltline that swept up over the top of the hood to the radiator cap and two-tone color schemes. The revised Lycoming straight-eight now developed 88 h.p. The roadster

carried a price of $1,695, with the coupe at $1,745, brougham at $1,795, and sedan at $1,995.

Cord was able to turn the company around. Sales increased rapidly, and in 1926, Cord became president of the company.[5]

Starting in 1926, Cord conceived a self-sufficient organization, similar to Ford, that could produce practically all the parts needed for automobiles, eliminating the need to buy a lot of material outside. He believed he could reduce costs this way. To accomplish this goal, Cord acquired control of Ansted Engine Company, Lexington Motor Car Company, and Central Manufacturing, all based in Connersville; Lycoming Manufacturing Company (and subsidiaries) of Williamsport, Pennsylvania; Limousine Body Company of Kalamazoo, Michigan; and Duesenberg Motors Company of Indianapolis. Growth in the company continued. In five years E.L. Cord had increased production 1,000 percent. On June 14, 1929, the Cord Corporation was organized with a capitalization of $125 million as a holding company to centralize growing activities.[6]

Starting in 1927, Auburn Model 8-88's began competing at various race venues across the country. In March, Wade Morton recorded 1,000 miles at almost 70 m.p.h. at the Culver City Speedway. In July, two roadsters and a sedan set new speed marks for fully equipped stock cars from five to 5,000 miles at the Atlantic City Speedway.

The powerful Auburn 8-115 with Lockheed four-wheel hydraulic brakes was introduced for 1928. Styling innovations were a trend at Auburn in 1928, with the introduction of the five-passenger Phaeton Sedan—a sporty touring car that could be converted into a closed sedan. Also premiering this year was the first Auburn boattail speedster designed by stylist Alan H. Leamy, who provided the genesis for Buehrig's version.

The aerodynamic Auburn Cabin Speedster was introduced in 1929. That year's catalog boasted, "Here is tomorrow's automobile design. Automobiles, as well as planes, must minimize wind resistance to attain increased speed. The Cabin Speedster is a subtle compound of racing car and airplane, sky-styled, and designed by the famous racing driver and aviator, Wade Morton."

In 1931, Auburn production concentrated on a single straight-eight engine, the Lycoming 8-98. Auburn's V-12 160 sold for less than $1,000, in 1932. This is probably the least expensive 12-cylinder automobile ever marketed. Another new feature for 1932 was the Columbia (a recent addition to the Cord Corporation) two-speed rear axle. That summer an Auburn V-12 speedster set additional speed and endurance records.[8]

The legendary designer Gordon Buehrig started to work for Auburn in 1934. He designed the Auburn 851 with a Lycoming straight-eight engine. The car was introduced in August 1934, which was one of the first mid-year introductions. Buehrig also designed the Auburn 851 boattail speedster with a Lycoming supercharged 150 h.p., straight-eight engine, and a price tag of $2,245. Its success was legendary. An 851 speedster became the first fully equipped American production car to exceed 100 m.p.h. for 12 hours at the Bonneville salt flats in Utah in July 1935. The Auburn 851 speedster with its tapering tail, pontoon fenders, and four chrome-plated exhaust pipes is regarded by many as one of the most beautiful cars ever built.

Unfortunately, critical acclaim and styling achievement did not add up to a commercial success. The Depression finally caught up with Auburn in the mid-thirties. The last Auburns were built in 1936.[9]

Some Auburn production totals[10]

1924	approx. 2,600	1925	5,600
1926	8,500	1927	14,000
1928	14,700	1929	23,509
1930	11,154		
1931	30,951 ranking 14th in U.S. retail sales		
1932	11,646	1933	5,038
1934	5,536	1935	5,163
1936	1,848		

New styling, illustrated by this 1926 sedan pictured below, allowed E.L. Cord to turn the Auburn company around for a significant sales increase.
ACDM

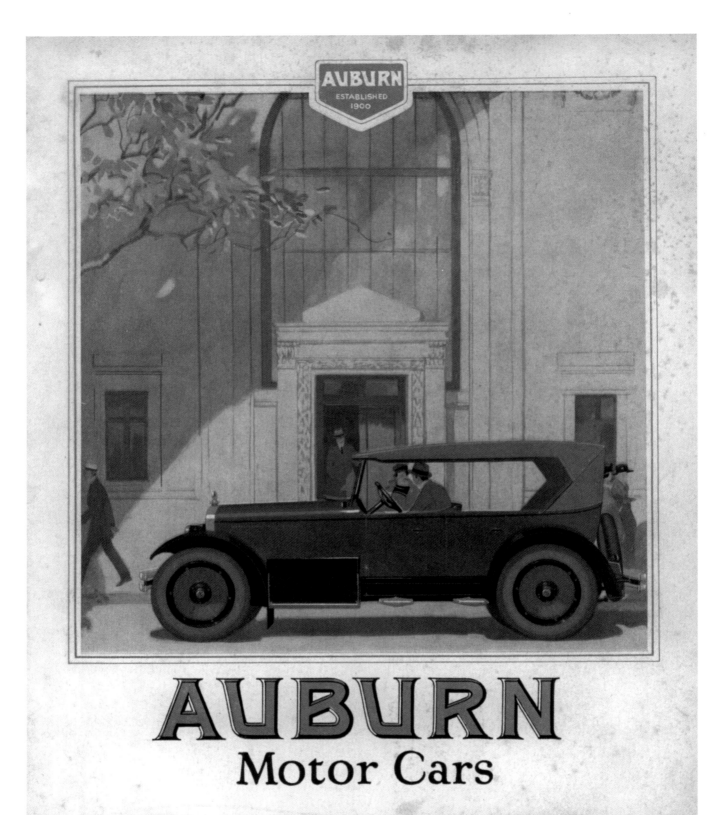

An early sales brochure illustrates Auburn's models as good, solid cars. By 1925, the line got an updated, flashier look.
TAC

The Cole Motor Car Company developed this ad on the Aero-Eight in 1921.
TAC

Additional specifications for selected models

The first Auburn automobile featured a one-cylinder, 6 h.p. engine, solid tires, and tiller steering, and sold for $800.

The entire aluminum body for the Auburn Cabin Speedster was 58 inches from the ground to its highest point. The two-passenger speedster had a 120-inch wheelbase with a 125 h.p. Lycoming Straight Eight engine. The bodylines tapered from front to the widest point and then tapered to the pointed tail. The entire car with gas, oil, and water weighed only 3,000 pounds.

The Lycoming 8-98's featured the first "X" braced center frame offered on a rear drive automobile.

Endnotes

1. Smith, John Martin, *"A History of DeKalb County Indiana 1837-1987,"* 1987, p 1007.
2. Smith, p 1021.
3. Smith, p 1023.
4. Smith, p 1023.
5. Betts, Charles L., *The Auburn Straight-eight,* Leatherhead, Surrey, England Profile Publications Ltd.," 1966, p 3.
6. Betts, p 5 - 8.
7. Two-Place Cabin Speedster, Auburn, IN, Auburn Automobile Co., © 1929.
8. Kowalke, Ron, Standard Catalog of Independents: *The Struggle to Survive Among Giants,* Iola, WI, Krause Publications," 1999, p 14.
9. Smith, p 1025.
10. Provided by the late Henry Blommel, automotive historian of Connersville, IN.

Cole, 1909-1925

The Cole Motor Car Company is one example of an automobile manufacturer that evolved from Indiana's carriage industry. By the end of the company's drive through history, it contributed several innovations to the automotive industry.

Cole's story starts with founder Joseph Jarrett Cole, who started working in the carriage business in about 1888. He served as a salesman and corporate executive for carriage makers Parry Manufacturing Company of Indianapolis and the Moon Brothers Carriage Company of St. Louis for about 16 years.[1]

In November 1904, Cole purchased a one-half interest for $25,000 in the Gates-Osborne Carriage Company of Indianapolis. He became president and changed the name to The Cole Carriage Company on December 4, 1905. The company was known for its full line of vehicles.[2]

Cole began to think seriously about building an automobile in early 1908 and secured the permission of the other board members to build a model for the company to manufacture. At about the same time, the company employed Charles S. Crawford, a graduate engineer from Washington University, to assist Cole in developing the automobile. The first Cole Solid Tire Automobile was ready for the board's inspection on October 9, 1908.[3]

The car was designed for the road conditions of the day. It was a modern high-wheeler with solid tires. During the next seven months, the company built 170 solid-tire cars retailing from $725 to $775.[4]

A second model was completed and shown to the directors on June 1, 1909. As a result of their favorable impression of this second car, board members voted to incorporate as The Cole Motor Car Company on June 22, 1909. They rented facilities for the company at 750 East Washington Street in Indianapolis.[5]

This conventional second model was known as the Cole Model 30. The company sold 112 units of the Model 30 by the end of 1909. In 1910, an additional 783 were sold and another 1,316 in 1911.[6]

During these years, Cole was also involved in the racing circuit. By 1910, Cole's two-passenger Flyer model soon lived up to its name with

The Cole Aero-Eight for 1920 was sold in nine different models. LDC

"Wild Bill" Endicott behind the wheel. By year's end, the Flyer captured the Massapequa Trophy in the Vanderbilt Cup Race, as well as making impressive showings in numerous other contests, including a 24-hour marathon at Brighton Beach.[7]

In 1911, the Cole Limousine, the company's first closed-car version, was introduced. The board also reviewed plans for the new 1912 Cole Model 40 in November 1911. This model included the latest innovations of the day—a Leonard Electric lighting

The 1921 Cole was sold under the slogan "There's a Touch of Tomorrow In All That Cole Does Today."
LDC

system, a Prest-O-Lite self-starter, a Bosch dual ignition, a Schebler carburetor, and Firestone pneumatic tires with demountable rims.[8]

At about the same time, Cole recognized the need for manufacturing space. The company constructed a four-story, reinforced concrete plant in 1911 covering 66,000 sq. ft. of space on the southwest corner of Market and Davidson Streets in Indianapolis. As demand increased, Cole decided to expand in 1913 and then again in 1919. The buildings remain today, although they were remodeled in 1997 to accommodate the Indianapolis/Marion County Jail Annex. All identification of the Cole Motor Car Company was removed from the buildings for the renovation.

One of the first models to be produced in Cole's new manufacturing space was The Colonial Coupe, a closed car that sold for $2,500 in 1912. During that year, the company also built the

Speedster for "the man who wants to get there first." The company tested every Speedster at the Indianapolis Motor Speedway and guaranteed that the car would reach 70 m.p.h.[9]

All of Cole's models were assembled cars. Parts included:

- the engine, clutch, and transmission from General Motors' Northway Division, which also built Cadillac's version,
- a Stromberg carburetor,
  - a Stewart speedometer and motor-driven tire pump,
  - Timken axle and bearings,
  - Firestone tires with demountable rims.

J. J. Cole believed that a supplier who specialized in making only one or a few parts could do a better job than a major manufacturer trying to be a jack-of-all-trades in making all components. He reflected his belief by adopting the phrase "The Standardized Car" for his product, thus indicating that Cole used components that were "the standard for quality in the industry."[10] He ran a six page ad in the July 26, 1913 issue of the *Saturday Evening Post*, which was the largest automobile ad ever purchased to that date.

That philosophy was still evident in 1913 when Cole introduced five 68 h.p., six-cylinder models. The company also continued manufacturing four four-cylinder models. Other major improvements for 1913 included shifting the driver's seat from the right to the left side of the car and the

NOTE OF INTEREST

Joseph J. Cole was so excited about the prospect of driving the first car of his design that he forgot to include one important accessory—the brakes.

He spent most of the afternoon on his initial test run driving around and around Monument Circle in downtown Indianapolis until the car ran out of gas, providing the necessary means to stop the car.

His company sold his first car—with brakes—in 1909.

adoption of the Delco starting, lighting, and ignition system.

Cole's production total of 3,547 cars for 1913 was an increase of 78 percent compared with 1912. The trend toward the low-priced, mass-produced automobile, however, was also starting to appear. The Cole Motor Car Company, however, was upgrading its cars, building them bigger and better—and more expensive. They ranged from a two-passenger roadster at $1,685 to a limousine at $4,250.[11]

With the introduction of the Cole Eight model in January 1915, the company became the second manufacturer after Cadillac to offer a V-8 engine. Cole also made the Berline Limousine, a large model that seated six in the spacious body. The early part of 1916 marked the shift to total eight-cylinder engine production. The year's total was 4,445 cars.

J. J. Cole and the board explored ways to reduce the cost of manufacturing. They were aware that lowering the cost in significant amounts could be accomplished only through large-scale production. In late 1916, Cole briefly considered a merger with 10 Indiana-based companies, including the Muncie-based Inter-State Motor Company and Warner Gear Company. In 1917, he turned down a second offer made by William C. Durant to become a General Motors subsidiary. Instead, Cole continued producing a high-end standardized automobile.[12]

The year 1917 saw the introduction of the unique Cole Toursedan, designed to give the motorist a closed car in the winter and an open touring car in the summer. The Toursedan had a permanent top and could be transformed to a touring car by storing all of the windows and the upper sections of the door frames in provided compartments. It was a seven-passenger automobile with two comfortable auxiliary folding seats—all for $2,495. The body was built by Springfield in Massachusetts.[13]

The following year's model, the all new Cole Aero-Eight, was displayed at the New York Auto Show. The body had low beveled panels, high cowl, massive fenders, and keen, sharp lines.

Cole manufactured the 1918 Aero-Eight with a Willoughby body. LDC

Due to the inflationary effect of World War I, by the end of 1918, prices for Cole cars ranged from $2,595 for an open model to $4,095 for a closed model. The 6,255 cars produced in 1919 marked a high point for the company and was very near the actual capacity of the plant. Cole was ranked second only to Cadillac among America's high-priced automakers.[14]

Following the new peak of 1919, Cole contracted for the necessary parts to produce a total of 15,000 cars for the year 1920. After reaching a production peak in March, the prices of commodities decreased. As a result, business activity fell off.

At first, the decline was very gradual, but it gained momentum as the 1920 season progressed. The market for high-priced automobiles suffered severely. By the end of 1920, the market had literally fallen out from under the Cole Aero-Eight. During 1920, Cole produced 5,838 automobiles—85 percent of these in the first six months of the year. The Cole factory was flooded with extra component parts.[15]

After enjoying many years of prosperity, Cole began losing money in the wake of the postwar recession. The recession brought a decline in all business activity as well as a serious curtailment of automobile sales. The success of the low-priced, mass-produced cars cut the volume of Cole cars approximately 50 percent. Price reductions for Cole in 1921 ranged from 23 to 33 percent. Production in 1921 totaled 1,722 automobiles, a decline of 70 percent compared with the preceding year.[16]

In 1922, Cole had all aluminum bodies on three of the five closed models. Cole added another first to its credit in September 1923 by introducing balloon tires as standard equipment on the Volante model. The Firestone Balloon Tire operated at 25 p.s.i. versus the 70 p.s.i. in a standard tire.[17]

The 1924 Master Models offered a newly designed multiple disc, self-adjusting clutch. By 1924 Cole finally used all the components purchased for the 1920 models. Cole auto production for the years 1922, 1923, and 1924 were 1,745, 1,522, and 632 respectively. Production ceased completely in October 1924. In January 1925, while his company was still solvent, J.J. Cole chose to liquidate rather than jeopardize the remaining assets of the corporation.

Cole made a total of 40,717 automobiles. Each model was a quality product, with the best material, craftsmanship and design available for the time.[18]

Cole "Firsts"

1909   Each and every automobile tested on the road and tuned-up under actual driving conditions.

1910   Offers Firestone demountable rims as standard equipment.

1911   Includes four doors as standard equipment .

1912   Adopts the Prest-O-Lite self-starter.

1913   Becomes known as "The Standardized Car."

1915   Introduces the first V-8 engine with detachable cylinder heads.

1923   Uses balloon tires as standard equipment on the Volante model.

1924   Has the first balloon-tire equipped car to pace the Indianapolis 500 Mile Race.

Additional specifications for selected models

The Cole Solid Tire Automobile had a 14 h.p., air-cooled, flat twin engine.

The Cole Model 30 used a 30 h.p., four-cylinder engine.

The Cole Model 40 had a 40 h.p. engine on a 122-inch wheelbase chassis.

The Cole Aero-Eight's V-8 engine was rated at 80 h.p. with counterbalanced crankshaft and aluminum-alloy pistons.

Endnotes

1. Delancy, Howard R., *History of the Cole Motor Car Company,* Bloomington, IN, D.B.A. dissertation, Indiana University, © 1954, p 18-28.
2. Delancy, p 30.
3. Delancy, p 35.
4. Delancy, p 36.
5. Delancy, p 82.
6. Delancy, p 117.
7. Delancy, p 86-91.
8. Delancy, p 118-123.
9. Delancy, p 124.
10. Delancy, p 132-137.
11. Delancy, p 142-145.
12. Delancy, p 156-174.
13. Delancy, p 186.
14. Delancy, p 181-182.
15. Delancy, p 232-235.
16. Delancy, p 243.
17. Delancy, p 255-256.
18. Delancy, p 259-265.

Cord, 1929-1932, 1936-1937

Renowned architect Frank Lloyd Wright once described the first Cord model as "the best design from my 'streamline' standpoint ever put on the market." Made in Connersville, the Cord L-29, with its long, sweeping fenders, did indeed set a new course in automotive design.

The Cord L-29 was introduced in August 1929 as a 1930 model. It was the first production automobile with front-wheel drive and was made to fill the gap between the low-priced Auburn and the top-of-the-mark Duesenberg in the Cord Corporation line of cars. The Cord sedan and brougham were priced at $3,095 each, and the cabriolet and phaeton were $3,295.

The L-29 also was the first among American automobiles with the "X" braced frame, designed by Herbert C. Snow. Project engineer Cornelius W. Van Ranst designed the new front-wheel drive system around the units in the successful Indianapolis 500 racecars. Harry Miller and Indianapolis driver Leon Duray served as consultants on the project. Alan H. Leamy was the chief stylist.[1]

Cord claimed advantages in safety, easy handling, comfort, and durability. Plus, front-wheel drive provided a lower body silhouette, allowing a distinctive and pleasing front end appearance that appealed to coachbuilders.

The L-29 was available in four models: a convertible Cabriolet with rumble seat, four-door convertible Phaeton Sedan, five-passenger Sedan, and the five-passenger Brougham. All four models sported a stylish cadet-type visor. The Cabriolet and the Phaeton Sedan stood only 58 inches high, some 12 inches lower than their competitors. They are known for their long, low, racy lines. Their narrow corner posts provided a clear field of vision.[2] The V-shaped radiator grille would inspire a throng of imitators, most notably the 1931 Chrysler Imperial.

The Cord Model 810 Westchester Sedan, pictured above, offered many innovations.
ACDM

The L-29 regularly won prizes in the European Concours d'Elegance, which was quite an accomplishment for an American manufacturer. A Cord L-29 Cabriolet was also the pace car for the 1930 Indianapolis 500 mile race.

Unfortunately, the Cord L-29, which was the first automobile to bear Errett Lobban Cord's name, was introduced only two months before the stock market crash in October 1929. Although praised for its quality, sales didn't reflect its popularity. The L-29 was built from 1929-1931 with only 5,010 units produced. The last cars were 1932 models.

After a lapse of four years, the Cord name was revived for 1936. Gordon M. Buehrig's original work on the Cord Model 810 began as a "baby Duesenberg" in 1933. By December 1934, the design of the new front-wheel-drive model was essentially complete and then shelved. When the project was revived in July 1935, there was less than four months in which to build and test a prototype, tool up, and get the cars into production for the New York Auto Show on November 2, 1935.[3] The company made the deadline, but without the transmissions in place. Plus, the phaetons were without any tops. The missing parts didn't matter. The Cord 810 stopped the show. People had to stand on surrounding cars just to get a glimpse of Cord's exciting new design. Cord received over 7,600 requests for more information on the 810. Unfortunately, due to unanticipated production start-up problems, almost six months would pass before any deliveries were made.

The Cord Model 810 was available in four models: the five-passenger Westchester Sedan, four-passenger Beverly Sedan, five-passenger Convertible Phaeton Sedan, and the Convertible Coupe with rumble seat.

The new catalog boasted, "The New Cord demonstrates that it is possible to build a radically different kind of motor car which is, nevertheless, completely in accord with the very highest standards of beauty and good taste. We predict that the New Cord will exert a pronounced influence upon the future offerings of the entire automotive industry." The company extolled further, "You will be constantly amazed that a car so low in design should be so spacious and provide so much head and leg room."[4]

The first Cord 810 rolled off the assembly line in Connersville on February 15, 1936. Innovations on the Cord 810 included disappearing headlights, concealed door hinges, rheostat-controlled instrument lights, variable speed windshield wipers, Bendix Electric Hand (steering column mounted-electric gear pre-selection unit), and factory installed radio. The model was the first automobile in the United States to adopt unit body construction in its full sense. (Chrysler Airflow and Lincoln Zepher used modified forms.)

In November 1936, the company introduced the Cord 812 for the 1937 model year. An example of the model's claim-to-fame was its use as the official chief observer's car for the 1937 Indianapolis 500 mile race.

The year, however, witnessed a soft auto market, and Cord production fell to around 1,100 units. In 1937, only the wealthy few could afford the $2,500 to $3,500 needed to buy this exceptional automobile. Some of the internationally known celebrities purchasing Cord automobiles were the movie stars Sonja Heine and Tom Mix. In fact, actress Jean Harlow ordered a Cord with paint and upholstery to match her platinum blonde hair.

When production of the Cord automobile was terminated in October 1937, fewer than 3,000 Model 810/812 units had been produced. The automotive operations of Cord Corporation died when E.L. Cord shifted his focus to other interests.

In their day, these Cords stirred the imagination of the motoring public. Their clean simplicity of line, exciting innovations, and luxurious appointments won much admiration and many awards. The Cord Model 810/812 is revered by many as one of the most popular classic cars of all time.

Endnotes

1. Borgeson, Griffith, *Errett Lobban Cord: His Empire, His Motor Cars,* Princeton, NJ, Automobile Quarterly Publications," 1984, p 84.

2. 1929 Cord catalog, author's collection.

3. Brown, Arch, *Great Cars of the 20th Century,* Lincolnwood, IL, Publications International Ltd.," 1998.

4. *The New Front Drive Cord,* Auburn, IN, Auburn Automobile Co., © 1936.

Additional specifications on selected models

The L-29 was powered by a 299 c.i.d., 125 h.p., L-head, Lycoming (a Cord-owned company) straight-eight cylinder engine.

The Model 810 convertible stood only 58 inches high. It was powered by a 287 c.i.d., 125 h.p., L-head, Lycoming V-8 engine. The new unit body construction featured the engine immediately behind the differential that was driven from the forward mounted transmission. This arrangement resulted in a weight distribution of 55 percent front and 45 percent rear that enhanced uphill traction. This was all accomplished by a trailing arm independent front suspension with transverse leaf spring.

The 1937 Cord 812 had a 190 h.p. supercharged engine and boasted chrome-plated external exhaust pipes. It was capable of speeds in excess of 100 m.p.h.

NOTE OF INTEREST

The town of Speedway was founded by Carl G. Fisher in 1912 as a "horseless city" to provide housing for workers at his Prest-O-Lite plant and future manufacturers' plants.

Fisher was also instrumental in founding the town's main attraction—the Indianapolis Motor Speedway. The first auto races were in August 1909, with the first Indianapolis 500 on Memorial Day, 1911.

The Cord 810 Phaeton, pictured alongside three sedans, was the Chief Observer car for the 1936 Indianapolis 500 Mile Race. ACDM

Cord Cabriolet

You cannot appraise the Cord with any rear drive automobile in terms of each other.

CORD
FRONT DRIVE

SEDAN $3095 . . BROUGHAM $3095 . . CABRIOLET $3295 . . PHAETON $3295   Prices F. O. B. Auburn, Indiana. *Equipment other than standard, extra*

AUBURN AUTOMOBILE COMPANY . AUBURN, INDIANA

This ad for Cord appeared in publications in 1931.
TAC

Duesenberg, 1920-1937

Whether you spell it "duesy" or "doozy," the meaning is the same. Thanks to Duesenberg, the word has become part of our vocabulary to describe something that is one-of-a-kind or simply the best. By the 1930s Duesenberg had become known as one of the world's finest cars. In fact, no two Duesies were ever identical.

The company came to Indianapolis in 1920 and eventually was incorporated under four names: Duesenberg Automobile and Motors Company, Inc. (1920-1925), Duesenberg Motors Company (1925-1926), Duesenberg Inc. (1926-1929), and Cord Corporation (1929-1937). The complex consisted of a 17-acre site at 1511 West Washington Street that opened for production in July 1921.

Prior to moving here, the Duesenberg brothers—Fred and August—built extremely high-quality and advanced engines and automobiles. The brothers, however, were seldom financially successful. Part of their reason for moving to Indianapolis was to return to their racing roots and be near the Indianapolis Motor Speedway where they had already enjoyed some success. The track could be used for testing their passenger cars as well as the racers.

The first Duesenberg-production car debuted in November 1920. This Model A was a luxurious car, which pioneered the use of straight eight-cylinder engines and four-wheel hydraulic brakes. Pricing on Duesenberg models ranged up to $8,300 for a seven-passenger deluxe limousine. The limo's price made it the second most expensive car built in America at the time. More than 500 Model As were built through 1927. Millspaugh and Irish, a local coachbuilder, built most of the later bodies for the Model A and served as an in-house finishing contractor for bodies from other coachbuilders.

Errett Lobban Cord of Auburn acquired control of the company in 1926. His mission, as he explained to Fred Duesenberg, was to develop the ultimate motorcar that would outclass all American makes.[1]

In 1927, the interim Model X represented a further perfection of the Model A, incorporating chassis changes to make it lower and engine improvements that increased output to 100 h.p. Only a dozen Model Xs left the factory.

The Model J, introduced at the New York Automobile Salon for the 1929 model year, was the most remarkable automobile in America: bigger, faster, more elaborate and more expensive than any other car of its time. The cost of the long, low-built chassis ranged from $8,500 for a Model J to $11,750 for a Model SJ. Details included the

Duesenberg's Model A pioneered the use of straight eight-cylinder engines and four-wheel hydraulic brakes. ACDM

radiator grille, headlamps, hood, fenders, firewall, steering assembly, dashboard with instrument package, and the famous "bow tie" bumpers.

Model J's were very popular with all leading coachbuilders, and the company preferred to sell cars complete with bodies designed and made by approved builders, such as Murphy, Bohman and Schwartz, Judkins, Derham, and LeBaron. The catalogued models cost up to $18,000. A later Model J—known as the Rollston SJ Arlington Torpedo Sedan and built as the 1933/34 Century of Progress show car—was nicknamed "Twenty Grand" for its reported price of $20,000.

Another special J—designed by Herbert Newport—was the one-of-a-kind 1934 Walker La Grande Rigid Coupe built for Eli Lilly pharmaceutical heir J.K. Lilly. This model was nearly $25,000.

Duesenberg's famed in-house designer Gordon M. Buehrig penned the "Twenty Grand" as well as the Brunn torpedo phaeton and the Weymann boattail speedster that would later be the prototype for his 1935 Auburn 851 speedster.

In 1932 a supercharged 320 h.p. version of the Model J, called the SJ, was added. The SJ could reach a maximum speed of 129 m.p.h. with an acceleration figure of 0 to 100 mph in 17 seconds. The SJ was the first stock car to be equipped with a centrifugal type supercharger.[2]

The 1930s saw even greater designs for Duesenberg thanks to E.L. Cord's edict to Fred Duesenberg: "Offer the world an automobile of undisputed rank—in fact, the finest thing on four wheels." The customer started with an engine and chassis that was twice as powerful as anything on the market, to which they added a body custom designed to their individual tastes. The result drew such celebrity buyers as William Randolph Hearst, Elizabeth Arden, Mae West, Gary Cooper and Clark Gable. Chewing-gum magnate Philip Wrigley

owned five Duesenbergs. In Europe, the Kings of Spain and Italy also bought Duesenbergs.

Market positioning played a large part in the Duesenberg aura. The cars were advertised in high-end consumer magazines like *Vanity Fair* with full-page spreads. An example of an ad depicts a woman leisurely talking to her gardener while overlooking a magnificent courtyard. The copy simply stated "She drives a Duesenberg." Instead of focusing on the product, this 1934-1935 advertising series was the first lifestyle campaign in the automotive field.

Customization was also a huge factor in Duesenberg's popularity. The early 1930s catalog displayed 18 models by seven different coach-builders. Yet these were just suggestions to get the process started. A salesman worked with the customer to discover general preferences for body style, color combinations, interior decor, and any other nuances. These selections were forwarded to the Duesenberg body engineer in Indianapolis. The body designer worked with the customer's aesthetics and the body engineer's technical specifications to develop one or more pencil outline sketches. Then these two in-house personnel decided which design best integrated engineering and art to develop a color rendering for customer

Film star Gary Cooper was one of the famous buyers of Duesenberg. He is pictured with a Model J Derham Tourster. ACDM

approval. The moment of truth always came when the customer accepted or rejected the final design. Afterward, scale layout drawings were made of the body and submitted to selected coachbuilders for bids.

Selecting the right coachbuilder was a discriminating task because some builders were specialists in certain styles. The body engineer served as liaison to coordinate preferences of Duesenberg, the customer, and the body builder. Then the body was shipped to Indianapolis for mounting on the chassis, painting, and final trim installation.

Duesenberg's attention to detail was evident throughout the process and went a long way toward achieving the Duesenberg mystique. The Duesenberg Model J existed at a time when the coachbuilding craft was at its peak in the mid-1930s. Yet, Duesenberg and coachbuilding declined and closed out the 1930s era.[3]

The make survived most of the Depression, but died in the collapse of the Cord Corporation in 1937. Model J production totaled 480 before the end, with 36 of the total being Model SJs. One fact is particularly remarkable: over 75 percent of the original Model Js built are still roadworthy some 70 years later. No other American marquee has been so fortunate.

Pete DePaolo drove a Duesenberg race car to victory in the 1925 Indianapolis 500 Mile Race. It was the first Indy car to average over 100 m.p.h. ACDM

Additional specifications for selected models

The Model A featured a 260 c.i.d., single-overhead camshaft engine, which cranked out 88 h.p. on a 134-inch wheelbase.

The Model Js 420 c.i.d., eight-cylinder engine, made by Lycoming (a Cord Corporation firm), had dual overhead camshafts operating four valves per hemispherically shaped combustion chamber. This version developed 265 h.p. at 4,250 r.p.m. The engine had well over twice the horsepower of its nearest rival, the Chrysler Imperial L-80 Six at 110 h.p. The rigid Model J chassis was equally impressive as the engine with 7/32-inch thick frame channels that were 8.5 inches at the center. Six cross members braced the ladder-type frame. Although the complete car weighed more than 4,980 pounds, it was claimed to be capable of 116 m.p.h. in top gear and 89 m.p.h. in second.

A Glance at Duesenberg's Racing History

One of Duesenberg's most famous racers appeared in 1920—a 183 c.i.d., eight-cylinder engine with single overhead camshaft and three valves per cylinder. It won the 1921 French Grand Prix. In the 1920s, Duesenberg's racing cars were serious contenders at Indianapolis Motor Speedway. Victory came in 1924 along with the adoption of a centrifugal supercharger. Duesenberg enjoyed repeat victories in 1925 and 1927. Yet, Duesenberg racing was not officially supported by the auto production branch. The racing operation was a separate entity headed by August Duesenberg. By 1932 Duesenberg racing was in a serious decline primarily because of rule changes and new track surfaces. The last Duesenberg car for serious contention at the Indy 500 was entered in 1934.

This Duesenberg Model SJ, pictured above, was nicknamed the "Twenty Grand." Built for the 1933/34 Century of Progress in Chicago, Illinois, the car was given the label because of its reported $20,000 price tag. The car was known for the understated elegance of the interior décor.
ACDM

Duesenberg's Crown Jewel
The Model J Series

Production of the Model J series from 1929 to 1937 encouraged a new era in American coachbuilding. The series provided a kind of inspiration for coachbuilders to produce their best work.

Duesenberg executives decided to farm out the body work to other companies because they believed that one company could not duplicate the innovation and craftsmanship of many specialists. So, Duesenberg provided the company's unique personality to the chassis—the radiator shell, the fenders, and lights. Coachbuilders then built around the chassis, anything from a speedster to a town car.

The Walter M. Murphy Company of Pasadena, California, made more Model J bodies than any other coachbuilder. In total, about 175 body styles were built by 14 different companies.

Today the Model J is one of the most valued of classic cars. Collectors probably still believe in the description of a Model J that Harold Blanchard provided in an 1928 Motor article: "The Model J possesses the same fine materials, fine workmanship, strength and precise construction commonplace in racing cars. It has the power, acceleration and speed of a racing car together with the size, comfort, flexibility and durability which must be prime features of any auto passenger car."[4]

Endnotes

1. Steinwedel, Louis William, *The Duesenberg: The Story of America's Premier Car,* Philadelphia, PA, Chilton Book Company, " 1970, p 17 - 33.

2. Steinwedel, p 34 - 70.

3. Steinwedel, p 71 - 120.

4. Holls, David, "The Crowning Touch," Automobile Quarterly, Volume 30, Number 4, p 58—69.

The Duesenberg Automobile & Motors Company, Inc.
INDIANAPOLIS

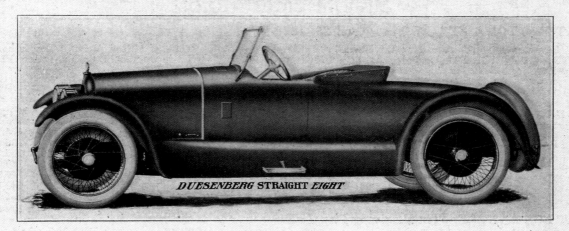

DUESENBERG STRAIGHT *EIGHT*

The
Duesenberg Straight Eight
An Opportunity for Investment

STOCK in The Duesenberg Automobile & Motors Company, Inc., offers an attractive investment feature which is commanding the attention of investors in every section of the country.

The Duesenberg Automobile & Motors Company is now erecting a large plant for the manufacture of Duesenberg Straight Eight Automobiles; the celebrated car developed by Fred S. Duesenberg, which has achieved a remarkable series of records in American motor competition. The plant is being erected in Indianapolis, Ind., on one of the best factory sites in that city.

The stock is an authorized issue of $5,000,000 par value cumulative preferred, and is selling in heavy volume, among both small and large investors. In Indianapolis, the home city of the corporation, the stock is enjoying a particularly active sale.

DUESENBERG STRAIGHT *EIGHT CHASSIS*

Duesenberg provided a brochure on the company for potential investors in early 1920.
TAC

Duesenberg was the first in the automobile field to advertise the lifestyle associated with its vehicle instead of focusing on the product. These ads are typical of those published in 1934 and 1935 in *Vanity Fair* and other publications that targeted the well-to-do consumer.
HAS&SM

Haynes,
1894-1925

Indiana's documented automotive history began with the Sintz engine that Elwood Haynes discovered at the 1893 Chicago World's Fair. Haynes ordered a one-horsepower engine for experimentation that fall. He mounted the engine on sawhorses in his kitchen and installed gasoline and battery connections. After much cranking the engine started. The machine "ran with such speed and vibration that it pulled itself from its attachments to the floor. Luckily, however, one of the battery wires was wound around the motor shaft and this disconnected the current."[1]

His wife suggested that he find another location for his experiments. Shortly afterwards, Haynes made arrangements with Elmer Apperson to work in the privacy of Apperson's Riverside Machine Works in Kokomo. Moreover, the intense vibration of the engine prompted Haynes to design and build a much heavier carriage frame than he had planned originally.

Haynes needed to determine the amount of rolling resistance on an ordinary road and calculate other engineering parameters. He conducted his experiments with a bicycle rider towed behind a light buckboard by a cord. The resistance and other engineering measurements were recorded with a spring scale. This experiment indicated how much power was necessary for every 100 pounds on a vehicle equipped with ball bearings and pneumatic tires. With this information, he then calculated the gearing for the Sintz engine. The total weight of the completed machine was about 820 pounds.

Indiana's first gasoline-powered auto was ready for testing.

Midway through the afternoon of July 4, 1894, three men silently rolled the strange-looking carriage out into Main Street in front of the Riverside Machine Shop. A crowd immediately gathered. Out of concern for public safety, Haynes decided to test the machine away from the crowd. He arranged for a team of horses to pull the vehicle out into the country. On the outskirts of Kokomo along Pumpkinvine Pike, they stopped, unhitched the horse team, and started the gasoline engine. Haynes and two passengers boarded the machine, and he eased it into gear. Off they went into the countryside traveling at a speed of seven miles an hour and drove about one and one-half miles further into the country. He then turned the auto around, and it ran the four miles into town without making a single stop. Haynes called his "little machine" the Pioneer.

"I remember as the little machine made its way along the streets we were met by a bevy of girls mounted on wheels," Haynes noted. "I shall never forget the expression on their faces as they wheeled aside, separating like a flock of swans and gazing wonder-eyed at the uncouth and utterly unexpected little machine."

According to author Ralph Gray, "Haynes had conceived the idea, drawn up the plans, purchased the engine, worked out the engineering problems—using the higher mathematics he had acquired so laboriously at Worcester Polytechnic Institute in Massachusetts—and financed the entire project. The Apperson brothers and their workmen built the car. The Appersons made modifications and offered various suggestions as the work progressed. But primary credit is usually attributed to Haynes."[2]

While there remains some question about who actually built the first car in America, only the Haynes was ever advertised as "America's First Car." This claim was based on the grounds that the 1893 Duryea was only a motorized buggy and the Haynes Pioneer was built from the ground up as a self-propelled vehicle.

NOTE OF INTEREST

Charles H. Black of Indianapolis was one of the first Americans to actually drive an automobile, a German-made Benz in 1891. That historic journey in Indianapolis also resulted in another automotive first, according to an account related by Black's mechanic. During this six-block drive, Black crashed into a surrey when the horses became frightened, thus causing the first automobile accident. At the next turn, the car drove into the Occidental Hotel shop window, creating the second automobile accident. The third happened when the auto destroyed another shop window a few feet away.

Acting on the advice of the police, Black and his passengers drove back to his carriage factory, ending one of the first automobile journeys in America.

HaynеS

AMERICA'S FIRST CAR

Model 28   Four-Cylinder   Roadster

Haynes advertised his company as having manufactured
"America's First Car."
NAHC

In 1895, Haynes and the Apperson brothers formed an informal partnership and set about building a new car especially for the *Times-Herald* race in Chicago, the first automobile race in America. This second car, Pioneer II, included a new horizontally opposed, two-cylinder, four h.p. engine and pneumatic tires. The Apperson brothers built the engine using an aluminum alloy developed by Haynes as a sturdy, lightweight substitute for cast iron. Haynes' alloy is the first recorded use of aluminum in an automobile engine. The Pioneer II auto was unable to start the *Times-Herald* race because it was damaged in an accident while proceeding to the starting line on race day morning. The entry, however, received a $150 prize for its meritorious design feature—the reduction of vibration by balancing the engine.[3]

The Haynes-Apperson Company was incorporated in 1898 and set out to dramatically increase its production. In 1900, the company produced almost 200 automobiles, when the total United States production amounted to nearly 4,200 units.[4] The 1901 Haynes-Apperson line included a two-passenger Run-About and four and six passenger "carriages." A Haynes-Apperson won the New York-to-Buffalo Pan-American Exposition run late in 1901.

Elmer Apperson resigned from the Haynes-Apperson Company in November 1901. Between 1901 and 1905, Haynes directed his full attention to the company.

Horseless Age reported on a few changes on the Haynes in 1903. Not only had a left-hand steering wheel replaced the tiller, but also the entire steering column could be tilted forward out of the way of driver or passenger upon entering or leaving the vehicle.[5] Today we might refer to this feature as the tilt steering wheel. In 1904, the two-cylinder engine was moved from under the seat to under a hood. Haynes produced two- and four-cylinder automobiles in 1905. By 1906 four-cylinder cars were the company's sole product.

In 1904 and 1905, Haynes conducted metallurgical experiments upon alloys of nickel and cobalt with chromium. At the same time, he searched for a suitable material for spark mechanisms. For this work, he received the patent for Stellite, one of his most significant metallurgical discoveries, in 1907.[6] Stellite is still used today in aerospace and other highly corrosive environments.

The firm was reorganized in 1905 with a new corporate name, Haynes Automobile Company. Haynes relinquished direct managerial control to V.E. Minich and devoted more time to metallurgical research.[7]

Near the end of 1908, Kokomo's *Morning Dispatch* reported that 600 Haynes employees were capable of producing 400 cars a year. Actual production for 1908 and 1909 amounted to approximately 350 cars each year. The "oldest automobile factory in the United States" manufactured two grades of automobiles—the five-passenger, 30 h.p. runabout selling for $2,500 and the seven-passenger, 50 h.p. touring car priced at $5,500. In 1911, Haynes became the first company to equip an open car with a top, a windshield, head lamps, and a speedometer as standard equipment.[8]

Elwood Haynes took one of these cars for the 1913 Indiana Automobile Manufacturers Association tour from Indianapolis to San Francisco and to Los Angeles, California.

During that year, a six-cylinder engine joined the Haynes line. The four-cylinder engines were dropped in 1914. The 1914 Haynes was one of the first to offer the Vulcan Electric Gear Shift as standard equipment.[9] The Haynes V-12 engine was in the line-up from 1916-1922. The Haynes six-cylinder soldiered on to the end of production.

By early 1915, the Haynes factory was working three shifts to keep up with demand. This kind of activity demanded upgraded facilities. A new four-story machine shop, three-story paint shop, test barn, and administrative building relieved the strain on assembly operations.[10]

Haynes automobile production was dramatically impacted by the U.S. entry into World War I in April 1917. Haynes produced 4,000 truck motors for the war effort. By September 1920, the company completed a new four-story assembly building, 500 feet by 150 feet, complete with a moving assembly line in the 1100 block of South Home Avenue.[11] The building stands today. At one point the assembly line reached a maximum production rate of 60 cars a day. The company also began to build its own automobile bodies in 1920, and in 1921 boasted that its cars were at least "90 percent Kokomo-made."[12]

On July 4, 1922, a commemorative plaque and granite monument along Pumpkinvine Pike—the route of Haynes first test drive—were dedicated in honor of the 28th anniversary of Elwood Haynes' notable invention of "America's First Car."[13] But the Haynes had already slipped into a gradual decline, producing only 1,500 units in 1924. Manufacturing at the Haynes plants ceased on September 2, 1924.[14] Elwood Haynes passed away in April 1925, a couple of months after the assets from the company bearing his name were sold at a receiver's sale.

Endnotes

1. Haynes, Elwood, *The Complete Motorist,* Kokomo, IN, The Haynes Automobile Company, © 1913, p 9.
2. Gray, Ralph D., *Alloys and Automobiles: The Life of Elwood Haynes,* Indianapolis, IN, Indiana Historical Society, © 1979, p 72.
3. Gray, p 80.
4. Gray, p 84.
5. Gray, p 106.
6. Haynes, p 14.
7. Gray, p 111.
8. Gray, p 113.
9. Haynes, p 15.
10. Gray, p 179.
11. Gray, p 183.
12. Gray, p 190.
13. *In Honor of Elwood Haynes,* Kokomo, IN, Indiana Historical Commission, 4 July 1922.
14. Gray, p 169.

The New, 1923 Haynes 55 Sport Sedan, 5 Passengers

ANNOUNCING THE
1923 HAYNES
FOUR SPORT MODELS

THE vogue of the sport-model car is established. Haynes has been responding to it, and now meets it completely with four new models of this type of car for 1923.

They are cars for those who love the thoroughbred—who want strength with beauty and power with comfort.

THERE ARE NO EXTRAS TO BUY. Each of these cars is fully equipped. The newest accessories are standard equipment. Front and rear bumpers, a spacious trunk, six disc wheels with six 32 x 4½ cord tires, sun and vision visor, polished protection bars at the rear of the body, handsome individual steps—everything that you naturally expect as an essential feature of a sport car. The open models are equipped with new design windshield wings and are trimmed in beautiful Spanish leather. All of the new 1923 Haynes 55 sport models have a 121-inch wheel base and are finished in a pleasing shade of deep maroon.

Graceful in design, they have the outstanding attractiveness of real individuality. Beneath their attractiveness is the famous Haynes-built six-cylinder motor and the sturdy mechanical perfection which characterizes the Haynes. The demand will be great without a doubt. We urge that you make your own reservation at once with your Haynes dealer.

THE HAYNES AUTOMOBILE COMPANY, *Kokomo, Indiana*
EXPORT OFFICE: 1715 Broadway, New York City, U. S. A.

Copyright 1922, by The Haynes Automobile Company

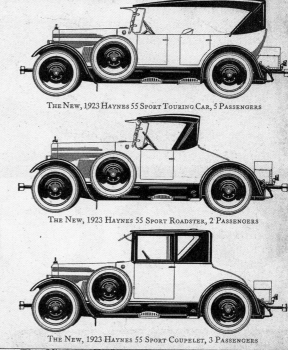

The New, 1923 Haynes 55 Sport Touring Car, 5 Passengers

The New, 1923 Haynes 55 Sport Roadster, 2 Passengers

The New, 1923 Haynes 55 Sport Coupelet, 3 Passengers

By the time this ad appeared in 1923, The Haynes Automobile Company was in a decline.
TAC

54

Haynes "Firsts"

- Automotive wire wheels fabricated by Elmer Apperson in 1894

- Recorded use of aluminum in an automobile engine in the 1895 Pioneer II

- Balanced horizontally opposed, two-cylinder engine in the Pioneer II, *Haynes-Apperson* catalog 1903

- 1,000-mile automobile trip in the United States in July, 1899. Kokomo; Portland, IN; Cleveland, OH; Buffalo, NY; and Brooklyn, NY, totaling 1,050 miles

- Installation of the tilting steering column in 1903

- An open car with a top, a windshield, head lamps, and a speedometer as standard equipment in 1911

- Vulcan Electric Gear Shift as standard equipment in the 1914 Haynes

Famed race car driver Ray Harroun is at the wheel of a 1910 Marmon.
NAHC

Marmon, 1902-1933

Prior to building a prototype automobile in 1902, the Nordyke & Marmon Company of Indianapolis had established its reputation as an outstanding builder of flour milling machinery. Since the firm's founding in 1851, it was known for its engineering prowess. It was a natural progression that the company's first automobile should spring from the fertile mind of Howard Carpenter Marmon, a practicing engineer. At an early age he exhibited an amazing mechanical ability and a curiosity concerning all sorts of machinery.[1]

Howard C. Marmon's first prototype car for Nordyke & Marmon was credited with development of the first side-entrance rear compartment with rear-hinged doors. Also significant was the forward placement of the engine under a hood. The water-cooled, two-cylinder V-2 engine had an aluminum crankcase. The body construction was cast aluminum, with the rear compartment being a one-piece casting, including an integral bustle trunk.[2]

A full field test of another seven prototypes in consumer hands preceded the actual public launch of the Marmon automobile. On December 24, 1904,

Horseless Age announced that Marmon would enter the automotive field for the 1905 season with a very unusual motor car. The Marmon offered two patented innovations: a "three-point-suspension" that incorporated a main frame and a propulsion frame, and an overhead valve, air-cooled, four-cylinder 90 degree V configuration engine with pressure lubrication.[3] The engine featured a gear-type oil pump, drilled crankshaft and connecting rod passages, a pressure gauge on the instrument panel, and a sump from which oil was recirculated through the engine bearings. This use of full-pressure lubrication was the earliest automotive application of a system that has long since become universal to internal combustion piston engine design.[4] Its cast-aluminum body construction avoided the cracked surfaces and chipped paint that traditional coachbuilders had with wood body construction. The model B touring car was priced at $2,500.[5]

At this time, most of the large manufacturers were still providing specifications of major components to be built by other firms. Fully integrated manufacturing would come in a few years.

Yet, Marmon was ahead of its time. The company could be classified as one of the first fully integrated auto manufacturers in America. The 1906 catalog notes, "We manufacture the Marmon Car, all of it from the ground up, excepting such items as the wheels, tires, lamps, ignition apparatus, etc. We make the pressed-steel frames, fenders, hoods, the axles, driving mechanism, transmissions, and other numerous parts. We make the aluminum castings for bodies and machinery parts; brass, bronze, and iron castings; do all machine work and gear cutting except cutting the bevel gears. We make our air cooled motor entirely, and in this we believe we have attained greater perfection than reached in any other air cooled motor. We build, trim, and finish the bodies, assemble and finish the cars complete ready to use."[6]

Highlights of the next three years included:

- 1906—A Marmon Model D won the Glidden Tour with a perfect score. Next year's model, the short-lived Marmon Eight Cylinder, was demonstrated to the public curbside at the Grand Central Palace Auto Show in New York in December.

- 1907—The Model F featured an exclusive all-aluminum body.

- 1908—Marmon's first closed model, the Model G Landaulet, and the Model H water-cooled Marmon were introduced.[7]

One of the company's historically interesting cars, the Model 32, arrived in 1909. "The new '32' is the result of an effort to produce a car of highest grade and most approved design which should be moderate in weight, power, and in initial and upkeep cost," according to a press release in 1909.[8] With this model, Marmon made the shift to water-cooled production. It also used torque tube drive with a rear transaxle that was currently in vogue at the time. When introduced, the "32" was offered in three open body styles on a 112-inch wheelbase. The five-passenger touring car, four-passenger Suburban and a two-passenger roadster were priced at $2,400. Also available on order were a limousine at $3,400, a landaulet at $3,500, and a coupe at $3,000.[9]

A Marmon Model D, similar to the one pictured below, won the Glidden Tour with a perfect score in 1906. TMH

MARMON SIXTEEN

The Marmon Sixteen is the modern automobile. Its beauty of line and appointment is the beauty of the simplicity and efficiency of today. Its 200-horsepower engine is an achievement of great importance. Both in action and appearance the Marmon Sixteen redefines the motor car in terms of the present. Wheelbase, 145 inches.

Prices under $5000. Marmon Motor Car Company, Indianapolis, Ind.

The ad above illustrates the 1931 Marmon Sixteen, one of the company's best models. Walter Teague's design for the Sixteen was considered a bold advance.
TAC

A six-cylinder racing variation of the "32" won the first Indianapolis 500 Mile Race in 1911. Ray Harroun drove the Marmon Wasp into Victory Lane. The 145-inch wheelbase, six-cylinder Model 48 was marketed in response to the public appetite for a Marmon Six performance automobile.

In 1912, Marmons sported a new Baby Wasp radiator ornament in commemoration of the Indianapolis victory. This miniature reproduction of the Marmon Wasp was cast in one piece, had a four-inch wheelbase and showed the clean lines and low-seats of the original.[10] In 1914, models ranged from a Model 32 two-passenger roadster at $2,900 to Model 48 seven-passenger berline limousine at $6,450.

The 1915 Marmon Model 41 was the first car with the full Bosch electric system. The magneto, generator, starter, and all switches, wiring harnesses, lamps and bulbs were procured from a single source.[11] This 12-volt system had many advantages over the common six volt circuits.

The 1916 introduction of the Model 34 marked the first example of styling the car as a complete entity versus the previous practice of component styling. All exterior surfaces were free of irregularities and sharp edges. The entire body and radiator shell were aluminum, as was the

An illustration of Marmon's 1922 Model 34 four-passenger Speedster is shown above.
TMH

six-cylinder engine cylinder block and most other engine components, including the push rods.[12] In the summer of 1916, a Model 34 completed a cross-country trip under AAA surveillance in five days. This beat the record set by Cannonball Baker in a V-8 Cadillac by 41 hours. The feat also led to the procurement of Marmon 34s for use by the U.S. Army and the French Army General Staff during World War I.[13]

In 1919, the Model 34 was known as "The Foremost Fine Car," basing the claim on the company's willingness to test all critical components. For example, engine crankshafts were statically and dynamically balanced. Plus, each new production engine was run for over three hours of power testing and finished the test sequence at wide-open throttle.[14]

A specially designed Model 34B speedster model was designed to pace the 1920 Indianapolis 500 Mile Race. Reportedly, Barney Oldfield brought the pack to the starter's flag reaching 80 m.p.h. Later in the summer the company offered a speedster inspired by the pace car to the public with a Marmon racing yellow body, hood, and wheels. For the 1924 model year, Marmon announced optional front brakes and balloon tires.[15]

When the Model 34s were first introduced in 1916, the seven-passenger touring car listed at $2,750. During the peak of the post-war expansion in the summer of 1920, the price for the same style had risen to $4,200. By 1923, a seven-passenger phaeton had fallen to $3,700.[16]

NOTE OF INTEREST

In 1933, the Marmon Company faced an ignoble end—bankruptcy. A major creditor was William Ansted, owner of Metal Auto Products, which manufactured auto parts for Marmon. The day that Ansted realized that Marmon received the final blow, he had all Marmon's overdue bills tallied for a total of $70,000. With the invoices in hand, Ansted went directly to the Marmon factory to negotiate some kind of settlement. Payment came in the form of some tools and the last Marmon car made, priced at $5,000. Anstead enjoyed relating the story and boasting about having purchased the most expensive car, a nearly $70,000 price tag, to date.

In May 1924, George M. Williams, former president of Wire Wheel Corporation of America, purchased a substantial block of Marmon stock and became its president. Howard Marmon remained as chief engineer and vice president. Together they debuted the refined Model 74 for the 1925 model year with the slogan "The New Marmon—It's a Great Automobile."

Marmon offered three open styles: a rumble seat roadster, five-passenger phaeton, and seven-passenger touring car. The company's five deluxe closed styles included a coupe, five-passenger sedan and sedan limousine, and seven-passenger sedan and sedan limousine. Later in the year "standard" styles entered the line with a seven-passenger sedan and a four-door brougham coupe. Marmon introduced its Model 75 to recognize the 75th anniversary of the firm in 1926. In this version, the styles ranged from the five-passenger town coupe at $3,485 to a custom-body, seven-passenger limousine at $4,600. This model closed out the generation of Marmon autos that started with the Model 34 in 1916.[17]

In 1926, Nordyke & Marmon reorganized the structure of the company and its operations. First the owners changed the name to Marmon Motor Car Company, a move that they felt reflected their future course. They sold stock to the public in the newly formed company. Next, they sold the milling side of the business. The Nordyke name was transferred to the Allis-Chalmers Company.[18]

The Little Marmon arrived in 1927, a straight-eight in the $1,795 to $1,895 price range. This model was Marmon's first entry into the mid-priced market. The company sought this entry because of the continuing erosion of the market for high-priced, high-quality automobiles. The Little Marmon survived for one season.

In 1928 two eight-cylinder models were offered. They were the Model 68 on a 114-inch wheelbase, in three body styles, selling for $1,395, and the Model 78 on a 120-inch wheelbase, in six body styles, ranging from $1,895 to $1,995.[19] Marmon then enjoyed a substantial production increase in 1929 because of a low-priced new straight-eight, called the Roosevelt. The 1929 Roosevelt had the distinction of being the first eight-cylinder car in the world to sell for less than $1,000. Marmon warranted a listing in the Guinness Book of Records for its factory installed radio, also in 1929. The Roosevelt appeared in the 1930 catalog as the Marmon Roosevelt and only lasted one more year. The 1930 Roosevelt was the only car in its price range to be offered with a full one-year warranty.[20]

The Marmon Big Eight was introduced in December 1929. It was powered by an all new straight-eight engine on a 136-inch wheelbase with an advertised price of $3,300, and a delivered price approaching $3,800.[21] Also for 1930, Models 8-69 and 8-79 replaced the previous Models 68 and 78, respectively. These three production models carried forward into 1931. The Marmon 70 replaced the Roosevelt as Marmon's mid-priced offering, with prices still starting below $1,000 in 1931.

Model year 1929 proved to be the highpoint for Marmon auto production at 29,216 units.

NOTE OF INTEREST

The original Nordyke and Marmon Plant 1 was at the southwest corner of Kentucky Avenue and West Morris Street in Indianapolis. In 1916, Plant 2 was constructed at the southwest corner of Drover and West York Streets. During World War I, this plant was expanded for production of the Liberty V-12 aircraft engine. Plant 3, the five-story structure measuring 80 x 600 feet parallel to Morris Street, was completed in 1919 (now Eli Lilly and Company's Building 314). The Marmon assembly plant was built adjacent to the Morris Street property line with Plant 3 behind and parallel to it (also part of the Eli Lilly complex).

It is noteworthy that in the summer of 1924, Plant 2 was reconfigured to promote what today would be called "just-in-time-manufacturing." Heavy components from outside suppliers arrived via rail at the west end of the building and flowed to the chassis line. Other machining operations were arranged in parallel lines to the assembly line. Assembled and machined components progressed down their lines at the rate required to deliver it to the proper point in the assembly line. At that time, with one exception, Plant 2 was the largest single manufacturing plant in the industry, with 261,800 square feet under one roof.[27]

Howard Marmon developed this 1933 model with a V-12 engine and demonstrated it widely about six months prior to his death. It was a futile effort to save the company. The car has been deemed an engineering masterpiece.
TMH

As the Depression deepened, however, Marmon auto production continuously fell from 10,115 in 1930 to 86 in 1933.[22]

With the introduction of the Marmon Sixteen in 1931, it appeared that Marmon had saved the best for the last. The Sixteen, a magnificent $5,000 automobile with a 491 c.i.d. V-16 engine produced 200 h.p. and was good for over 100 m.p.h.

Howard C. Marmon and his group of engineers started development of the V-16 automobile in November 1926, but shelved the project in 1928 when the company's finances were lagging. Unfortunately, Cadillac introduced a similar model one year later. With this impetus, Marmon enlisted Walter Dorwin Teague's firm to design eight exceptional body styles for the Sixteen in 1930. The first production Sixteen shipped in February 1931. The V-16 was honored by The Society of Automotive Engineers as "the most notable engineering achievement of 1930." The society was especially impressed by the extensive use of lightweight aluminum, generally a difficult metal to work and maintain in automobile power plants.

The Marmon V-16 warrants recognition as the largest American passenger car engine of its era.

However, the timing was not right. America's weak economy was not kind to the Sixteen, with only 390 built in the three-year period ending in 1933.[23]

The promise of the Roaring Twenties proved hollow for many automakers across the nation, including Marmon. Marmon stock that had peaked in May 1929 at more than $100 per share dipped to slightly more than $3 three years later.[24] In addition, the luxury-car market had shrunk drastically, and lower-price competitors already secured a solid hold on the mass market. Marmon executives were forced to go to Eastern bankers for working capital to keep the company afloat.

At the very end, Howard Marmon built the HCM Special at his own expense. This prototype auto had a 150 h.p. V-12 engine, independent front suspension, DeDion rear axle and tubular backbone frame, with styling by Teague. Yet, it never saw production.[25] In May 1933, Marmon Motor Car Company entered receivership.

Marmon's cumulative production from 1902 to 1933 approached 110,000 autos. The mid-point of producing 55,000 autos was reached at the end of the 1927 model year. It is interesting that in 1929 and 1930, Marmon production exceeded Cadillac in the luxury market: 1929—Marmon 22,323 vs. Cadillac 14,986 and 1930—Marmon 12,369 vs. Cadillac 12,078.[26] A number of automotive enthusiasts over the years have praised Marmon as a fine automobile.

A popular open-type body, the 4-passenger, 4-door touring car.

New standards of performance and long life

THIS concrete expression of faith in the practical advantages to be secured by Marmon fine workmanship affords convincing proof that the new series Marmon 34 has met with as instant recognition as did the light-weight scientific construction introduced in the Marmon 34 four years ago. It constitutes an impressive note of confidence in Marmon engineering and Marmon reliability.

There is now a sufficient number of the new series Marmon 34 in the hands of owners to warrant conclusions being drawn as to performance. From owners everywhere come enthusiastic reports. It is unanimously agreed that all predictions made at the shows have been fulfilled. The new series Marmon 34 has set new standards of performance and long life.

And it is a significant fact that so many Marmon 34 owners are men prominent in the automotive and allied industries. These men know fineness of mechanical workmanship. They know motor car values. Their choice of the Marmon 34 as the car they prefer to drive constitutes a strong endorsement of Marmon engineering and manufacturing excellence.

The dealer who is a part of the Marmon selling organization has an immeasurable advantage. If you are in a position to handle such a car as the Marmon, it may be well worth your while to write and find out whether there is a possibility of your securing the agency.

The High Efficiency Motor is so rigidly constructed and accurately balanced that it operates smoothly at all speeds.

NORDYKE & MARMON COMPANY
Established 1851 :: :: INDIANAPOLIS

This ad for the Marmon 34 appeared in 1920 and indicated that the model had grabbed the hearts of auto aficionados.
TAC

Endnotes

1. Hanley, George and Stacey P., *The Marmon Heritage,* Rochester, MI, Doyle Hyk Publishing Co., © 1985, p 26.
2. Hanley, p 34.
3. Hanley, p 35.
4. Carson, Richard B., *The Olympian Cars: The Great American Luxury Automobiles of the Twenties & Thirties,* New York, NY, Alfred A Knopf, © 1976, p 242.
5. Hanley, p 38.
6. Hanley, p 30.
7. Hanley, p 39 - 43.
8. Hanley, p 78.
9. Hanley, p 81.
10. Hanley, p 86.
11. Hanley, p 100.
12. Hanley, p 150 -154.
13. Hanley, p 149.
14. Hanley, p 158.
15. Hanley, p 167.
16. Kimes, Beverly Rae, Standard Catalog of American Cars: 1805 - 1942, Ioli, WI, Krause Publications, © 1996, p 927.
17. Hanley, p 170 - 181.
18. Hanley, p 456.
19. Hanley, p 225 - 229.
20. Hanley, p 230 - 235.
21. Hanley, p 237.
22. Kimes, p 925.
23. Hanley, p 272 - 290.
24. Hanley, p 462.
25. Hanley, p 301 - 311.
26. Hanley, p 405 - 411.
27. Hanley, p 427.

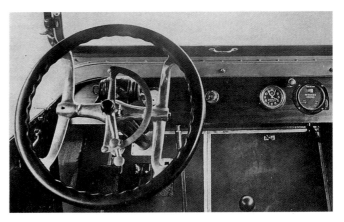

McFarlan introduced an electrically warmed steering wheel to the 1917 line. The wheel also was one of the first applications of tilt steering.
(factory photo)

McFarlan, 1910-1928

Connersville started its move into the automotive age when John B. McFarlan converted part of the family farm in 1886 into one of the first industrial parks in the country. In his desire to expand his carriage business, he lit the spark for what turned out to be a center for automobile production and automotive component manufacturing.

The automotive saga in Connersville actually starts in 1856 when John McFarlan moved to the small town and combined several small buggy companies to form the McFarlan Carriage Company. After building his industrial park, various industries moved in to form what eventually became the nucleus of Connersville's automotive industry.

The idea for a McFarlan motor car was conceived by John's grandson, Alfred H. (Harry) McFarlan. Harry designed the McFarlan Six in 1909 and enlisted his grandfather's approval and financial support. Ironically, John B. McFarlan

died two weeks before the first experimental car rolled out of the plant.

McFarlan's policy was to concentrate only on a six-cylinder car selling in the $2,000 price range. Further policy dictated that its product would be one of quality using McFarlan's own fine coachwork, a carefully selected six-cylinder engine, and the best in standard components—all at a fair price. The company backed up its policy with over 50 years of experience in the construction of quality, rugged carriages and in the contacts for excellent equipment suppliers.

The preliminary catalog of 1910 offered two body styles—the Model 26 five-passenger touring car and the Model 28 four-passenger pony tonneau. Both were priced at $2,000. Pricing changed in 1911, however, when these two models were listed at $2,100, including lamps and top. Three larger models were offered at prices up to $2,600.

About 15 other manufacturers offered six-cylinder autos ranging from $3,000 to $6,000. Indiana manufacturers Premier, Apperson, and National were among McFarlan's competitors.

All 1912 McFarlan models had compressed-air self-starters as standard equipment. The starter was of McFarlan's own make. Some of the optional items of equipment included a windshield, speedometer, spare rim, and electric lighting systems.

McFarlan began using 572.5 c.i.d. engines from the Teetor-Hartley Engine Company of Hagerstown in 1914. Also in 1914, McFarlan ceased its carriage-building operations. McFarlan models' wheelbase increased to 132 inches and offered a

Westinghouse electric starter in 1915. Pricing for the 1915 models ranged from $2,590 to $4,310.

An interesting option was reported in the June 15, 1916 issue of *Horseless Age:* "In order to facilitate entrance or exit to or from the front compartment on the left side, the steering wheel is so arranged that it may be tilted out of the way. An ingenious idea has been carried out providing the steering wheel with segments which may be heated from the electrical system for winter driving." Touring cars and companion models listed at $3,500 and closed models from $4,600 to $5,300.

The McFarlan Twin Valve Six series was introduced on September 9, 1920. Eleven different models ranged from $5,350 to $9,000. The most spectacular McFarlan was the Model 154 Knickerbocker Cabriolet. One of these models with gold-plated trim was featured at the 1923 Chicago Auto Show and listed at $25,000.

In 1923, McFarlan began contract manufacturing for all Auburn closed bodies. McFarlan introduced its lightweight Single Valve Six in 1924. Single Valve Sixes were available in six body styles from $2,500 to $3,150. Four-wheel hydraulic brakes became standard equipment on the Twin Valve and Single Valve series for 1925.

In October 1925, an eight-cylinder engine joined the McFarlan offerings. The price on the five-passenger touring car was $2,650, the same as its equivalent SV Six. For 1926, the SV and the Eight five-passenger sedans priced at $3,180 were priced close to Hoosier competitor Marmon. The Twin Valve sedan was in the $6,000-$6,999 bracket, which mirrored pricing for another Hoosier manufacturer—Duesenberg.

By 1927, McFarlan production was decreasing, down 61 percent for the year. Like many other small independent manufacturers, McFarlan became a casualty of economic times. On August 8, 1928, R.S. Springer was named trustee, and the plant

machinery was sold. On April 1, 1929, the Auburn Automobile Company bought the McFarlan plant and used it to store leather upholstery materials, small parts, and finished Auburn and Cord cars.

Total estimated production for the life span of McFarlan is 2,087 automobiles.

Additional specifications for selected models

The 1910 models were priced at $2,000 and were available with royal blue bodies and running gear (with an option of cream running gear) of "torpedo gray, dull finish." The cars had a 248 c.i.d. valve-in-head, six-cylinder, 35-40 h.p. engine; a 120-inch wheelbase; 36-inch artillery type wheels with demountable rims; and a water-jacketed Stromberg carburetor. The guaranteed speed was listed as from three to sixty miles per hour on direct drive.

In 1911, three larger models were offered with a 128-inch wheelbase and with a 377 c.i.d. engine.

The 1912 McFarlan Twin Valve Six series had 120 b.h.p. engines with 24 valves and 18 spark plugs and rode on a 140-inch wheelbase.

The 1925 model had a wheelbase of 131 inches with a 298.6 c.i.d. Lycoming straight-eight engine. The car had Lockheed hydraulic brakes and the new duPont "Duco" paint.

Endnotes

Reference material: "What was the McFarlan?", Keith Marvin, Alvin J. Arnheim, and Henry H. Blommel, New York, NY, Alvin J. Arnheim, ©1967

McFarlan's 1923 TV Knickerbocker Cabriolet offered a considerable design change from previous models. Rear-panel windows permitted more light to enter the cab. Plus, entrance steps replaced running boards, and coach lights were stationed behind the front doors.
(factory photo)

Pratt and Elcar, 1908-1933

The company eventually known as both The Elkhart Carriage and Motor Car Company and the Elcar Motor Company serves as an excellent example of the typical firm that made the transition from a successful buggy builder to a respected manufacturer of quality-assembled automobiles. After 25 years in the direct-sale buggy and harness business, the Elkhart-based company introduced its first motorized buggy in 1908.

The story actually begins with the Elkhart Carriage and Harness Manufacturing Company, whose predecessor was started in 1873 to produce buggies and carriages. In 1906, Elkhart Carriage founders William B. and George B. Pratt developed their first experimental model. In 1908, they began manufacturing the Pratt-Elkhart, described as "A standard automobile along modern lines."[1]

The company's first motor buggy reflected its roots. It was typical of many other highwheelers of the day offering a high-ground clearance to clear obstructions encountered while driving in the country.[2]

By early summer 1909, the brothers recognized that providing a more conventional shaft-driven automobile was the market's direction. This new medium-sized Pratt-Elkhart Model 30-35 automobile was offered as a 1910 model with only a five-passenger touring car available. The price was $1,600. By 1911, the line included the five- and seven-passenger touring car, five-passenger vestibule touring car, and two-passenger roadster. Pratt-Elkharts were sold in all 46 states by the end of 1911.

New models soon followed:

- The 1912 Pratt Forty at the end of 1911
- The Pratt-Thirty by mid-1912
- The Pratt-Fifty at the end of 1912
- The 1914 Pratt-Sixty at the end of 1913
- The 1915 Pratt Six-Fifty
- The 1915 Pratt Four-Forty
- The 1915 Eight-Fifty series.

In August 1915, William and George Pratt invited a number of individuals to invest in their company.

The brothers made 40 percent of the shares available for sale to generate additional cash to fund capital improvements. The corporate name was changed to Elkhart Carriage and Motor Car Company and the car's name of Pratt to Elcar.[3]

The new executives realized that the firm's wealth lay with producing a popular-sized car versus a mid- to high-priced car like the predecessor Pratt, which was priced around $2,000. They designed the new 1916 four-cylinder Elcar for the low price of $795 and advertised it as "The Car for the Many." Additional models in the 1917 line-up were a two-passenger roadster and a five-passenger all-weather sedan with removable glass frames that were priced at $995. As a result of World War I, the company contracted to produce military ambulance bodies for the army in May 1918.[4]

Automobile production resumed in 1919 with a carryover of the 1918 models. The line-up consisted of four four-cylinder and four six-cylinder models. Elcar, like most other manufacturers, enjoyed the immediate post-war boom in 1919 with record production. The company, however, was restrained by material shortages from their suppliers just as the demand for automobiles increased in the immediate post-war boom. This rising demand and supplier shortage forced dramatically increasing prices. At the end of 1919, the Federal Reserve implemented a tightening of credit. Thousands of cars across the nation were held in storage because banks would not finance dealer inventories. The recession of 1920 quickly followed. In the last quarter of 1920, Elkhart began offering sales

To accommodate public demand for lower-priced cars, The Elkhart Carriage and Motor Car Company decided to offer a four-cylinder Elcar Model B for about $800 in 1916. It was advertised as "The Car for the Many."
WSL

incentives to dealers. By the end of the year, the company had reported its first loss during one of its greatest sales years. The company continued in spite of its loss. The 1921 line-up consisted of 11 standard models in six body styles. By 1922, 16 models were being produced ranging from $1,195 to $2,495.[5]

On June 29, 1922, the Pratts retired and sold their operating control of the company to a group of executives from the Auburn Automobile Company. At the same time, the corporate name changed to Elcar Motor Company. In late 1922, Elcar also entered the taxicab market. The company produced cabs under many names including El Fay, Martel, Paragon, and Royal Martel.

Elcar's new line-up debuted at the January 1923 auto shows. Popular options for the 1924 model year were balloon tires and four-wheel brakes. Elcar's eight-in-line offering debuted as the 8-80 in summer 1924. In 1925, Lycoming engines powered Elcars across the line-up in fours, sixes, and eights.

Beginning in 1926, Elcar executives began to concentrate on its six- and eight-cylinder offerings because of their larger profit margin versus the highly competitive four-cylinder market. By the end of the year, they ceased offering four-cylinders.

The model line-up started with the Model 6-70 Brougham at $1,295 in 1927. In 1927, hydraulic brakes were available across the entire line. The announcements for 1928 showed 28 models, with the emphasis on the eight-cylinder lines for 22 models. Elcar continued to pride itself in its adaptability in essentially custom building various body styles. For 1929, Elcar introduced the Model 75 Club Sedan, a six-cylinder offering that started below $1,000. At the other end was the Model 96 seven-passenger Fleetwing Sedan at $1,695.

By mid-summer 1929, Elcar—as well as most auto manufacturers across America—saw a drastic slow down. The stock market crash of October 1929 hit simultaneously with Elcar's introduction of its 1930 models. The company had so much material on hand that some of it was not used up until 1931.[6]

For 1930, Elcar announced 36 models across six different series. The models ranged from $995 for a Series 75A two-passenger roadster to $2,750 for a Series 140 5-passenger convertible sedan. Severe reduction across the model line-up manifested in 1931. Elcar offered two model series 86 and 100 on

117- and 123-inch chassis, respectively. The company struggled to hold on, but entered receivership in October 1931. Elcar Motor Company ceased operations in 1932. A few more cars and taxicabs were built from parts on hand until late 1933.[7]

Elcar's last model, the Model 140 offered the third most powerful standard American production car for 1930, trailing only Cadillac's V-16 and the Duesenberg Straight 8. Elcar's offerings could match the best-built American autos of the day, but quality-assembled automobiles could not match economically the cars built by mass producers.

Endnotes

1. Hampton, Charles C., *The Automobile Industry in Elkhart*, monograph, © 1977.
2. Locke, William S., *Elcar and Pratt Automobiles: The Complete History*, Jefferson, NC, McFarland & Company, Inc., © 2000, p 16-22.
3. Locke, p 23-37.
4. Locke, p 41-49.
5. Locke, p 50-67.
6. Locke, p 76-92.
7. Locke, p 117-121.

Additional specifications for selected models

The 1908 Pratt-Elkhart had a 12 h.p. horizontally opposed two-cylinder engine mounted under the seat with dual-chain drive to the rear wheels.

The 1910 Pratt-Elkhart Model 30-35 included a right-hand drive and a Waukesha four-cylinder engine out front under the hood. It was built on a 117-inch wheelbase with pneumatic tires.

The 1912 Pratt-Forty offered 40 h.p. and a 120-inch wheelbase. It was available in a two-passenger runabout, four-passenger demi-tonneau, and five- and seven-passenger touring cars—all selling for $2,000 each. The car was also equipped with a Prest-O-Lite starting system.

The 1914 Pratt Sixty had a 421 c.i.d. Buda six-cylinder engine and was offered as five- and seven-passenger touring cars. Prices started at $2,550.

The 1915 Pratt Six-Fifty with a left-hand drive had a Continental six-cylinder engine and a 132-inch wheelbase. The price was $2,250.

The 1915 Pratt Four-Forty with a four-cylinder engine had a 122-inch wheelbase and shared as much of bodies and equipment of the Six-Fifty as possible. The price was $1,950.

The 1915 Eight-Fifty series offered a 283 c.i.d., 74 h.p., V-8 engine and a 125-inch wheelbase.

The 1915 Elcar was available as a five-passenger touring car and two-passenger runabout with a 192 c.i.d. Lycoming engine and a 114-inch wheelbase.

The three models in the 1923 Four-Forty series had a 40 h.p. Lycoming engine and a 112-inch wheelbase.

The 1923 Six-Sixty series came in five models with a Continental engine and a 118-inch wheelbase.

The 1924 Six Fifty line was on a 112-inch wheelbase.

Sound Reasons for ELCAR *Amazing Performances*

SUCH a success as that of the present Elcar Sixes and Eights-in-Line naturally follows performance so impressive and exceptional.

The sensitive, powerful, instantaneous motor response that gives mastery in traffic, leadership on the road, a fine disregard of distance—such characteristics are no accidental achievement.

They are the fruit of the vast composite experience which the Elcar and the Lycoming organizations have pooled to create the Elcar-Lycoming Motor.

To a knowledge accumulated through 17 years of building sound value into cars, was added the seventeen years of motor-building experience, the facilities for precise and accurate manufacturing on a large scale and the engineering and technical equipment of the great Lycoming plants and organization.

The motor that has resulted from this co-ordination of effort is added assurance of service in a car already noted for its unusual merit.

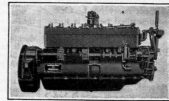

The Lycoming-Elcar 8-in-Line Motor

The unusual performance records made by this motor are characterized by a reserve of power, a responsiveness to the throttle and an economy of operation that are amazing even in this day of motor progress.

Full force feed lubrication; large water passages over combustion chambers; an unusual degree of accessibility; gas economy; these are some of the features which are combined with the quality materials and Lycoming workmanship noted for seventeen years.

ELCAR MOTOR COMPANY — BUILDERS OF FINE VEHICLES SINCE 1873 — ELKHART, INDIANA

LYCOMING
Motored
ELCAR

This ad for Elcar ran in 1926 and promoted an urbane elegance for the vehicle and driver.
TAC

Studebaker, 1902-1963

Studebaker, the longest-lived Indiana automaker, stands out among America's independent auto producers for many reasons. For example, the company was the only top-rated carriage builder to make a direct transition to being a top-rated auto producer. In addition, during its first two decades, Studebaker vied with Ford and other manufacturers for the top four spots in auto production. Between 1909 and 1953, Studebaker enjoyed a top-ten rating among America's auto producers with the exception of only four years. And, Studebaker made the transition from one of the larger manufacturers to one of the last independent U.S. auto producers.

The Studebaker saga actually began with the founding of a small blacksmith shop in 1852. During the next 50 years, The Studebaker Brothers Manufacturing Company in South Bend produced more than 750,000 wagons, buggies, and carriages. The company became known as "The Largest Vehicle Builders in the World." Studebaker carriages were sought after by the rich and famous. For example, President Abraham Lincoln had one, which he used to ride to Ford's Theater on the night of his assassination in 1865. President Benjamin Harrison's White House stable was also fully stocked with Studebaker Brothers vehicles and tack. In addition, Studebaker vehicles played important parts in the Boer War and the Spanish-American War.

In 1896, Chairman Frederick S. Fish obtained the board's permission to build and test a "horseless vehicle." In the next couple of years, the company entered into a number of contracts to build bodies for electric car manufacturers.[1]

Studebaker's first recorded sale of a car was to F.W. Blees of Macon, Missouri, on February 12, 1902.[2] Auto production for the year was 20 electric cars. The cars had a top speed of 13 miles per hour and an approximate 40-mile range between charges with two passengers riding along. If this top speed seems ridiculously low, the standards of the age need to be considered. Electrics were primarily used in urban areas, where their main competition was horse-drawn carriages and buggies. Horse-drawn vehicles had a normal cruising speed of four or five miles per hour. Speed limits were very low in most urban areas, some major cities were as low as four miles per hour. For 1902, the Studebaker electric was quite competitive.[3] The line offered three models: a runabout, a trap, and a Stanhope.[4]

One famous buyer of a Studebaker electric car was the inventor Thomas Alva Edison, who bought an early Stanhope, probably in late 1903 or early 1904. (A two-passenger Stanhope in 1902 cost $1,100.)[5] This was about the time when Studebaker switched from wire wheels to wooden-spoked artillery wheels. This purchase may have been simultaneous with his introduction of the Edison battery, which occurred in 1904. Studebaker was one of the first to adopt Edison's new batteries. There is also an unsubstantiated story that Edison designed the Studebaker electric. Studebaker produced 1,841 electrics over 10 years with production ending in 1912.[6]

The gasoline auto market, however, grabbed Fish's attention in 1903. Unlike electric cars which were a natural outgrowth of carriage building and assembling manufactured components, gasoline automobiles were another matter. The engine and other mechanical components for gasoline automobiles needed to be designed. Studebaker lacked the requisite expertise. So, the company contracted with an existing manufacturer of automobiles. Fish also understood that one of Studebaker's strengths was its coast-to-coast distribution network, with offices in all major cities. Drawing on their strengths, Studebaker's objective became to sell gasoline automobiles and use the distribution network to its advantage.[7]

On July 22, 1904, Studebaker recorded its first gasoline auto sale, a Studebaker-Garford Model C five-passenger touring car with detachable tonneau.[8] The Garford Company of Elyria, Ohio, built the chassis. Studebaker continued this arrangement with Garford until 1912. Some 2,481 Studebaker-Garfords were built during the eight-year association.[9]

Sales for 1906 totaled $6.8 million, an increase of nearly $3 million from 1902 when sales of wagons, carriages, and 20 electric autos were $4.1 million. By 1907, the total rose to $7.8 million, with most sales coming from horse-drawn vehicles. However, sales of automobiles over the past five years accounted for most of the increase.[10]

Early in 1908, Fish began researching Studebaker's options for expanding its sales beyond

STUDEBAKER
"The Automobile with a reputation behind it"

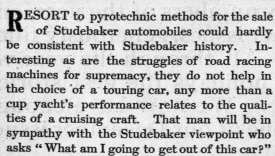

R ESORT to pyrotechnic methods for the sale of Studebaker automobiles could hardly be consistent with Studebaker history. Interesting as are the struggles of road racing machines for supremacy, they do not help in the choice of a touring car, any more than a cup yacht's performance relates to the qualities of a cruising craft. That man will be in sympathy with the Studebaker viewpoint who asks "What am I going to get out of this car?"

Model "L" has a record which will furnish an interesting answer. Ask us about it.

This car, as is true with every Studebaker production was a "known quantity" before we offered it to the public. No guesswork, no experiment about it—but a car well built, on well proved principles, for the rational motorist. It is a successful attempt to achieve lightness and efficiency through simplicity.

Model "L." 28=32 H. P.
Price $3000 to $4000 According to Body

Storage battery, jump spark ignition with La Coste coil. Vertical motor, 4 cylinders. Three speeds forward and one reverse. Weight 2600 pounds.

Each car thoroughly equipped with headlights, generator, taillight, sidelights and horn, also the best tried out type of shock absorber, a conveniently placed tool box and irons for carrying extra tires.

Write for our catalog.

STUDEBAKER AUTOMOBILE COMPANY
South Bend, Ind.

Members Ass'n of Licensed Automobile Mfrs.

Studebaker Branch Houses

NEW YORK CITY	SAN FRANCISCO, CAL.
CHICAGO, ILL.	SALT LAKE CITY, UTAH
KANSAS CITY, MO.	DENVER, COLO.
PORTLAND, ORE.	DALLAS, TEXAS

T HE Studebaker Electric Stanhope has earned a wide and honorable reputation. It is extensively used in cities on account of its convenience, graceful proportions and simplicity of control. It admirably serves the purposes of physicians, and provides a conveyance which women can operate with ease. A Studebaker electric car can be driven by a novice through crowded streets without difficulty or danger.

The Stanhope, like our other electric cars, has the distinctive Studebaker feature of location of both battery and motor above the springs. Its delightful riding qualities are partly due to this arrangement.

Model 22b Stanhope
Price $1250

Four speeds from 3 to 14 miles per hour. Forward and backward speeds equally divided. Will carry two passengers over average streets, 40 miles on one charge. Steered by side lever; speed regulated by controller handle on the left. Has cut out switch, permitting leaving the car unattended. Meter indicates energy in battery. Each car equipped with special close top; also set of necessary tools, tire pump, repair outfit and charging plug with 15 feet of cable.

See our exhibit at Madison Square Garden, New York, January 12th to 19th

WRITE FOR COMPLETE CATALOG

This Studebaker 1907 advertisement featured both gasoline and electric automobiles.
TAC

the level possible using the Garford operations. In September, Fish contracted with the EMF Company of Detroit for part of the fledgling operation's production. The initials EMF reflected three individuals: Barney Everitt, William Metzger, and Walter Flanders. The three men had gained some fame early in the decade with other auto manufacturers before venturing out on their own.

By the spring of 1909, Studebaker entered into a three-year agreement with EMF to handle sales and distribution for the entire production. On March 9, 1910, Studebaker purchased outright control of EMF. In its two years of existence, EMF had racked up $21 million in sales and had become the second largest automobile manufacturer in the country. EMF production for 1909 totaled 8,132 cars, and in 1910 jumped to 15,300.[11]

Studebaker was finally in control of its automotive destiny. The assets of the Studebaker Brothers Manufacturing Company and the Everitt Metzger Flanders Company were combined into a new entity called the Studebaker Corporation. It was incorporated on February 14, 1911. With incorporation, a series of other events helped strengthen Studebaker:

- Production was concentrated on the increasingly successful medium-priced gasoline auto market.

- High-priced gasoline autos were discontinued, and electric car production was phased out over two years.

- Horse-drawn vehicles took on a lessening corporate role.

At the end of 1911, production totaled 22,555 gasoline autos and electrics, placing Studebaker second in the marketplace after Ford. Sales of motor vehicles rose to a total of 28,523 in 1912. The last Studebaker electric was built in 1912 when the company commented "the ultimate superiority of the gasoline auto had become apparent."[12]

The new six-cylinder Model E was introduced for 1913. It featured the first six-cylinder monoblock engine casting (concurrently introduced by Premier of Indianapolis) and electric starting and lighting. The Model E was rated at 40 h.p. and rode on a 121-inch wheelbase. Prices started at $1,550 for a touring car, while the limousine listed

for $2,500. Studebaker claimed that its six-cylinder model for less than $2,000 was another American first.[13] A four-cylinder Model SA started at $875.

Studebaker's 1938 President was one of Raymond Loewy's first designs for the company. The model year also saw the premier of Studebaker's innovation of windshield washers. SNM

Between 1912 and 1914, Studebaker was the third best-selling brand in America after Ford and Willys-Overland. In the $625 to $1,500 price class, Studebaker ran even with Buick and only slightly behind Willys-Overland. A total of 35,410 cars were sold during calendar year 1913.

The next year marked Fish's last as president of Studebaker Corporation and introduced an up-rated Model S four-cylinder at 30 h.p., listed at $1,050. The Six started at $1,575. The year also witnessed the move of the steering wheel to the left side. Production hovered around the preceding year's mark at 35,460 units.[14]

Albert Russel Erskine was promoted to the Studebaker presidency in 1915. After serving as Studebaker's treasurer, Erskine was astute concerning the financial details of automotive marketing. He instituted a series of fiscal controls, which allowed price cuts to be passed on to the customer. This thinking mirrored Henry Ford's philosophy for passing on price reductions to the consumer to widen the appeal of autos to a broader market. Fully equipped Studebaker four-cylinder prices were cut from $1,290 in 1913 to $885 by the summer of 1915. Production totals rose from 35,410 in 1913 to 46,845 in 1915.[15]

Another benefit for consumers was Studebaker's introduction of installment purchasing to the American auto market in 1916. The purchaser paid an initial 25 percent down payment with the balance spread out over 12 equal monthly payments.[16]

The decade's high point in production also came in 1916 with a total of 65,536 units. Late in 1916, Studebaker started construction of a new auto plant in South Bend.[17]

In April 1917, Studebaker made a major shift to production of goods for the U.S. War Department. Government orders for horse-drawn vehicles amounted to 73,000 units in 1917. Automobile production was 42,357, and Erskine's eye was still on automotive sales. He assembled a new engineering team under the direction of Fred Zeder, who recruited Owen R. Skelton from Packard and Carl Breer from Allis-Chalmers.

The new 1918 cars—the Light Six starting at $1,295 and the Big Six starting at $1,695—were the first automobiles designed from scratch as Studebakers. A new three-speed transmission with aluminum-cone clutch replaced the transaxle and a new frame facilitated the use of Hotchkiss drive. The styling was more contemporary with the model's feature line, which began at the radiator and flowed across the entire length of the automobile.

Auto production reached its low point for the decade at 18,419 units. Late in 1918, Studebaker finally decided to closeout the horse-drawn vehicle operations. Company officials knew the government contracts would taper off in 1919. About this time, Zeder, Skelton and Breer left Studebaker to set up a consultancy that later would form the engineering keystone for Walter P. Chrysler's new venture in 1924.

The 1939 Loewy-designed Champion was made specifically for the low-price market. Prices started at $660.
SNM

With the closing of the carriage operation, Studebaker geared up for more sales of its automobiles. Plant 2, designed for production of the Light Six, opened in early 1920. That year Studebaker recorded sales of 51,474 automobiles.

By 1921, the company set a new sales record of 65,023 cars sold. This ranked them as fourth among America's auto builders. As the decade progressed, production shifted from aging facilities in Detroit, Michigan, to new plants in South Bend. In 1926, Studebaker constructed an 840-acre proving ground just west of South Bend. This was the first test facility in the industry.[18]

In 1927, Studebaker introduced a new European-influenced model with the Erskine. Studebaker's European dealers had been clamoring for a smaller car with a high-revving, small-bore engine to take advantage of their laws, which taxed higher horsepower. The Erskine offered those desired qualities at an introductory price of $975. Unfortunately for Studebaker in 1927, Chevrolet announced its competing Capitol series four-cylinder model at $525 and outsold Ford for the first time. One year later Ford also introduced a competitor— the all new four-cylinder Model A for $525.

The Erskine was like a fish out of water, a high-end offering in the low-price field. Erskine sales barely peaked at over 25,000 units in 1929 before being discontinued in 1930.[19] Traditional Studebaker models entered the 1927 year with the new Dictator starting at $1,195, Commander at $1,530, and, and President at $1,810. Today, the Classic Car Club of America recognizes most of these cars built from 1929 through 1933 as full classics.

Many enthusiasts regard the high-end President to be the finest prewar Studebaker. Studebaker's chief engineer, Barney Roos, designed the President and debuted the new 337 c.i.d. 109 h.p., straight-eight President engine in mid-1928. In fact, a President Eight sport roadster paced the 1929 Indianapolis 500 Mile Race. In 1930, Studebaker introduced freewheeling. A freewheel refers to an overriding clutch that automatically disengages the drive shaft when needed.

With the onset of the Great Depression, Studebaker cars ranged from $935 for a Six (the renamed Erskine) to $2,795 for a President.[20] Albert Erskine reported in the 1930 annual report, "Last year was a very poor one for profit making in the automobile industry." That would be an understatement for Studebaker. Sales of $86.1 million were the lowest since 1919, and profits dropped to the lowest figure since the company went public in 1911.[21]

For 1931, all models were downsized across the line. Erskine and other Studebaker executives began discussing the need for a low-priced six-cylinder car sometime in early 1931. The 1932 Rockne nameplate was announced with two models numbered 65 and the 75 to roughly correspond to their horsepower ratings. Prices started in the $600 range. Again, like the Erskine, The Rockne would compete with the new Ford V-8 with two more cylinders and prices starting at $460.

NOTE OF INTEREST

Work at the Studebaker plant was interwoven into the fabric of life in South Bend as evidenced by this account in *Studebaker: Less Than They Promised* by Michael Beatty.

"By 1900 South Bend was a bustling city of 36,000 residents, one out of every four born in a foreign country mostly from eastern Europe. South Bend was never a one-company town. Nevertheless, Studebaker was the largest employer, and many hundreds of Polish and Hungarian workers lived in neighborhoods to the west and southwest of downtown South Bend, where their small but well-kept homes were located within the sound of the factory's steam whistle which called them to work early in the morning and signaled lunch time and the end of the ten-hour work day.

"Many sons followed their fathers in the bustling factories while their daughters often worked in the clothing plants which were located in South Bend because there was an ample supply of female labor. The census of 1920 showed that the booming city of South Bend had almost doubled its population in 20 years, to 71,000. Almost one out of every five residents was born outside the United States, and the proportion of immigrants among industrial workers was even greater."

The Rockne accounted for 22,223 of 44,711 Studebaker's cars for 1932.[22]

In 1932 Studebaker reported a $5.1 million loss. The company's cash on hand as a percentage of sales stood at 1.2 percent. It was a poor showing compared with 38.6 percent and 142 percent at General Motors and Nash, respectively. GM and Nash were the only auto companies to report an after-tax profit that year.

Studebaker's financial picture placed it in an especially precarious position if any of its major creditors demanded payment of outstanding debts. In March 1933, Studebaker entered receivership. Later in the spring, Rockne's Detroit plant merged production with South Bend, and the nameplate was no more. Studebaker's dilemma may have played a part in the decision of 62-year-old Erskine to commit suicide in July 1933.[23]

Two names rose to acquire the Studebaker Corporation helm. Harold S. Vance, former vice-president in charge of production, and Paul G. Hoffman, a previous vice-president of sales, were named trustees. In April, their first full month, they made an operating profit of $20,000. This may not seem like a lot of money, but it was a step in the right direction. Studebaker's loss for the year was $1.4 million, which was a 72 percent improvement over the previous year. In December 1933, Hoffman and Vance filed a reorganization plan of the corporate affairs.[24]

In addition to reviving the corporation in receivership, the duo oversaw the development of entirely new models for 1934. The line consisted of the Dictator Six, the Commander Eight, and the President Eight. The President was smaller, lighter, and less expensive than previous models. Prices ranged from $720 for a Dictator Special coupe to $1,510 for a President Land Cruiser Sedan. Studebaker was also America's ninth ranked manufacturer in 1934 with sales of 46,103 automobiles.[25]

In January 1935, the new Studebaker Corporation was incorporated under the laws of the State of Delaware. Harold Vance was named chairman of the board, and Paul Hoffman as president. A short time later, Studebaker began designing a complete new line of cars for 1936. The Commander was dropped from the line up for a short time.

The 1950 Commander arrived in time to celebrate Studebaker's centennial year in the vehicle business. The company started making wagons, carriages, and buggies in 1852.
SNM

Dictator models now ranged in price from $665 to $775, and the top-end Presidents from $965 to $1,065. Many of the 1936 Studebakers had independent front suspension. In fact, Studebaker was one of the first independent auto companies to develop their own independent front suspension in 1936. Again Studebaker was America's ninth ranked manufacturer in 1936 with sales of 85,026 automobiles.[26] A reversal of fortune was also evidenced in 1936. The company reported a profit of $2.8 million on sales of $68.9 million.

During 1936, the United Auto Workers (UAW) was making its final push to unionize the industry. In an effort to promote labor relations, Studebaker was not opposed to unionization of its plants. South Bend UAW Local No. 5 was one of the first established in the nation in May 1937.[27] This early capitulation to the union would affect Studebaker in later union negotiations.

The 1938 model year marked the beginning of one of the most famous affiliations in Studebaker's history. Raymond Loewy, one of America's most famous industrial designers, consulted with Studebaker and developed the all-new line-up.

These full-width bodies were offered in Commander and President versions. Studebaker's innovation of windshield washers premiered in this model year. Obviously, Loewy's design helped sales. Industry-wide sales of passenger cars were off by 55 percent in 1938. Studebaker bucked this trend with sales off by 43 percent, thanks in part to the popularity of Loewy's designs. Studebaker moved to tenth place in domestic auto sales with 92,200 units.

Spring 1939 saw the introduction of the Loewy-designed Champion. The lightweight Champion was designed specifically for the low-price market with prices starting at $660. Champion accounted for around 60 percent of Studebaker's 106,470 cars sold for 1939. The corporation placed a strong eighth for the year and reported a $2.9 million profit.[28]

For 1941, the new Loewy staff designed bodies for the Commander and President models. The President Skyway coupe premiered America's first one-piece curved windshield. The company did a brisk business in 1941 with 133,900 cars produced and profits just short of $6 million. This season, Studebaker was ninth in U.S. auto sales.

As Studebaker was preparing for the 1942 model year in the summer of 1941, the nation was concerned about involvement in the war in Europe. The American government began restricting strategic materials for military use. On January 1,

1942, civilian sales of passenger cars were halted. Studebaker showed an eighth place ranking in American sales during the shortened model year.[29]

Studebaker Corporation was already conducting military production. The company had been producing multi-wheel-drive military trucks since 1940. By January 1942, crews were ramping up production of Cyclone aircraft engines at three plants. By the end of the year, the company was building the M-29 amphibious cargo carrier known as the Weasel. The Weasel was a track-laying vehicle powered by the Champion engine. General Douglas MacArthur used a Weasel as his personal vehicle during the Philippine campaign. In total, the company built 197,000 US6, 2½ ton, 6x6 trucks; 64,000 Cyclone aircraft engines; and 15,000 Weasels for the war effort. Studebaker alone completed $1.2 billion in war contracts. The net profit was $26.9 million before the costs of reconversion to civilian production was calculated.[30]

These military contracts strengthened Studebaker's financial position. On May 11, 1945, production of civilian automobiles was authorized to begin on July 1. The first postwar Studebaker Champion rolled off the line on October 1. During the 1946 model year, Studebaker was only able to produce 43 percent of its production target of 265,500 due to material shortages and labor strikes at supplier plants. The Champion was a carryover of the 1942 design while the corporation ramped up for America's first all new automobiles of the postwar era. This process started as noted in the 1943 annual report: "a few men in our organization can be assigned to postwar planning without any detrimental effect to our current war production."

The 1947 Studebaker line—advertised as "First by far with a postwar car"—debuted in the spring of 1946. Designed by Raymond Loewy and Virgil Exner, these autos were different from bumper to bumper than any of Studebaker's previous cars. A wide, narrow grille spanned the entire front end, and the front fenders were flush with the body. Plus, horizontal taillights were divided into two sections, and the five-passenger coupe featured a wrap-around rear window. The Champion was available in two trim levels, Regal and Deluxe, and started at $1,446. The Commander began at $1,661 for a three-passenger coupe and ranged up to the Land Cruiser Sedan at $2,043. On the strength of the 1947 model year, 161,498 autos were produced. Studebaker attained a 4 percent market share, a level that it would remain at for almost five years.[31]

In 1948, Studebaker set a new record with 164,753 cars sold. Pre-tax profit was $32.3 million on sales of $383.6 million. Studebaker's 1949 automotive offerings were mildly restyled versions of the previous models.

Working on expertise gained during the war, the company realized some of the pent-up demand for trucks. The company decided to introduce the all new Studebaker R-series truck line for 1949. This offering boosted Studebaker to nearly a 5 percent market share in trucks. Studebaker set another record in 1949 with 228,402 cars and 64,971 trucks produced and nearly half-a-billion dollars in sales.[32]

The renowned "bullet-nose" Studebaker was introduced in 1950. Customer acceptance of these Loewy-styled models set the high watermark for Studebaker auto production in 1950 with 268,099 cars produced. The "bullet nose" front end featured two lower grilles, and the flush front fenders flowed back to the rear fenders with vertical taillights. The Champion Custom coupe started at $1,414, with the Commander Land Cruiser sedan closing out the line at $2,187. These pricing levels placed Studebaker squarely in the market against Chevrolet, Ford, Plymouth, and Pontiac. In mid-year, Studebaker ranked as one of the first independents to develop its own automatic transmission while working with Borg-Warner of Muncie.

The big Studebaker news for 1951 was the introduction of the 232 c.i.d. overhead valve, V-8 engine. This small-block, overhead-valve offering marked a first in the low-priced market. Ford and Chevrolet would follow the lead in three and four years, respectively. The 1951 and 1952 offerings were restyles of the previous models.

Studebaker was the first auto company to mark its centennial in the vehicle business in 1952. To highlight this event, the company cast a bronze commemorative medallion, produced a film titled *The Studebaker Story,* and published *A Century on Wheels,* a book by Stephen Longstreet.

The all new "Studebaker Century Models of 1953" were previewed to dealers in January of that year. The Loewy-influenced Starliner hardtop coupe

Actual color photograph of 1947 Studebaker Champion Regal De Luxe 4-door sedan

Get real distinction for your new-car money...
get this thrilling new 1947 Studebaker

Home-town pride and family pride go into Studebaker craftsman-ship—And its high quality is evident in the way Studebaker cars and trucks stand up year after year, mile after mile. Most Studebaker craftsmen have made a lifework of their jobs. Unique father-and-son teams, such as Clayton L. and James J. Ash, shown above, are numerous.

EVEN people you don't know come up and enthuse over the distinction of your far advanced new 1947 Studebaker.

So many heads turn to look, your first trips around town, you know for certain you were smart to wait and get this Studebaker's real postwar styling.

Envious motorists everywhere give this revolutionary automobile the kind of attention and admiration that only a celebrity usually receives.

And more gratifying still, the advanced designing of its chassis, as well as its body, assures ease and comfort you never enjoyed before in an automobile. This new Studebaker is low-to-the-ground for safety as well as for looks.

Most of its weight is down where the laws of gravity work in your favor.

You ride cradled between the axles where road jolts can't reach. And thanks to its unique automatic controls, variable ratio steering and exclusive self-adjusting brakes, this 1947 Studebaker is a magnificently behaving car.

Production isn't adequate yet—so please be patient until your Studebaker dealer can schedule your delivery.

STUDEBAKER
First by far with a postwar car

© The Studebaker Corporation, South Bend 27, Indiana, U. S. A.

Following World War II, Studebaker proudly advertised that it was the "First by far with a postwar car."
TAC

The 1957 Golden Hawk had a sporty design and easily accommodated a family of four.
SNM

is probably one of Studebaker's most recognizable post-war offerings. The coupes are known for their sleek low profile that flows in an unbroken line from front to rear. They have improved weight distribution and a reduced center of gravity. Visibility was improved by about 33 percent with wrap-around windows at the front and rear. The sedans were not quite as stylish and complicated the engineering requirements for working on the same chassis. When the dust settled, a total of 186,484 cars were built, a little over 55 percent of the 1950 record mark. These were heady times for Studebaker, but cracks were starting to show in the financial picture.[33]

The demand for automobiles in the postwar seller's market masked a pending concern—poor labor productivity. During the war and reliance on government programs, productivity got out of line. Ford, GM, and Chrysler—with their larger cash positions—were able to suffer some labor unrest in order to get their production costs in line. Studebaker had always enjoyed cozy labor relations and chose not to stand up to the union. The company did not demand higher levels of productivity. As the automakers' supply approached consumer demand in the early 1950s, Studebaker's productivity imbalance became a drag on profits. This posed a problem for Studebaker and the other independents as time advanced. Studebaker's pre-Korean War profit margin was 4.72 percent of sales. In 1951, the government issued price controls and material allocations similar to those in World War II. When Studebaker closed out 1951, the profit margin shrank to 2.51 percent of sales. Studebaker held on to a 4 percent market share, but profits slid to $23 million, barely half of the 1949 profit level.

By the end of 1953, profits were only $2.7 million with a declining market share at 2.4 percent. Much as it had in the early 1930s, Studebaker continued to distribute large dividends to shareholders. In 1949, dividends amounted to about 21 percent of after-tax profits. By 1951, that figure rose to 56 percent. Although profits declined, dividends rose. This trend would have a detrimental impact on Studebaker's liquidity in the early 1950s. Studebaker again stood at the brink of insolvency.

As 1954 began, Studebaker officials began negotiations with the UAW Local 5 to bring

Studebaker's labor costs in line with the Big Three. The talking points were piece rates, manpower requirements, and work standards.[34] During 1954, however, the company did continue many of the same body styles as offered in 1953. Plus, the 1954 line added a two-door Conestoga station wagon.

At about this time, a series of mergers were taking place in the American auto industry. Studebaker began merger talks with Packard Motor Car Company in the spring of 1954. On June 22, 1954, Packard reached an agreement for a takeover of Studebaker. One of the most attractive parts of the merger was a $70 million line of credit extended to the corporation. James Nance was named president and chief operating officer of the new Studebaker-Packard Corporation on October 1, 1954. Hoffman and Vance retained seats on the executive committee. At once, Nance attempted to come to grips with the corporation's nagging financial problems. Executive efforts to persuade the union to increase productivity and decrease manpower were promptly answered by wildcat strikes throughout 1955. As the New Year approached, a new labor contract was reached.[35]

In 1955, after an absence of 13 years, the top-line President series returned. The high-end, tri-color President Speedster hardtop debuted in January 1955 and retailed for $3,253. These Loewy restyles featured a wide trim stripe from the character line all the way to the tail lights with an engine-turned instrument panel. All the excitement in the showroom didn't translate to profit for Studebaker-Packard in 1955. The corporation posted a $29.7 million loss on 182,059 cars produced. Like the rest of the independents, Studebaker continued to lose ground to the Big Three. Studebaker and Packard finished the year at 13th and 14th, respectively.

Styling in 1956 saw new front and rear sections on the Studebaker sedans with the small-block V-8 engine's displacement being increased to 289 c.i.d. and rated at 210 h.p. The year also marked the introduction of the Hawk series to replace the Speedster.

By the spring of 1956, Studebaker-Packard was again looking at liquidation. In May 1956, the Curtiss-Wright Corporation gave Studebaker-Packard (S-P) a capital infusion of $35 million in exchange for long-term leases on certain S-P facilities and the remnants of the S-P defense contracts.

Studebaker enlisted Raymond Loewy again to design the 1963 Avanti.
TAC

In December 1956, Studebaker's former engineer and division head Harold Churchill replaced Nance as president and chief operating officer. Hoffman and Vance also resigned from the board. Studebaker revenue for 1956 came in at $303 million. That amounted to a reported loss of $43.3 million on 82,406 cars.[36]

The 1956 financial crisis overshadowed planning for the 1957 model year. However, sedan styling was freshened up with a wraparound grille and larger tail lights. The Golden Hawk and the Silver Hawk, with large tail fins, represented the majority of the coupe offerings. In mid-year, the Scotsman models were introduced with painted grille and hub caps, no side trim moldings, and basic equipment offerings. This was Studebaker's attempt to offer the lowest priced model of any standard car in America at $1,776 for a two-door sedan. Yet, Studebaker still reported a loss of $11.1 million on 72,889 autos built. The 1958 mild restyle featured quad-head lights, tail fins, and a new hardtop roofline on all models. The Hawk line remained nearly the same. Studebaker produced 56,869 automobiles, which would mark the company's low point in the postwar era. Luckily, the corporation was working on a new model for the 1959 line.[37]

Based on the success of the 1957 Scotsman line, Churchill ordered engineering of the new Lark. With the introduction of the 1959 Lark, Studebaker entered the compact market and dropped all other models with the exception of the Silver Hawk. The

Lark retained the basic mid-body structure of the 1958 models with over two feet of length lopped off from front to rear. This "all new" model was an engineering master stroke considering the limited funds available for the design. The Lark line-up consisted of a two- and four-door sedan, a two-door hardtop, and a two-door station wagon. The lift that the Lark gave Studebaker was immediately felt, with 153,823 autos produced and a calendar-year profit of $28.5 million. That was the first profit since 1953.

New for 1960 was a Lark convertible and a four-door station wagon. The "Silver" name was deleted from the Hawk title, and the line soldiered on with few changes. Compact offerings from the Big Three, however, also appeared in 1960, and Studebaker immediately felt the competition. By fall, corporate executives were forecasting a loss for the coming year with the model-year production coming in at 105,902 units. At the end of December, Sherwood Egbert of McCulloch Corporation was elected chief executive officer.[38]

New to Studebaker's 1961 automotive line-up was the Lark Cruiser. Yet, production continued to drop. The year closed out at 78,664 cars produced. Studebaker eked out a scant profit of $2.5 million. For 1962, the Lark models were restyled. Quad headlights flanked a new egg crate grille, and the rear overhang was lengthened and round taillights incorporated. The new Gran Turisimo Hawk was another masterful design with a squared-off roof line. The tail fins were also deleted. The design by Brooks Stevens was an elegant update of the basic 1953 theme that had worn well over the past years. In 1962, Studebaker production amounted to 86,974 cars and showed a slim profit of $2.6 million.[39]

In retrospect, it appears that Studebaker saved its best for the last—the Avanti. In early 1961, Egbert began concept drawings for a new car that would repair Studebaker's tarnished image. With his desire to introduce a new car at the New York International Auto Show in April 1962, he enlisted Loewy to look at his drawings and return with a new model proposal. In the first part of April, Loewy's one-eighth scale clay model and styling drawings were in South Bend. Egbert introduced the Avanti full-scale styling model to the board of directors on April 27, 1961. By the fall of 1961, orders were placed with outside suppliers for items

Studebaker Milestones

- 1910 & 1911—Ranked fourth among American automobile producers
- 1911—Ranked second only to Ford
- 1912-1914—Ranked third after Ford and Willys-Overland
- 1913—Introduced a six-cylinder engine featuring monobloc engine casting (concurrent introduction along with Premier of Indianapolis)
- 1916—Introduced installment auto purchasing
- 1921—Ranked fourth place after Ford, Buick, and Dodge, and remained among the top 10 American producers through 1953 with the exception of four years
- 1926—Built the first automotive proving ground
- 1928—Set 160 endurance records
- 1930—Introduced free-wheeling
- 1931—Produced helical-cut transmission gears that almost completely eliminated gear whine
- 1936—Developed its own independent front suspension, one of the first independents to do so
- 1938—Introduced windshield washers
- 1940—Survived the Depression
- 1941—Introduced America's first one-piece, curved windshield on the President Skyway coupe
- 1947—Introduced the Champion, the first "all new" postwar car, and became the largest independent automobile producer in the post-World War II period
- 1950—Developed its own automatic transmission while working with Borg-Warner of Muncie
- 1951—Introduced a small-block, overhead valve, V-8 engine for the low-priced market
- 1963—Created the Avanti personal luxury car, which was one of the first American passenger cars to use caliper-type brakes

that Studebaker could not produce internally. The Avanti is best known for its under-the-bumper air intake and "Coke-bottle," wedge-shape design. The fiberglass body sat on a modified Lark Daytona convertible chassis. Avanti's safety theme was prominent throughout with a recessed and padded instrument panel with red lights for night vision, built-in roll bar, and safety-cone door locks. The car was also one of the first American passenger cars to use caliper-type disc brakes.[40]

In January 1962, Studebaker suffered the longest strike in its history over "personal-time" per shift. The company and labor union finally settled on 34 minutes per shift, which still exceeded the industry norm by 10 minutes. When the new Avanti was unveiled to the public in April 1962, production problems crept up with the fiberglass body. Production for 1962 moved up a little to 86,974 units produced. In addition to the Avanti, another unique model debuted for 1963—the sliding rear-roof, four-door, Wagonaire station wagon. Plus, the Lark and Hawk lines were slightly restyled.

As the 1963 calendar year opened, Studebaker started with a little over $50 million cash on hand. Production of the 1964 models started in August. The Larks, with a squared-up design and new model names, were the only new additions. The Hawk and Avanti remained unchanged for 1964.

Sales for the 1963 model year closed out at 67,918 cars produced, but the cash position shrank to $8 million. In October 1963, with an 86-day supply of unsold cars on hand, the production lines were stopped. On November 25, Egbert resigned. The halt of production in South Bend was made public on December 9, 1963. Automotive operations would shift to Hamilton, Ontario, closing there in March 1966.[41]

The demise of Studebaker also marked the end of the independent U.S. auto manufacturer.

Endnotes

1. Bonsall, Thomas E., *More Than They Promised: The Studebaker Story,* Stanford, CA, Stanford University Press, © 2000, p 23 - 37.
2. Kimes, Beverly Rae, *Standard Catalog of American Cars: 1805 - 1942,* Iola, WI, Krause Publications, © 1996, p 1411.
3. Bonsall, p 49.
4. *Studebaker Automobiles,* South Bend, IN, Studebaker Brothers Manufacturing Co., © 1902.
5. Kimes, p 1411.
6. Bonsall, p 49 - 52.
7. Bonsall, p 53.
8. Kimes, p 1411.
9. Bonsall, p 57.
10. Bonsall, p 58 - 62.
11. Bonsall, p 70 - 77.
12. Bonsall, p 85 - 88.
13. Kimes, p 1410.
14. Bonsall, p 96 - 99.
15. Bonsall, p 100 - 102.
16. *Increase Your Commercial Car Sales,* South Bend , IN, Studebaker Corporation © 1916.
17. Bonsall, p 104.
18. Bonsall, p 106 - 129.
19. Kimes, p 540.
20. Bonsall, p 138 - 148.
21. Bonsall, p 150.
22. Bonsall, p 154 - 161.
23. Bonsall, p 165 - 171.
24. Bonsall, p 179 - 182.
25. Bonsall, p 181 & 182.
26. Kimes, p 1434 & 1435.
27. Bonsall, p 187.
28. Bonsall, p 189 - 200.
29. Bonsall, p 203 - 208.
30. Bonsall, p 215 - 229.
31. Bonsall, p 234 - 246.
32. Bonsall, p 248 - 255.
33. Bonsall, p 257 - 265.
34. Bonsall, p 235 - 283.
35. Bonsall, p 283 - 291.
36. Bonsall, p 293 - 316.
37. Bonsall, p 317 - 333.
38. Bonsall, p 333 - 344.
39. Bonsall, p 350 - 365.
40. Avanti by Studebaker, South Bend, IN, Studebaker Corporation, © 1916.
41. Bonsall, p 369 - 380.

Additional specifications for selected models

The 1902 electric vehicles offered three models: a runabout, a trap, and a Stanhope. Specifications included a 24-cell, 96-ampere hour battery in the rear compartment; a single 24 amp., 40 volt Westinghouse vehicle motor; a controller that provided four speeds forward and reverse; a 15-foot charging cable; two electric side lamps; tiller steering; mechanical rear wheel brakes; an emergency drive brake; 30 x 3 inch pneumatic tires on wire wheels; a 61-inch wheelbase with a 54-inch tread; and a standard signal bell. Optional equipment included a choice of a stick or panel seat and a leather top. A two-passenger Stanhope without top was priced at $1,100.

The Garford Model C touring car was a mid-sized model with a 16 h.p. two-cylinder engine, chain drive, 82-inch wheelbase, right-hand-drive, and retailed for $1,600. A 20 h.p., 212.3 c.i.d. four-cylinder, shaft-driven touring car with a list price of $3,000 was introduced in 1905. In 1908, a 40 h.p., T-head, four-cylinder engine, touring car entered the line up at $4,300.

The Erskine used a 146 c.i.d. six-cylinder Continental engine rated at 40 b.h.p.

The Hawk featured a square-shaped grille and a flat-backed deck lid. The Golden Hawk featured the Packard V-8 rated at 275 h.p.

The Lark had a six-cylinder engine as standard equipment with a detuned V-8 as optional equipment.

Lark Regal models had Cruiser Quad head lights. The base Studebaker six-cylinder engine was improved with the adaptation of overhead valves and the horsepower rating increased to 112. Cruiser and Hawk models were available with the 289 c.i.d. V-8 rated at 225 h.p.

The 1961 Avanti was offered with a choice of two engines: the normally aspirated 289 c.i.d. V-8 rated at 240 h.p. or with the same engine with a supercharger rated at 289 h.p.

The Stutz Bearcat first appeared in 1912 for a run of 10 years. TSC

Stutz, 1911-1934

During his 30 years in the automobile industry, Harry Clayton Stutz had a hand in many of the automobiles that crossed the American landscape. The one bearing his own name, the Stutz, is the most well-known among his contributions.

In 1899, Harry Clayton Stutz founded the Stutz Manufacturing Company in Dayton, Ohio, to perfect and construct gasoline engines for stationary and vehicular purposes. Stutz sold his operations to the Lindsay Automobile Parts Company of Indianapolis in late 1902. Stutz's involvement with the Lindsay firm was short-lived. Around this time, he also met Frank H. Wheeler and George Schebler and encouraged the two to form the Wheeler-Schebler Carburetor Company in 1904. Stutz soon became chief salesman for the new firm.

In late 1905, he joined the new American Motor Car Company and designed the firm's inaugural four-cylinder conventional chassis automobile.

Stutz began a four-year involvement with the Marion Motor Car Company as chief engineer and factory manager in 1906. It was at Marion that Stutz began racing in competition as a promotional device for automobiles. Marion racers were involved in the 1907 Glidden Tour, the July 1909 Indiana Trophy race in Crown Point, the 1909 and 1910 races at the Indianapolis Motor Speedway, and the October 1909 and 1910 Brighton Beach races.

In 1910, Marion introduced the Marion Special Roadster specifically for racing. The Special had a number of Stutz-engineered features. One feature was the transaxle, which combined the transmission and rear differential. This innovation would form the basis of his next venture, The Stutz Auto Parts Company.

Stutz opened his new company in Indianapolis during November 1909 to manufacture and sell the transaxle he had designed and patented. Early auto manufacturers were making the transition from chain to shaft drive, and some thought it efficient to purchase the whole unit from a specialized manufacturer like Stutz. The 1911 Model 20 of the Empire Motor Car Company reflected Stutz's influence as consulting engineer with the implementation of new features, including the transaxle. Also in 1911, Stutz had a short association with the Nyberg Automobile Works in Anderson.[1]

It was during this time that Stutz formulated his dream of a quality sports car built from assembled, high-quality components manufactured by outside suppliers at a price below $2,000. The first Stutz was built in just five weeks and was immediately taken to the Indianapolis Motor Speedway for the inaugural running of the 500 Mile Race. Gil Anderson drove the car to an eleventh place finish.

In the summer of 1911, the Ideal Motor Car Company was organized for manufacture of the Stutz Model A, a duplicate of the Indy race car. New Stutz models were offered as a two-passenger roadster, a four-passenger toy tonneau, and a five-passenger touring car. Each was priced at $2,000. Lighting was provided by a Prest-O-Lite system.

Stutz produced this 1923 model called the Speedway Four Coupe. TSC

Stutz emphasized its 1911 record of competing without any adjustments in two additional "great races" in Philadelphia, Pennsylvania, and Santa Monica, California. A Stutz Model A torpedo roadster served as the pace car at the Indianapolis 500 in 1912.

The famous Stutz Bearcat sports car appeared in 1912 for a run of 10 years. It followed the usual Stutz recipe of a low-slung chassis, a large engine, and other bare necessities—hood, fenders, a right-hand raked steering column, two bucket seats, a fuel tank behind the seats, and wooden spoke wheels. The Stutz Bearcat was a popular car in the $2,000 price range.[2] Its appeal was boosted by Stutz's success at the race track. Bearcats finished fourth and sixth at the Indianapolis 500 in 1912 and won numerous other races that same year. The next year a Bearcat finished third at the Indianapolis 500, and by late fall Stutz driver Earl Cooper was crowned the National Champion after winning six consecutive races.

In June 1913, the Ideal Motor Car Company was reorganized as the Stutz Motor Car Company, with Harry Stutz as president. The demand for Stutz motor cars prompted the construction of a new manufacturing facility at 1002 North Capital Avenue in Indianapolis.

The Stutz White Squadron racing team did extraordinarily well in 1915 (its last under factory sponsorship), with victories at several tracks.[3] Also in 1915, Cannonball Baker drove a stock Bearcat cross country from San Diego, California, to New York City, New York, in a record-breaking time of 11 days, 7 hours, and 15 minutes.[4]

In the years preceding World War I, Stutz's sales increased nearly ten-fold—from 266 cars in 1912 to 1,873 five years later.[5]

Increasing sales necessitated an expansion of manufacturing facilities in 1916. Part of the new facilities included an 18,000 square foot building for the production of the Stutz-built, 16 valve, T-head, 80 h.p., four-cylinder engine.

Stutz also decided to sell stock in his company in 1916. A group of Wall Street investors headed by Allan A. Ryan bought controlling interest in Stutz. Unhappy with the new direction of the company, Stutz sold his remaining interest in the company that bore his name in June 1919, and founded two new automotive ventures—the Stutz Fire Engine Company and the H.C.S. Motor Car Company. *(See Stutz Fire Engine Company and H.C.S. for the continuation of the Harry C. Stutz story.)* At the end of 1919, with rapidly increasing sales, the Stutz company further expanded its manufacturing facilities to cover the entire city block.[6]

The boom following World War I provided Stutz with one of its best years ever, with 2,816 cars sold in 1920. Unfortunately, the recession of the early twenties took its toll on many auto companies, and Stutz was no exception. This reversal of events, from increasing to decreasing sales, was a new challenge. The Stutz company reacted promptly with a price reduction in July 1921. The year's production still exceeded demand with only 1,181 cars sold, and Stutz reported a loss for the year. Competitors in the luxury field were promoting six-, eight-, and 12-cylinder models while Stutz's proven four-cylinder was aging in the marketplace. In January 1922, Allan Ryan resigned as chairman. Ryan soon filed for bankruptcy after manipulating the market for Stutz stock.

On May 1, 1922, Stutz President William N. Thompson announced that the recessed market conditions of 1921 caused a substantial decrease in business volume. On August 2, 1922, control of Stutz passed to Bethlehem Steel President Charles M. Schwab and his associates. On August 15, Schwab announced a price reduction on selected models. The popular Bearcat model was no longer listed after this date. Stutz's car sales had dropped from a record 3,001 units in 1919 to around 1,200 during 1921-1922.[7]

On February, 17, 1925, Fredrick E. Moskovics (formerly of Remy Electric Company, Nordyke and Marmon, and the H.H. Franklin Company) was named president of Stutz, with the provision to proceed with his plans to design, develop, and manufacture a low European chassis with an eight-cylinder overhead cam engine.

The new Vertical Eight Series AA was introduced in January 1926. All models were priced at $2,995. This car was marketed as the Safety Stutz because of its innovation of safety glass windows. Other safety features included four-wheel hydraulic brakes, a low center of gravity, and a strong frame. The base of the car was Charles R. "Pop" Greuter's 92-horsepower straight-eight engine with chain-driven, single-overhead cam-shaft, and dual ignition, including two spark plugs per cylinder. The chassis featured an underslung worm-drive differential and centralized chassis lubrication. This configuration allowed the fitting of low-built, attractive bodies with safety glass. In 1926, the company set a sales record at 5,069 units.[8]

In late 1926, the Stutz Company formed collaboration with the Weymann American Body Company, a subsidiary of the French Weymann firm. The Weymann American built a plant near the Stutz factory to manufacture a flexible, fabric-covered body. Reportedly, Stutz helped with some of the plant's financing and was its largest customer. Weymann-American would also build bodies for Cord, Duesenberg, Marmon, Packard, and Pierce-Arrow.[9]

In 1927, the Stutz company introduced another new model, the Black Hawk speedster. The low-and-short open model reduced coachwork with scant cycle fenders. Step plates replaced the running boards. The models' fast looks proved to be no illusion when they won the American Automobile Association Stock Car Championship in 1927 and 1928. A privately entered Blackhawk placed second at the 1928 Twenty-Four Hours of LeMans after leading the Bentley team much of the way.

That same year, the company newsletter, *The Splendid Stutz,* announced the optional availability of a dash-mounted radio.[10] This predates the Marmon Roosevelt listing of a factory-installed radio by one year. Stutz introduced the six-cylinder Blackhawk marque starting at $2,345, in January 1929, at the National Automobile Show in New York City. By July, the company reduced the price to $1,995 in hopes of being more competitive in the market.

The 1933 DV-32 Cabriolet Coupe was one of the last cars made by Stutz.
TSC

Stutz also made a name for itself on the racing circuit. One of the company's race cars won the American Automobile Association Stock Car Championship in 1927.
TSC

Stutz embarked on another program of factory-sponsored racing, with an impressive record of accomplishments from 1926 to 1931 at Pike's Peak, Colorado: Atlantic City, New Jersey; Charlotte, North Carolina; Daytona Beach, Florida; Brooklands, England; and Mexico City, Mexico.

In January 1929, Moskovics resigned from Stutz. By year's end, the company saw declining sales and higher prices than its rivals in the luxury market. The events of the Depression further compounded Stutz's concerns in the marketplace. Combined Stutz and Blackhawk production for 1929 totaled 3,630 cars, with the senior marque contributing 2,320 of the total.[11]

In May 1931, Stutz introduced the DV-32, designed to compete with the new multi-cylinder cars being brought out by Lincoln, Cadillac, Marmon, and others. DV-32 prices started at $4,895. The single-camshaft eight with two valves per cylinder was renamed the SV-16. Along with the DV-32, a new Bearcat was listed in speedster form and on a shorter chassis as the Super Bearcat.

Meanwhile the Depression was taking its toll on the smaller manufacturers who lacked the financial resources to survive. After record sales of 5,069 cars in 1926, the Stutz company business declined to 110 autos in 1933. Stutz auto production effectively ended with the final six cars built in 1934. The company continued to manufacture a light delivery van called the Pak-Age-Car until April 23, 1938, when a federal court ordered liquidation.[12]

Additional specifications on selected models

The Stutz Model A had a 120-inch wheelbase chassis and used a 390 c.i.d. Wisconsin, T-head, four-cylinder engine producing 60 h.p. at 1,500 r.p.m. with the patented Stutz transaxle.

The DV 32 had a dual overhead-camshaft, four-valves per cylinder, and a 156 h.p., straight-eight engine.

Endnotes

1. Katzell, Raymond A., *The Splendid Stutz: The Cars, Companies, People and Races,* Indianapolis, IN, The Stutz Club, © 1996, p 7 - 17.
2. Katzell, p 31 - 39.
3. Katzell, p 57 - 62.
4. Katzell, p 45.
5. Katzell, p 36 - 83.
6. Katzell, p 79 - 83.
7. Katzell, p 84 - 107.
8. Katzell, p 131 - 136.
9. Carson, Richard B., *The Olympian Cars: The Great American Luxury Automobiles of the Twenties & Thirties,* New York, NY, Alfred A. Knopf, © 1976, p 214.
10. Katzell, p 179.
11. Katzell, p 139 - 185.
12. Katzell, p 191 - 237.

The NEW STUTZ *vertical eight*

All New Stutz bodies designed and constructed under the supervision of Brewster of New York

TOP
50"
70"
20"

THE NEW STUTZ is an automobile which, in its entirety, is distinctively different and notably advanced. The features that make it so have never before been combined in a single car. One or two have already become standard in certain expensive foreign cars; all have been thoroughly proved before their incorporation in this car.

SAFETY—Among the features that make the New Stutz an unusually safe car are: Extreme low center of gravity, great stability, ease of control, high brake-efficiency, rapid acceleration, pressed steel running board side-bumpers, safety-glass windshield, and narrow front corner-posts.

APPEARANCE—Pure motor car design, with its every low-hung line eloquent of power, speed, comfort, beauty and smartness.

EASY RIDING—Long, flat, low-rate, shock-compensated springs, combined with extreme low center of gravity, give the New Stutz a riding ease that eliminates all side-sway and all impression of contact between the wheels and the road bed. This is a thoroughly new engineering principle impossible of application to conventional design.

STUTZ 8 SAFETY CHASSIS

Body five inches nearer the ground
—yet providing full road clearance and headroom

Radically lowered center of gravity
—giving greater safety, comfort and roadability

Quiet, long-lived, worm-drive rear axle
—permitting lowered body; it improves with use

90 H.P. motor; with overhead camshaft
—novel design; smooth, flexible, vibrationless

New, non-leaking hydrostatic brakes
—inherently equalized; quick-acting and positive

ROADABILITY—The New Stutz has a remarkable quality of "road-adhesiveness." The result can be likened to a strong magnetic attraction exerted by the earth upon the car's wheels.

SMOOTH AND QUIET IN OPERATION—

First, a motor from which vibration has been eliminated and in which the conventional noise-producing parts operating the valves are done away with by a simplified overhead camshaft design.

Second, a worm-drive rear axle which does not become noisy with use.

PERFORMANCE — The motor actually develops over 90 H.P. A speed of over 75 miles per hour is available when desired; likewise, acceleration from 10 to 50 miles per hour in less than 15 seconds. The tremendous, eager energy of the car is exerted so smoothly and so graciously that the speedometer readings are at times truly incredible.

LOWER CENTER OF GRAVITY—The floor of the car is five inches or more nearer the ground than in conventional chassis design. This is made possible, while maintaining ample road clearance and full headroom, by the worm-gear drive.

WORM-DRIVE REAR AXLE—The adoption of this costly type of rear axle, in combination with a lowered center of gravity, represents its first appearance in any American passenger car, although it is standard in the more expensive foreign chasses. The worm-drive improves rather than deteriorates with use. Worm and gear are guaranteed by us for two years.

VERTICAL EIGHT MOTOR—This motor shows a performance unparalleled by any other stock motor under 290 cu. in. piston displacement. The camshaft, actuated by an exclusive form of automatic silent-drive, operates directly on the tappets of overhead valves.

NON-LEAKING, HYDROSTATIC BRAKES—These are four-wheel brakes of an entirely new design. Nothing on them to adjust. No working parts to get out of order. They are inherently equalized. Each brake is divided into six shoes, which are uniformly actuated by an expanding circular tube, giving equalized braking pressure at every point on every wheel.

CHASSIS LUBRICATION SYSTEM—All working parts of the chassis are lubricated by an entirely new self-lubricating system, non-clogging, self-cleansing, troubleless and positive.

OIL RECTIFIER—A triple-duty rectifier keeps the crankcase oil at its original purity and consistency, eliminating all foreign matter, gasoline and water.

IGNITION—The Delco dual ignition operates two spark plugs in each cylinder from opposite points. Knocking is eliminated, acceleration is improved, greater speeds are attainable, and longer and harder "pulls" may be negotiated.

FRAME—Most rigid frame on any car, with integral steel running boards (actually, side bumpers). Seven cross-members; double drop, torsion-resisting construction.

UPHOLSTERY—Rich and luxurious, employing fine, high-grade fabrics and genuine leathers of distinctive beauty.

BODIES—Six models. Designed and constructed under the supervision of Brewster of New York.

All models are equipped with bumpers, front and rear, Watson Stabilators and full-balloon cord tires. Ventilating eaves on all closed-body doors.

STUTZ MOTOR CAR CO.
OF AMERICA. Inc.
Indianapolis

The new Vertical Eight series by Stutz was introduced in 1926.
TAC

"The Car of
Quality."

Makes of Note

Crosley, 1940-1941 and 1947-1953

Owner Powel Crosley debuted his new automobile to the public in April 1939 at the Indianapolis Motor Speedway. The diminutive 925-pound Crosley featured an air-cooled, two-cylinder Waukesha engine, and an 80-inch wheelbase. The price started at $325. Plants in Cincinnati, Ohio, and Richmond, Indiana, produced the car.[1]

Crosley's sales techniques were as different as the car itself. The car sold through large department and appliance stores that handled other Crosley products, such as radios and refrigerators. The 1940 model line consisted of a convertible coupe, convertible sedan, and a station wagon. For 1941, a convertible station wagon known as the Covered Wagon entered the line-up. The 1942 Crosleys were produced for a short time prior to the cessation of manufacturing during World War II.[2]

During the war, Crosley purchased the rights to an overhead-camshaft, four-cylinder CoBra (copper-brazed) sheet steel engine. The complete engine weighed 59 pounds and produced 36 h.p. from 44 c.i.d. Crosley produced this engine under contract for Naval applications as generator sets and refrigeration units.

Production of the postwar Crosleys began in Marion, Indiana, in early summer 1946. These offerings consisted of a two-door sedan and a convertible coupe with prices starting at $905. The 1946 Crosley used a modified CoBra engine that produced 26.5 h.p. with a mileage rating of 50 m.p.g. The new car was 28 inches longer than the previous model and weighed about 1,000 pounds.[3] Prices in 1947 started at $888, which was about $300 less than its nearest competitor.

For 1948, Crosley added an all-steel-bodied station wagon. This was an industry first and predated a similar offering by Plymouth by a year. Crosley reached its production peak in 1948 with 27,707 cars produced, with 23,489 of the total being station wagons. Crosley proudly claimed the title, "World's largest producer of station wagons."[4]

In 1949, a new cast iron block engine replaced the CoBra engine. Mid-year, Crosley introduced hydraulic disc brakes on all four wheels. The famous Hotshot sports car debuted in mid-summer. This was America's first mass-produced postwar sports car. It was a sporty proposition with an overhead cam engine and four-wheel hydraulic disc brakes.[5]

The Super Sports roadster debuted in 1950, with upscale trim, a higher horsepower rating, and a price about $50 more than the Hotshot. Super

Pictured above is the 1939 Crosley convertible coupe. NAHC

Below is an illustration of the 1949 Crosley known as the Hotshot. HAS&SM

Sports and Hotshots enjoyed some motor sports success in the early 1950s. Crosley sales overall in 1951 were slightly over 6,500 units.

Crosley's declining sales came as a direct result of providing an economical, no-frills offering in a market that didn't value this feature. In the early 1950s, American motorists expected more than basic transportation in their automobiles. Longer, lower, and more power was the mantra of the Big Three.

Crosley production ground to a halt in July 1952 after a production run of 1,522 cars. Between 1949 and 1952, Powel Crosley invested more than $3 million of his own money trying to save his venture. Finally, Crosley Motors was sold to General

Tire and Rubber Company. The car was no more, but the Crosley engine lived on in various applications into the 1970s.[6]

Empire, 1909-1919

Major players in the development of the Indianapolis Motor Speedway—Carl C. Fisher, James A. Allison, and Arthur C. Newby—also had an interest in the Empire Motor Car Company.

They, along with Robert Hassler, built a two-passenger car known as "The Little Aristocrat" in April 1909. This was about the same time that they were developing the two-and-a-half-mile oval race track on the west side of Indianapolis.

Their primary interest was in developing Speedway, which diverted their attention from the Empire auto firm. However, the first car to try out the new paved surface at the track was the first Empire off the line of the Indianapolis plant. After that, they concentrated their efforts on making the race track a paying proposition. Although a few shorter races occurred, the first 500 Mile Race was on Memorial Day 1911.[7]

They sold their interest in The Empire Motor Car Company late in 1911 to another group of Indianapolis businessmen who renamed it Empire Automobile Company. This company decided to contract for all parts and final assembly of their Empire Automobile by two Connersville firms. Central Manufacturing Company received the contract to build the bodies, and the Rex Manufacturing Company made the tops and enclosures. Rex Manufacturing completed Empire final assembly in the building just east of Central Manufacturing. Later models had Teetor-Hartley four-cylinder and Continental six-cylinder engines. In 1919, The Greenville Car Company of Greenville, Pennsylvania, bought the Empire name and designs and moved production out of state.[8]

Ford, 1914-1932

The Detroit-based Ford Motor Company opened its four-story, Indianapolis assembly branch (known as Plant 215) at 1315 East Washington Street in the fall of 1914. Production of Ford cars and trucks continued unabated for nearly two decades, except for a period during World War I and model changeovers.

An Empire is photographed here on a 1913 auto tour. NAHC

In May 1924, the new Car Delivery Unit was erected at the rear of the site fronting on Southeastern Avenue. The plant layout was expanded twice in the mid-1920s to allow more space for assembly operations. These expansions increased the plant's capacity to 300 assembled cars per day. With this capacity, the Indianapolis assembly branch had the highest output of any Indiana auto manufacturing site in its era.

Ford body assembly and finishing operations commenced at this plant in 1929. The Great Depression, however, also took its toll on Ford. As a result, Ford discontinued production operations in December 1931. Limited operations resumed at the site as a Ford parts service and automotive sales branch in July 1934. The plant operated on this basis into the 1940s.[9]

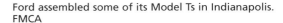

Ford assembled some of its Model Ts in Indianapolis. FMCA

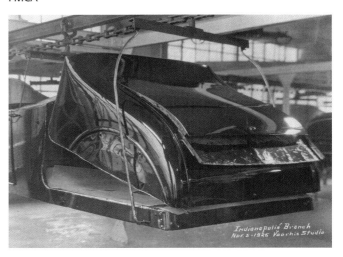

EMPIRE
"The Little Aristocrat"

Now $900
Completely Equipped

New Series Model 31, Five-Passenger Touring Car

Here in the 1914 EMPIRE is offered an automobile value that is really exceptional—a value that experienced car owners will be quick to see—one that by actual comparison will make an instant appeal to those about to buy their first car—a value that has won the acclaim of dealers everywhere.

See it—"The Little Aristocrat" of motordom. A full-fledged 5-passenger touring car.

A light-weight car with a surplus of strength and service that endures—a surplus that always means utmost safety.

But judge the EMPIRE by even more than the merely visible attributes of beauty, distinction and serviceability.

Judge it by what it has done as an actual touring car under road conditions that few other cars have ever attempted.

Five-Passenger, 110-Inch Wheel Base, Completely Equipped $900, Including

Demountable Rims	Rain Vision Windshield	Stewart Speedometer	Eisemann Magneto	Turkish Cushions
Mohair Top	Tool and Tire Kits	Prest-O-Lite Tank	Side and Tail Lamps	Oil Sight Feed
Top Envelope	Extra Rim	Gas Head Lights	Double Tire Irons	Dash Air Adjustment

The Empire Idea

The first EMPIRE Car was built five years ago for one of the wealthiest men in Indianapolis. He wanted a compact car of big efficiency. A car that would "stand up" under heaviest touring conditions. A car that would be associated with low-priced cars only in point of *price and minimum upkeep.*

Now the yearly output is many thousands. This year's model is enlarged, improved, and more refined than ever. But the basic principles that make for EMPIRE service remain unchanged.

The EMPIRE is distinctly a "one-policy" car. Every effort is concentrated in the making of this one model alone. The chassis is standard. That's why we can make it so well.

And the men behind it are all successful business men of large affairs. Every one of their enterprises is a permanent success.

What It Has Done

The EMPIRE is the car that traveled 3,766 speedometer miles across the continent with the "big fellows" in the Indiana-Pacific tour. Because of its light weight, surplus strength and power, it negotiated hundreds of miles of rough roads that no other tour ever attempted. The first and only car of its class to accomplish the feat. It was the sensation of the run.

Send for the Story

Write for the story of this great achievement. It comes to you free in the 9 x 12 book shown at the right. Profusely illustrated. This book is the last word in trans-continental travel. It will appeal to every car owner interested in American touring.

With it you will learn of the many unusual features that make the EMPIRE a car of exceptional value—a real touring car without excessive weight or heavy cost of maintenance.

Dealers

We regret that even our quadrupled output will not go all the way around. We want only the most successful and efficient automobile merchants to handle the EMPIRE—and those only who will render service in keeping with EMPIRE policy.

We want to hear from progressive Motor Car Sellers in the small towns as well as in big centers in open territory.

Our national advertising campaign will continue to tell the story of EMPIRE efficiency everywhere. This is the car that will help you take care of the inquiries you receive for a light weight, roomy car at this low, new price of $900.

FREE!

The Story of the Indiana-Pacific Tour, 9x12 Inches, Profusely Illustrated.

EMPIRE AUTOMOBILE COMPANY
Empire Corner INDIANAPOLIS, U. S. A.

(18)

Empire touted its Little Aristocrat possessing not only beauty but also "a surplus of strength and service that endures." The company emphasized its performance by the car's participation in the Indiana-Pacific tour.
TAC

H.C.S., 1919-1923

With the boom following World War I in full swing, Harry C. Stutz sold his interest in the Stutz Motor Company and left to form H.C.S. Motor Car Company in 1919. The H.C.S. was a moderate-sized, quality-assembled automobile similar to its predecessor, the Stutz. The H.C.S. factory was constructed at 1402 N. Capitol Avenue in Indianapolis, just across the street from another newcomer, the Stutz Fire Engine Company. The H.C.S. Indianapolis showroom was in the Charles E. Stutz Sales Company premises at 848 N. Meridian Street.

A 1921 H.C.S. is illustrated above.
NAHC

In late 1919, a H.C.S. prototype was built. The car had an upright nickel-silver radiator, drum-style headlights, cycle-type fenders, aluminum step plates in place of traditional running boards, and self-supporting side-mounted spare tires. A modified 50 h.p., Weidley four-cylinder engine was standard equipment. The prototype used a Delco generating, starting, and lighting system. The valve cover, side covers, bell housing, and finned oil pan were all of cast aluminum. The initial offering price of a roadster was $2,725 with a top price of $3,650 for the sedan.

H.C.S. was selected as the pace car for the 1921 Indianapolis 500. Then in the 1923 Memorial Day classic, The company-sponsored, straight-eight race car obtained the pole position and finished in first place.

Stutz's timing on the H.C.S. was unfortunate because of the economic recession of 1921-1922. In 1921, prices on H.C.S. open cars were reduced to $2,400, and the sedan dropped to $3,150. About 800 cars were produced in 1920 and around 650 cars in 1921.

Then in 1923 Stutz introduced the new six-cylinder Model 6 on a 126-inch wheelbase. A roadster was priced at $2,250. Early Model 6s also used Weidley engines, while later models used Midwest engines. Both were rated at 80 h.p. An interesting feature on the 1923 models was the use of 10-inch diameter drum headlights with six-inch tilting reflectors. A switch mounted on the steering column permitted deflection of the headlight beam.

This was an early application of headlight dimming. In 1923, four-cylinder production amounted to about 500 cars, with another 500 of six-cylinder cars.

With declining auto sales in mid-1924, Stutz decided that the company should concentrate on taxi cab production across the street at the Stutz Fire Engine Company building. As the H.C.S. Cab Manufacturing Company, it survived until January 1927.[10]

Henderson, 1912-1914

The Henderson automobile would probably never have existed without the initial contact with Cole Motor Car Company.

In July 1909, Charles P. Henderson and his brother R.P. Henderson were named directors of the Cole Motor Car Company. They soon formed the Henderson Motor Sales Company, which served as the selling agent for the Cole Motor Car Company.[11]

On June 30, 1912, Cole's exclusive contract with the Henderson Motor Sales Company expired, and the Henderson brothers left to manufacture their own automobile. The Henderson Motor Car Company was organized with capital of $100,000 to produce a low-priced standard automobile. Charles P. Henderson served as the company's president and sales manager and R.P. Henderson as vice-president and general manager.[12] The Henderson was announced to the public prior to the Indianapolis 500 on May 29, 1912.

The company leased an entire floor of the former Hume-Mansur building for office space in Indianapolis. Regarding their design, the Hendersons said, "In selecting the parts, accessories, and equipment, only those were chosen which were recognized as *standard* and which combined effectively with other parts and features to make the *Henderson* a new unit of motoring efficiency."

The Series One Henderson was offered as a four-cylinder automobile. In August 1912, after introduction of the 1913 models, the company erected a circus-style tent as temporary warehouse prior to road testing and final finishing. The Series Two Henderson featured Buda engines in two four-cylinder lines and one six-cylinder line. Coupe bodies were optional on the De Luxe and Six-Cylinder chassis.[13]

On July 1, 1913, renowned race car driver Ray Harroun left Indianapolis in a Henderson DeLuxe Four-Cylinder touring car—fitted with an optional carburetor. He drove along with 17 other Indiana-built cars as part of the I.A.M.A. Indiana to Pacific Tour. They traveled across country entirely on kerosene. This car successfully negotiated the heavily mired roads of Missouri, passed through the hot winds of Kansas, reached an altitude of over 11,300 feet, and plowed through the great American desert. As a result, the Henderson became the first automobile to cross the American continent on kerosene.

Unfortunately, Henderson's slogan, "The Car of Your Dreams," must not have appealed to enough dreamers because its final year was 1914. Lack of sufficient working capital plagued the company from the beginning. Preferring not to sell their operation, the Hendersons chose to liquidate it.

In August 1914, the Hendersons were welcomed back by the Cole Motor Car Company with C.P. as sales manager and R.P. as his assistant.

Inter-State, 1909-1919

Large-scale automobile manufacturing in Muncie started in 1909, thanks to the efforts of the Commercial Club of Muncie (forerunner to the Chamber of Commerce). A group spearheaded by the five Ball brothers—George, Frank, William, Edmund, and Lucius—along with J.M. Marling and Tom Hart formed the Inter-State Automobile Company. A two-building, three-block-long plant was built at the end of West Willard Street.[14]

Claude E. Cox, formerly with the Overland Automobile Company, designed the 1909 Inter-State

Henderson sold the Deluxe Model 54-W Roadster in 1913 for $1,785.
LDC

four-cylinder models. The cars were priced at $1,750. In 1912, features included electric lighting and starting, with an electric fuel pump. These four-cylinders came in 30, 40 and 50 h.p. Inter-State built four- and six-cylinder automobiles for 1913. The six-cylinder Model 45, rated at 38.4 h.p., had a 132-inch wheelbase and sold for $2,750.

In the late fall of 1913, Inter-State entered voluntary receivership. Frank C. Ball reorganized the company as the Inter-State Motor Company in early 1914. A new four-cylinder Model T on a 110-inch wheelbase was offered for $1,000 in 1915. From 1916 to 1918, Model T prices ranged from $850 to $1,325. Inter-State acknowledged that it was the same car with new pricing for the roadster and touring models.

Inter-State discontinued automotive operations for the duration of World War I in early 1918. General Motors acquired the Inter-State plant in early 1919. A division of GM called Sheridan Motor Car Company then produced the Sheridan at this site during 1920 and 1921.

William C. Durant took over the facility in 1921 to form Durant Motors of Indiana, Inc. Durant

A 1915 Inter-State has been restored for modern use.
NAHC

90

The Automobile for Women

Electrically Started and Lighted	*Inter-State*	Controls Itself Pumps Its Own Tires

THE advent of the Inter-State, with its marvelously simple mechanism, its electrical self-starter and its self-controller has brought a revolution in motoring. Now the powerful and magnificent Inter-State starts and obeys the will of the woman driver as readily, as easily and as simply as an electric coupe. Without moving from the driver's seat or shifting gears she starts the engine by a turn of the switch — regulates the mixture by a simple movement of the lever on the steering column, and the magnificent Inter-State is under way

No labor to start the Inter-State

and under perfect and absolute control, with no more trouble than turning on an electric light. The Inter-State electric self-starter is **part of the system** and **built into it,** and the motor dynamo turns the engine itself until it picks up under its own power.

Electric Lights as in Your Own Home

Any or all lights on by turning switch

ONE of the greatest features of the Inter-State is its electric light system—not a single light or two—but an entire and reliable system, front —side—rear, all correlated and so arranged that by a turn of the switch, without leaving the driver's seat, any or all of the lights may be turned on in all their brilliancy. No more gas tanks, no more oil filling, no more lamp trimming or adjusting. The system is simply perfect. The front head-lights are provided with a dimming feature so that driving in city streets may be done with a medium diffused light.

Write Today for Art Catalog

This describes fully the six 40 and 50 H. P. completely equipped Models which cost from $2,400 to $3,400. Gives complete details of all the equipment and features, and also shows the Inter-State Models 30-A and 32-B, 40 H. P., costing $1,750 and $1,700 respectively.

THAT greatest nuisance of motoring—tire pumping—is *totally eliminated* with the Inter-State equipment. Any woman can attach the valve to the tire, turn on the pump and in a few minutes have tires just as solid and as perfectly filled as if done by the greatest tire expert in the world.

The Inter-State *does* the work. You *direct* it. There is nothing to it at all and you are fore-armed for any emergency with the complete and thorough equipment of the Inter-State.

Inter-State Tire Pumping—No Work

Motoring Now All Pleasure

THIS great car performs all the labor itself— electrically self-started—electric lights and ignition, tire pumping and the automatic regulation of fuel consumption.

For the first time in the history of the automobile, electricity plays its *real part* in the entire mechanism. The Inter-State Electric System is really the *nerve system* commanding the energy and motion of the powerful steel muscles that make the Inter-State such a masterpiece of construction. Every conceivable accessory and feature is built into or included in the Inter-State. The Inter-State is truly the *only complete car* in this country or abroad —and this statement is made advisedly.

The *Only Complete Car*—Equipment and Features Unequalled

INTER-STATE AUTOMOBILE COMPANY, Dept. B   Muncie, Indiana

Boston Branch: 153 Massachusetts Avenue   *Omaha Branch:* 310 South 18th Street

The Inter-State claimed its "simple mechanism, its electrical self-starter and self-controller" made it "The Automobile for Women." TAC produced two makes of autos in this plant from 1922 to 1928, Durant (1922-28) and Princeton (1923-24). The Durant and Princeton used Ansted engines from Connersville. The Princeton was Durant's attempt to produce a car between his Flint and Locomobile lines. Auto manufacturing in Muncie ended in 1928.

LaFayette, 1919-1922

Charles W. Nash of Nash Motors formed the LaFayette Motors Company in Indianapolis as a luxury manufacturer in October 1919. A large cadre of former Cadillac executives were involved with this venture, including chief engineer D. McCall White, who also penned the 1915 Cadillac V-8.

The LaFayette was a luxurious, lavishly equipped V-8 design. Its L-head engine developed 90 h.p. at 2,750 r.p.m. The LaFayette utilized a unit engine construction with the engine, clutch, and transmission comprising a single unit. The unit engine assembly was set in the frame at such an angle that it transmitted power in a straight line to the torque tube axle. It had a patented device for removing water and sediment from the oil. LaFayette pioneered thermostatically controlled radiator shutters for engine cooling.[15]

Production began in August 1920 with the introduction of the 1921 LaFayette. The company produced a variety of open and closed body styles ranging from $5,000 to $7,500. LaFayette only sold 700 cars in the first year and about 350 cars in 1922. In July 1922, LaFayette Motors moved to Milwaukee, Wisconsin, to geographically consolidate Nash operations.

LaFayettes, illustrated below, were luxurious and lavishly equipped. TAC

The Four-Door Coupé

A 1924 Lexington is pictured above. NAHC

Lexington, 1910-1927

Knisey Stone, a Kentucky race horse promoter, founded The Lexington Motor Company in 1909 in Lexington, Kentucky. Several months later the company outgrew its building. In 1910, a group of Connersville businessmen noted that the community had too much tied up in the buggy and carriage industry, which was being displaced by the growing use of the automobile. The group enticed the infant Lexington Motor Car Company to relocate from Lexington to a new plant at 800 West 18th Street in the McFarlan industrial park.

John C. Moore, the company's chief engineer, immediately started on improvements to the Lexington to keep the company ahead of its competition. His 1911 multiple exhaust was reported to give 30 percent more power on less fuel. Each cylinder had a separate exhaust. Dual exhaust pipes and mufflers were used.

The company was promotionally minded and entered both the Glidden Tour and the Indianapolis 500 in 1912 to attract attention.

Financial difficulties of 1913 were solved when E.W. Ansted acquired Lexington to assemble the six-cylinder Howard for a contract with a Chicago distributor. The company was renamed Lexington-Howard. In 1915, the name reverted to Lexington Motor Company. At this time, the four-cylinder engine was supplemented by a light six and a supreme six. With the new Ansted engines, Lexingtons became modern and powerful.

Lexingtons—like most other Indiana-built automobiles—were assembled cars, being built with components from many different suppliers. Lexingtons became popular with the release of the Thoroughbred Six and Minute Man Six models.

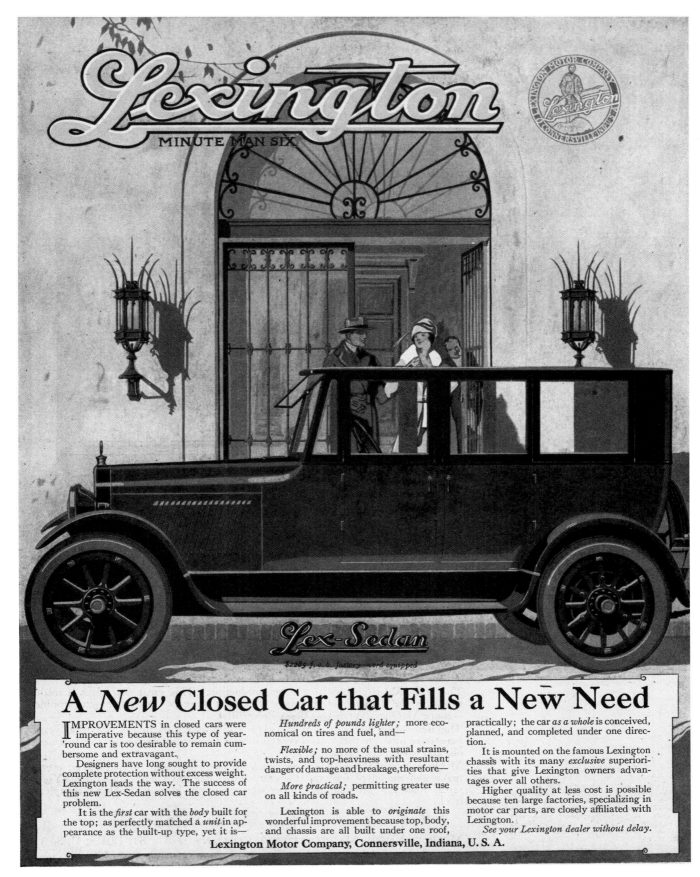

A *New* Closed Car that Fills a New Need

IMPROVEMENTS in closed cars were imperative because this type of year-'round car is too desirable to remain cumbersome and extravagant.

Designers have long sought to provide complete protection without excess weight. Lexington leads the way. The success of this new Lex-Sedan solves the closed car problem.

It is the *first* car with the *body* built for the top; as perfectly matched a *unit* in appearance as the built-up type, yet it is—

Hundreds of pounds lighter; more economical on tires and fuel, and—

Flexible; no more of the usual strains, twists, and top-heaviness with resultant danger of damage and breakage, therefore—

More practical; permitting greater use on all kinds of roads.

Lexington is able to *originate* this wonderful improvement because top, body, and chassis are all built under one roof,

practically; the car *as a whole* is conceived, planned, and completed under one direction.

It is mounted on the famous Lexington chassis with its many *exclusive* superiorities that give Lexington owners advantages over all others.

Higher quality at less cost is possible because ten large factories, specializing in motor car parts, are closely affiliated with Lexington.

See your Lexington dealer without delay.

Lexington Motor Company, Connersville, Indiana, U. S. A.

This ad for a Lexington appeared in early 1920.
TAC

93

Lexington's first Connersville plant expansion was in 1915. A factory building was erected just north of the office. The company also built a 100-foot smoke stack with the Lexington name in lighter-color bricks. Four years later the company built a 106,050 sq. ft. assembly building west of the office.

In 1917, Moore put together a new frame with a rigid box cross-section that eliminated the problem of jammed doors caused by frame flexing. The car using this new frame also had an emergency brake affixed to the drive shaft. Lexington autos featured hardtop enclosures made by the Rex Manufacturing Company of Connersville in 1918.

Also in 1918, the newly formed Ansted Engine Company acquired the Teetor-Hartley Motor Corporation of Hagerstown. In 1919, the 85,306 sq. ft. Ansted Engine building was erected just north of the Lexington plant and extended to 21st Street. The combined Lexington and Ansted facilities measured three blocks long and two blocks wide totaling 270,000 sq. ft. of floor space.

Lexington built two short-wheelbase race cars with the powerful Ansted engine for the 1920 Pikes Peak hill climb. The cars placed first and second in their initial outing and brought home the Penrose trophy. Again in 1924, Otto Loesche won in 18 minutes and 15 seconds. He brought the trophy home for keeps. The Penrose trophy is on display at the Reynolds Museum on Vine Street.

Frank B. Ansted, president, announced the formation of the United States Automotive Corporation at the New York Auto Show on January 12, 1920. It was a $10 million merger with the Lexington Motor Car Company, the Ansted Engineering Company, and The Connersville Foundry Corporation from Connersville, plus the Teetor-Hartley Motor Corporation of Hagerstown.

The high point of Lexington production arrived in 1920 with over 6,000 cars built.

On December 16, 1921, William C. Durant, founder and former president of General Motors, ordered 30,000 Ansted engines for his new Durant Six that was being built in Muncie by Durant Motors of Indiana, Inc.

Late in 1921, Alanson P. Brush (designer of the Brush runabout and consulting engineer to General Motors) sued the company, alleging that the Ansted engine infringed on a number of his patents. The negative publicity hurt.

Records show that in 1922, United States Automotive Corporation—Lexington's parent company—owned 10 different factories that were building parts for its cars. Historian Henry Blommel notes in his writings "It was a great alliance of parts-making plants that found the culmination of its efforts in the finished Lexington car."

Lexington Motor Car Company and United States Automotive Corporation were affected by recessionary events in the early 20s. Production in 1922 plummeted to roughly a third of the 1920 total.

In 1923, The Ansted Engine Company entered receivership with William C. Durant as a principle shareholder. Lexington Motor Car Company also entered receivership in 1923.

In 1926 and 1927, E.L. Cord's Auburn Automobile Company purchased Ansted Engine and the Lexington Motor Car Company, respectively. The Lexington was soon phased out.[16]

McIntyre, Kiblinger, and Imp, 1907-1915

The W.H. Kiblinger Company, an established manufacturer of buggies and wagons in Auburn, established its auto department in 1907. The Kiblinger was a highwheel vehicle that sold for as little as $250, which was extremely reasonable at the time. Kiblinger's initial catalog went on at length to trumpet that its highwheeler was more satisfactory than a horse and buggy: "The Kiblinger is the only gasoline automobile that any woman or even a boy can feel safe to drive."

The first Kiblingers were available in two models—A and B. The main difference between the models was that the Model B had a slightly larger

Two men demonstrate the light-weight advantage of the Imp. (c.1913-1914).
ACDM

A young John McIntyre was behind the tiller of this early Kiblinger model (c. 1908-10).
ACDM

engine displacement and cost $50 more. The bodies were described as "Piano box type." Wire spoke wheels with cushion tires were available for an additional charge of $25. The entire vehicle weighed 450 pounds.[17]

In 1909, after Kiblinger's death, the company name changed to W.H. McIntyre Company. Early McIntyre models continued to be highwheelers. By early 1909 a McIntyre advertisement boasted of "21 Models to Choose From." This ad was still comparing the McIntyre to a horse and buggy: "McIntyre motor vehicles never fail—never get tired—cost no more than a good horse and buggy—cost far less to keep—do more work in less time than three horses." The company was pitching the highwheeler to rural customers for use over any kind of road in all kinds of weather. The top-of-the-line, Model M four-passenger runabout, featured a four-cylinder engine for $850.

By 1910, highwheeler popularity began to wane. The McIntyre Company noted this market change and began to offer conventional front-engine automobiles and commercial vehicles. The new conventional model was offered in six body styles, all priced from $1,400 to $1,750. One highwheeler model survived in the line through the 1911 model year. For 1912, McIntyre offered a four-cylinder auto with roadster, touring, and landaulet bodies priced at $1,125. By 1912, the commercial truck line was available in a variety of ton capacities in every conceivable body style.

The rising popularity of six-cylinder autos prompted McIntyre to offer one as a five-passenger touring car

for the moderate price of $1,485 in 1913. McIntyre continued to make conventional models through 1915.[18]

Cyclecars were introduced in Europe in 1909, and the novelty transferred to the United States by 1913. The Imp Cyclecar subsidiary of the W.H. McIntyre Company produced one of America's first cyclecars in November 1913. The Imp's 10-12 h.p. V-2 engine utilized a friction transmission and belt drive. The cyclecar rode on a 100-inch wheelbase, weighed only 600 pounds, stretched 50 miles from a gallon of gas, and cost only $375. The Imp was offered in two models: a tandem seat passenger car and a single seat parcel delivery van for only $20 more.

By 1914, cyclecars became a fad. There were over 50 different cyclecars manufactured in the United States. Prices ranged from less than $300 to over $600. Indiana-built cyclecars included Comet, Hoosier Scout, and Spacke. A 1914 Imp advertisement was particularly boastful: "The only car in the world that any Woman, Boy, or Girl can Operate, Care for, and Handle with Ease."

In the summer of 1914, Imp the Second was introduced for $695. This new model had a four-cylinder, water-cooled engine, and a roadster body with side-by-side seating. Approximately 6,000 Imps were built during 1914.

Cyclecar construction techniques used a wood frame and many wooden components. Due to this light construction, the vehicles were not very durable. The belt-drive system was another source of mechanical headaches. The cyclecar fad passed as fast as it began.

DeKalb County's first female doctor, Bonnell Souder of Auburn, also was one of the firsts to drive a McIntyre automobile. She is pictured in a McIntyre Physician's Runabout (c. 1912).
ACDM

McIntyre

The Practical Car for Practical People

The McIntyre is "the car you can afford to own after you've bought it"
Built in 25 Models, a car for every purpose at a price to suit every pocketbook.
Two and four cylinder. Shaft and chain drive. Solid Rubber Tires. Air cooled. Ten to Thirty horse power.

Not what we say but here is what others say

What the Car Does.

"We were in mud and water several times and once I stopped in the mud and water when the hubs were out of sight just to test the car and it pulled out without a bit of trouble. Use it in all kinds of weather and on all kinds of roads. Run it on roads that no low wheeled automobile on the face of the earth could run. Run this high wheeled machine through mud and soft gravel where it was so deep until it struck the step and the muffler. Never struck a road yet but have gone over it, good or pad, snow or mud."

"To date have covered a distance of 8800 miles. Have averaged 21 miles to the gallon of gasoline. Made sand any depth, hills any height, never towed any distance."

"7137 miles in 66 days. Repair account $4.67.

"Very durable and always reliable. No tinkering, no repairing. Always ready to go when I am, day or night."

W. H. McINTYRE CO.,

AUBURN   INDIANA

The W.H. McIntyre Co. relied on testimonies to help sell its vehicles in this 1909 ad.
HAS&SM

In summer 1915, the W. H. McIntyre Company filed for bankruptcy. In its time, the company produced the largest range of vehicles of any company in Auburn. An example of the Imp resides at the Auburn Cord Duesenberg Museum.[19]

Maxwell, 1906-1916

When Maxwell-Briscoe (predecessor of DaimlerChrysler) built its New Castle facility in 1906, it was the largest automobile plant in the nation. The company's Model L—a two-passenger, twin-cylinder runabout—sold for $780 when the plant opened. Four-cylinder versions followed with the Model M five-passenger touring car priced at $3,000.

Maxwell sold 12,000 autos by 1909. A 1909 *Motor Age* advertisement proclaimed, "When you buy a Maxwell you buy a car of established value." The ad called the Model LD, "The Aristocrat of Runabouts."

By the spring of 1910, Maxwell boasted of over 25,000 cars sold. An April 21, 1910 *Motor Age* ad claimed of the Model E five-passenger tonneau: "Here is a 'Big Car' the wealthiest man will be <u>proud</u> to own—and the man of moderate means can <u>afford</u> to <u>maintain</u>. This 'Big Car' can be run 5,000 miles a year at an average <u>total</u> cost of <u>$3.98 a week</u>." A customer's unsolicited testimonial letter backed up the claim. These were heady times for Maxwell-Briscoe. They ranked third in industry sales after Ford and Buick.

The model pictured below is one of the first autos manufactured by Maxwell in 1906.
NAHC

In 1910, the company became part of the United States Motor Company, which later collapsed in 1912. In 1913, Jonathan D. Maxwell salvaged what was left and continued to make inexpensive four-cylinder autos.

The Maxwell line consisted of three models in 1914: The 25-4 five-passenger touring car for $725, 35-4 five-passenger touring car for $1,085, plus the one-year-only 50-6 seven-passenger touring car for $2,350. From 1915 onward, the line concentrated on the Model 25 four-cylinder offering.[20]

Total production of cars and trucks topped the 100,000 mark in 1917. The postwar recession in the early 1920s hit Maxwell particularly hard. At one time, there were 17,000 unsold Maxwells sitting on factory lots.

In 1923 Walter P. Chrysler took over control of Maxwell and Chalmers, its associated company. The Chrysler Six, introduced in 1924, outsold Maxwell's four-cylinder autos. The 1925 Maxwells were the last, being replaced by the Chrysler four-cylinder car.

Chrysler has enjoyed a long association with the New Castle community. Today the facility at 18171 I Avenue manufactures auto and truck parts.

National, 1900-1924

L.S. Dow and Phillip Goetz founded the National Automobile & Electric Company in Indianapolis during 1900. The first National vehicles were light electric vehicles offered in a plethora of body styles. A 1901 advertisement boasted, "The electric vehicle is always ready, requires no mechanical knowledge to run it, and among electric vehicles, the 'National' is pre-eminently simple, powerful, elegant, and excellent."

In 1904 the company was reorganized as the National Motor Vehicle Company. Its first gasoline auto premiered in 1903. By 1905, a National car employed the powerful four-cylinder Rutenber engine, with a round radiator that served as a distinguishing feature. The company stopped electric car production in 1906.

National introduced a six-cylinder Model E seven-passenger touring car in 1906, one of the first sixes in America. The 1906 catalog stated, "It was placed on the market to supply a growing demand for a high-powered commodious touring car of

Victories for National Cars

In the Three Days' Meet, Opening the Great Indianapolis Motor Speedway, August 19-21, were recorded the following

The best known racing cars and the most famous drivers of the world were on the new circular track and made the competition the hottest ever known. No one make of car has ever made such a handsome clean-up as did the National with its "Forty" and "Sixty."

August 19th

Ten Miles Free-for-All Handicap
National Sixty, 3rd; Jno. Aitken. Time 8:36.2.

250 Miles Prest-O-Lite Trophy
National Forty, 3rd; C. C. Merz. Time 4:57:07.1
National Forty, 4th; Thos. Kincaid

August 20th

Ten Miles Stripped Chassis, 301 to 450 Cu. In.
National Forty, 1st; C. C. Merz. Time 9:16.3

Ten Miles W & S Trophy Competitors
National Sixty, 1st; Jno. Aitken. Time 9:26.6
National Forty, 4th; Thos. Kincaid

Ten Miles Free-for-All, Open
National Sixty, 2nd; Jno. Aitken. Time 8:32.6

Five Miles Free-for-All Handicap
National Sixty, 1st. Jno. Aitken. Time 4:25
(World's Record Standing Start)
National Forty, 2nd; C. C. Merz. Time 4:35

August 21st

Fifteen Miles Free-for-All Handicap
National Forty, 1st; Thos. Kincaid. Time 13:23.5

Three Hundred Miles, Wheeler & Schebler Trophy (unfinished)
National Sixty, John Aitken, made 25 miles in 21:27.6

and the

World's Record for 50 Miles. Time 44:21.2
World's Record for 75 Miles. Time 1:09:34.6
World's Record for 100 Miles. Time 1.31:41.9

The National "Forty" cars driven by Merz and Kincaid are the first stock cars built by the National Factory for 1910. There are 500 more, precisely like them in every particular of design, workmanship and materials, coming through the 1910, to sell at the remarkable list of **$2,500.**

We are making the allotments right now! Get in early if you want to handle them.

National Motor Vehicle Company 1006 East 22d St. Member A. M. C. M. A. Indianapolis, Ind.

This 1909 ad touted National's performance at the Indianapolis Motor Speedway.
HAS&SM

The auto pictured above is one of a variety of four- and six-cylinder models manufactured by National in 1912. NAHC

extremely flexible control, in which vibration is reduced to a minimum." Its cylinders were cast separately until 1908, when National produced engines with cylinders cast in pairs.

The U.S. shield-shaped radiator design debuted in 1908. In 1908 and 1909, National offered two models each with higher h.p. ratings in the four- and six-cylinder lines range from $2,750 to $5,000.

Immediately after a strong showing at the inaugural races at the Indianapolis Motor Speedway during August 1909, National featured the 1910 Model Forty in a two-page advertisement in Motor Age magazine: "The National 'Forty' this year is the fastest, the most powerful, and most capable car that has ever been offered at anything under $4,000 heretofore." The price was $2,500.

During this period, racing played an important part in National's plans. National finished seventh in the Inaugural 500 Mile Race on Memorial Day 1911. Additional 1911 competition road race victories include Elgin, Illinois; Santa Monica, California; and the Cactus Derby from Los Angeles, California, to Phoenix, Arizona. Joe Dawson driving a National won the Indianapolis 500 Mile Race in 1912 with an average speed of 78.7 m.p.h.

In 1912 the company focused on production of a variety of fours and sixes with pricing starting at $2,500. Eleven models were available in the 1914 line with prices ranging from $2,375 to $4,800.

In 1916 a new range of six body styles were announced with a Highway Six or the Highway Twelve in the same chassis. The 12 was dropped in 1920, and National soldiered on with six-cylinder cars for its final four years. A merger in 1922 between National, Dixie Flyer and Jackson led to a range of three cars for 1923 and 1924. In January 1924, the company entered receivership.[21]

Overland, 1903-1911

Claude E. Cox demonstrated the first Overland automobile at the Standard Wheel Works at 13th and Plum streets in Terre Haute on February 12, 1903. The Wheel Works was the largest manufacturer of wheels in the world at the time with three plants in Ohio, and one each in Michigan, Fort Wayne, and Indianapolis. General offices were in Terre Haute along with a facility that specialized in heavy wheels for wagons and trucks.

Cox designed the Overland as part of his thesis while he was a student at Rose Polytechnic Institute. Cox worked at the Wheel Works as a salesman while he was studying at the nearby college. The runabout used a five h.p., single-cylinder engine, and planetary transmission. His design had several innovations and received an unusual amount of attention. Cox placed the engine of his car in the front, remarking that it was the "logical" place for it. Cox also improved the seating arrangement by making the entrance to the rear seat compartment through the sides rather than through the rear of the auto as in earlier models.

The Wheel Works devoted the second story of one of the new buildings to manufacturing Overlands. Demand for the autos increased to the point that it was difficult to produce the necessary quantity at the Terre Haute facility. In January 1905, Overland operations moved to Indianapolis facilities at 900-1300 West Henry Street. Cox went to Indianapolis as manager of the Overland Automobile Department of the Standard Wheel Works. He improved the 1905 models with the addition of a shaft drive and a steering wheel.

More financial backing was required when Standard sold the car and manufacturing rights to David M. Parry who formed The Overland Automobile Company on March 31, 1906. Parry previously had made a personal fortune manufacturing buggies and carriages.[22]

Shortly before the national panic of 1907, John North Willys contracted with Overland to manufacture 500 cars in 1908 and paid $10,000 to bind the agreement. This gave the factory the financial ability to increase its facilities. During the panic, Overland noted that it could not fill its contract nor meet its current payroll. Over a weekend, Willys raised the $350 and deposited it to the credit of the Overland Company.

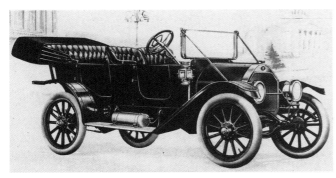

A 1912 Overland Model 59-T is illustrated above.
HAS&SM

Bankruptcy was stalled for the moment on the pledge that the company would be reorganized with Willys as president, treasurer, general manager, sales manager, and purchasing agent. Overland resumed production. In 1908 Willys built 465 four-cylinder Model 24 automobiles, paid the most pressing debts, and showed a profit of $58,000.[23]

In early 1909, Willys purchased a controlling interest in the Marion Motor Car Company of Indianapolis, which he later sold in 1912. By September 1909, with the inevitable improvement in credit and the available cash, he took over the plant of the Pope auto manufacturing facilities in Toledo, Ohio. This became the home of his Willys auto empire and production started on a new automobile that he named the Willys-Overland.

Willys assembled Willys-Overlands in Indianapolis through the 1911 model year. Then the plant produced component parts for Willys-Overland until 1923.[24]

Claude Cox continued to be affiliated with the automobile industry all of his life. In 1909 he left Indianapolis and joined the Inter-State Automobile Company in Muncie. In two years he left Muncie for the Wilcox Motor Car Co. in Minneapolis, Minnesota. Then, in 1912, he became the director of research for General Motors Company in Detroit, Michigan. At the time of his death in 1964, Cox was president of Bartlett Research, Inc., an automotive research firm in Detroit.[25]

Parry, 1910-1911; New Parry, 1911-1912; Pathfinder, 1912-1917

Prior to starting the Indianapolis-based Parry Auto Company in summer 1909, David M. Parry was president of the Parry Manufacturing Company and a principal stockholder in the Overland Automobile Company. He offered the Parry as a two-passenger roadster and five-passenger touring car with four-cylinder overhead valve engines. A December 9, 1909 *Motor Age* article stated that Parry planned to build 5,000 autos in 1910. Parry production did not meet this benchmark, thus forcing the company into receivership due to heavy equipment outlays.

After reorganizing the firm as the Motor Car Manufacturing Company, the car name was changed to New Parry. The only thing new in this offering was the name. The two-passenger roadster and five-passenger touring car were essentially a duplicate of the previous offerings. Additional models were a four-passenger touring car and a four-passenger demi-tonneau. These four-cylinder models were priced from $1,350 to $1,750.[26]

The Pathfinder introduced in 1912 succeeded the New Parry as a boattail speedster. It was noted for several advanced body innovations, such as the disappearing top and a spare wheel cover. Initially, Pathfinders had four-cylinder engines, followed by sixes with V radiators.

The company was reorganized as The Pathfinder Company in 1916. The year also saw the introduction of a model with a Weidley 12-cylinder engine called Pathfinder the Great, King of Twelves. In December 1917, the company was liquidated in receivership.[27]

The New Parry was essentially the same as the old Parry. The name change resulted after reorganization of the firm.
HAS&SM

Plymouth, 1935-1959

Chrysler Corporation purchased Dodge Brothers, Inc. and became part of the Evansville manufacturing scene in the spring of 1928. Chrysler operated the plant for the assembly of Dodge-built trucks until 1935. In 1935, the demand for Plymouth automobiles was so great that Chrysler's entire Evansville plant converted to Plymouth assembly.

Briggs Indiana Corporation also became involved when it acquired the former Graham Auto body plant on East Columbia Street in 1936 and dedicated it to the production of auto bodies for the adjacent Plymouth plant. Plymouth and Briggs soon employed 4,000 people producing 300 cars per day, which was an economic boon in the later part of the Great Depression.[28]

During World War II, all civilian production ceased to make room for war production. Chrysler's Evansville Ordinance Plant produced over three billion rounds of small arms ammunition, 1,660 reconditioned Sherman tanks, 4,000 rebuilt Army trucks, 800,000 tank grousers (track overshoes that made tanks more maneuverable on muddy terrain), and 100,000 incendiary bombs. Chrysler employed over 12,000 people during its peak wartime production.[29] Briggs' Indiana plant built wings for the Navy torpedo bomber known as the TBY. In early 1944, the Briggs plant employed 3,700 people.

Postwar demand for cars encouraged the plant to turn out as many as 400 cars per day. On March 25, 1953, the one millionth Plymouth came off Evansville's assembly line. During this time, more than 3,300 made up the Chrysler payroll, which totaled over $8 million annually. Production rates varied from 500 to 800 cars per day.[30]

In the spring of 1951, Chrysler obtained a contract to build the 60-foot Albatross aircraft hull at the Evansville plant. At one time, construction of the aircraft hull occupied about one-half of the plant floor space. Completed hulls were shipped by a specially-built truck to Long Island, New York,

A 1952 Plymouth model is pictured below being assembled alongside a Grumman Albatross.
DCHC

for final assembly into finished air-sea rescue planes.[31]

Chrysler was Evansville's largest employer in 1959, when the company moved and consolidated Plymouth operations at a new plant in St Louis, Missouri.

A 1919 Premier was notable because of the use of the Cutler-Hammer Magnetic Gear Shift.
NAHC

Premier, 1903-1926

George B. Weidley and Harold O. Smith organized the Indianapolis-based Premier Motor Manufacturing Company in 1903 with a capitalization of $50,000 for the production of air-cooled cars. Premier's claim to fame was the use of the oak leaf on its radiator badge, which the company said was the first use of an emblem as an automobile trademark.

Premier made the transition to water-cooled engines in 1908. When Premier completed the 1909 Glidden Tour, it had established an unprecedented record of three perfect scores. In a 1909 *Motor Age* advertisement, Premier boasted, "Do not judge the Premier by its best performance. Judge it by its average performance." The company introduced its first six in 1908. Starting in 1913, Premier built only sixes.

On October 15, 1914, Premier entered receivership. In December 1915, the company was reorganized as the Premier Motor Car Company. The 1918-1920 Premier was notable mainly for its use of the Cutler-Hammer "Magnetic Gear Shift," an electric transmission system controlled by a push button arrangement mounted on the steering column. The overhead-valve, 295 c.i.d. engine was an advanced six, with a one-piece aluminum block, crankcase and pistons, and cast-iron cylinder liners.

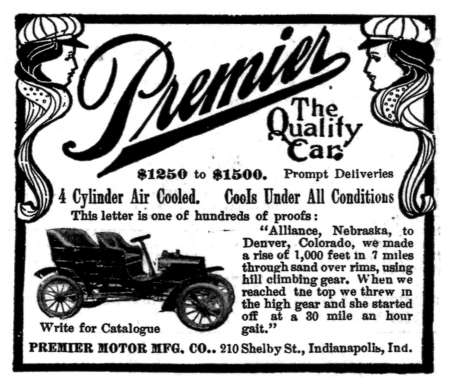

In 1905, Premier promoted the car's ability to travel the terrain from Nebraska to Colorado.
HAS&SM

Reeves offered an option to its Octoauto—the six-wheeled Sextoauto—in 1912.
HAS&SM

In 1920 L.S. Skelton reorganized the company as the Premier Motor Corporation. Troubles followed the company through the spring of 1923 when the company emerged from another receivership as Premier Motors, Inc. In the same year, Premier obtained control of the Monroe Motor Company and then marketed the Monroe four-cylinder car as the Premier Model B in 1924. The Premier six-cylinder car remained as the Model D through late 1924.

Late in 1923 the company received a contract for building 1,000 Premier taxicabs. From then on, taxicabs were the firm's only products. In October 1926, Premier sold out to the National Cab & Truck Company of Indianapolis.[32]

Reeves, 1896-1899, 1905-1910, 1911-1912

A number of automobiles sprang from the fertile mind of Milton O. Reeves of the Reeves Pulley Company in Columbus between 1896 and 1912. Reeves called his first car the Motocycle, which he tested on September 26, 1896. The Motocycle, like many other early autos, used a two-cycle, two-cylinder Sintz gasoline engine. One notable feature of his Motocycle was its use of a variable speed transmission. Reeves' variable speed transmission may have been one of the earliest automotive applications.

The third Motocycle, a lightweight four-seater, was built for Claude Sintz in 1897. In all, five Motocycles were built in a two-year period. Reeves was extremely satisfied with the operation of his

Reeves introduced the eight-wheeled Octoauto with the intent to produce a smooth-riding automobile that would "float" over rough streets and roads.
NAHC

variable speed transmissions, but said that gasoline engines were unreliable and not satisfactory for this application.[33]

M.O. Reeves and Girney L. Reeves obtained the company's permission to investigate the possibilities of building complete automobiles in mid-1904. By January 1905, the board of directors approved manufacturing air-cooled, four-cylinder autos. The 12 h.p. Model D and the 18-20 h.p. Model E used a cone clutch, a sliding-gear transmission, and a shaft drive.

In the summer of 1906, Reeves introduced its first water-cooled, four-cylinder engine and an air-cooled, six-cylinder engine. The 1906 Reeves "Big Six" was one of the first six-cylinder autos built. In late 1906, Reeves began to shift away from the high-end market.[34]

In summer of 1907, Reeves introduced the Go-Buggy, a utilitarian high-wheel runabout. It was designed for the rural Midwest market that did not need high-priced automobiles. The Go-Buggy used an air-cooled, opposed two-cylinder engine mounted under the floorboards of a buggy-type chassis. During 1910, the Reeves Pulley Company decided to concentrate on its variable speed transmission and industrial pulley business and divested itself of the automobile and gasoline engine operation.[35]

Thereafter, M.O. Reeves took on the duties of producing two unique automobiles called the Octoauto and the Sextoauto. He introduced the Octoauto, an eight-wheeled vehicle, in 1911. It resulted from his desire to produce a smooth-riding automobile that would "float" over rough streets and roads. The Octoauto had two axles each at front and rear with six of the eight wheels steerable on a 180-inch wheelbase. The main advertising claim for the Octoauto was its increased comfort provided by the eight-wheels. Noted writer and editor Elbert Hubbard called the Octoauto, "The only easy riding car in the world." Basically, it was an Overland engine, transmission, rear end, extended frame, and body, with Reeves modifications. The total length of the car was 248 inches.

The Sextoauto, introduced in summer of 1912, had two wheels in front and four wheels in the rear. Reeves built the Sextoauto on a modified Stutz six-passenger touring car chassis. It was aimed at the luxury market with a price of $5,000. Neither of these cars found a willing market. The prototypes were later returned to their original configurations and sold as used cars.

At the time of his death in 1925, M.O. Reeves held over 100 patents. His proudest possession was a medal presented to him by the Edison Institute in 1910 for the design and development of the variable speed transmission.[36] Variable speed transmissions are seeing a rebirth in automotive applications at the beginning of the 21st century.

ReVere, 1918-1926

Logansport-based ReVere Motor Car Corporation was incorporated in 1917 with $1,500,000 capital stock issued. Auto racers Gil Anderson, Tom Mooney, and Adolph Monsen collaborated on the design of the high-powered, high-performance ReVere. The car utilized the Duesenberg four-cylinder, 103 h.p., "walking-beam" engine, which was so named for the horizontal valve arrangement that used extremely long vertical rocker arms (walking-beams). Production began in 1918. The price for a five-passenger touring car on the 131-inch wheelbase was $3,850.

During the summer of 1918, Cannonball Baker drove a ReVere touring car for 17,000 miles on an endurance and speed run. He broke all records for this distance. Baker experienced no trouble with his ReVere on the trip.[37]

ReVere's 1919 "Foursome" was the epitome of sportiness with bullet head lamps, slanted windshield, step plates, cycle fenders, wire wheels, and side-mounted tires. An example of an avid fan of the ReVere was King Alfonso XIII of Spain who ordered a white, custom-built Foursome with Victoria top for $7,800.[38]

Innovations for 1925 included an optional Continental six-cylinder engine. The last model in 1926 may have anticipated power steering with dual steering wheels, one for normal driving and one for parking. Between 1918 and 1926, ReVere built about 2,700 automobiles.

By 1920, the corporation's capital stock increased to $3.5 million. Yet, in January 1921, creditors petitioned ReVere into bankruptcy. The ReVere organization saw six changes of management in eight years and faded from view after 1926.[39]

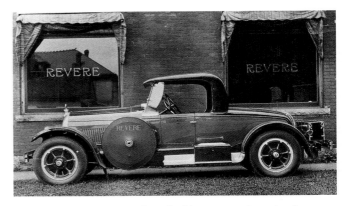

This 1926 ReVere was equipped with two steering wheels—one for normal driving and the other for parking. NAHC

Waverley, 1898-1916

Waverley electric vehicles were built in Indianapolis under four different corporate names: Indiana Bicycle Company (1898-1901), International Motor Car Company (1901-1903), Pope-Waverley (1903-1907), and The Waverley Company (1908-1916). The first Waverley electric car was a two-passenger Stanhope with tiller steering, 36-inch wheels with pneumatic tires, and a single headlight.[40]

Waverley exhibited one Stanhope, four dos-a-dos, and one delivery wagon at the New York Auto Show in May 1899. This line-up showed that its factory was—at that time—manufacturing in quantities for a variety of needs. All of the cars—with the exception of one dos-a-dos—were sold and delivered after the show.[41]

Waverley offered a number of other models like the piano box runabout and an open road wagon. About 2,000 vehicles were sold by 1903. Waverley then built the first coupe body ever constructed for an electric vehicle. The popularity of this type of closed car was so great that all the electric manufacturers soon devoted their attention to closed passenger cars.[42] The demand for coupes, broughams, and limousines steadily increased, to the neglect of the smaller open cars. By 1909, the Silent Waverley Electrics used a "noiseless" shaft drive from the traction motor to the rear wheels.

The 1911 Model 81 Brougham's interior was finished in broadcloth, broad lace and "Goat Morocco." It used either solid or pneumatic tires with side-lever steering and ran on Exide, Waverley, and Edison batteries. Standard luxuries included a flower vase, two vanity cases with watch and salt bottles, a match safe and cigar holder, and an umbrella holder. In 1912 Waverley offered the first front-drive electric.

The 40-page 1914 catalog gave copious descriptions of six models including the Roadster Coupe that rode on a 104-inch wheelbase and looked like a conventional gasoline roadster with a long hood and a false radiator. The four-passenger Brougham was offered in three versions: front-drive, rear-drive, and front-and-rear-drive. To help promote sales, the company published "A day with a Silent Waverley." This pamphlet charted the day of a fictitious woman as she rolled up the miles in the Silent Waverley traveling from the office, school, shopping, and other engagements. She was able to travel, according to the pamphlet, without the fussing and fuming of gasoline autos.[43]

Most electrics, though almost noiseless, were annoyingly slow (5-25 m.p.h.) and their batteries needed recharging after a few hours of use. Suitable for densely populated areas, electrics were seldom seen in the open country because of their limited traveling range (up to 75 miles). Although later Waverleys furnished a range between charges sufficient for about two-day's use, the popularity of electric cars began to wane. Waverley electrics were no longer produced after 1916.

Endnotes

1. *Crosley the car of tomorrow,* Cincinnati, OH, Crosley Corporation, © 1939.
2. Gross, Robert, *Timeline: Crosley 1937-1952,* Special Interest Autos, April-May 2001, p 48.
3. Cronin, J.F., *Crosley Streamlining Car,* The Cincinnati Enquirer, 20 January 1946.
4. Gross, p 48.
5. *The Crosley Hotshot,* Cincinnati, OH, Crosley Motors, Inc., © 1949.
6. Gross, p 49.
7. Kimes, Beverly Rae, Standard Catalog of American Cars: 1805-1942, Iola, WI, Krause Publications, © 1996, p 533.
8. Blommel, Henry, *Connersville: The "Little Detroit" of Indiana,* Antique Automobile, March-April 1969, p 4.
9. *History of the Indianapolis Branch,* Indianapolis, IN, Ford Motor Company, © 1941.
10. Katzell, Raymond A., *The Splendid Stutz: The Cars, Companies, People and Races,* Indianapolis, IN, The Stutz Club, © 1996, p 321-334.
11. Delancy, Howard R., *History of the Cole Motor Car Company,* Bloomington, IN, D.B.A. dissertation, Indiana University, © 1954, p 82-83.
12. Delancy, p 124-126.
13. *The Henderson Accelerator,* Indianapolis, IN, Henderson Motor Car Company, October 1912, p 2-11.
14. Lenmasters, Ron, *Inter-State Brought Muncie Into Auto World in 1908,* Muncie Star, 3 July 1976.
15. *Introducing The LaFayette—An Eight,* Motor Age, 8 January 1920, p 12-17.
16. Blommel, Henry, *Indiana's Little Detroit,* Connersville, IN, n.d., p 12-15.
17. Smith, John Martin, *Ride With Us In A Kiblinger Automobile,* Auburn Dekalb Vanguard, Auburn, IN, April 1971, p 24-25.
18. Smith, John Martin, *McIntyre Motor Vehicles,* Auburn Dekalb Vanguard, Auburn, IN, April 1971, p 15-20.
19. Smith, John Martin, *Imp America's First Compact Car,* Auburn Dekalb Vanguard, Auburn, IN, April 1971, p 11-14.
20. *Three Maxwell Models,* Detroit, MI, Maxwell Motor Company, © 1914.
21. Kimes, p 1032-1033.
22. Calvert, Judy Stedman, *First Overland Motor Car Built In Terre Haute,* The Terre Haute Journal, 4 January 1985.
23. Glasscock, Carl Burgess, *Motor History of America,* Los Angeles, CA, Floyd Clymer Co, © 1946.
24. Charlie Weaver, President of The Willys-Overland-Knight Registry, letter to C. McCord Purdy, 16 August 1973, Hoosier Auto Show & Swap Collection.
25. Calvert
26. *New Parry 1911,* Indianapolis, IN, The Motor Car Manufacturing Co., © 1911.
27. Kimes, p 1156.
28. Mellon, Steve, *Evansville Then & Now,* Scripps Howard Publishing, © 1995, p 90.
29. Stout, Wesley W., *Bullets By The Billion,* Detroit, MI, Chrysler Corporation, © 1946, Forward.
30. Mellon, p 90.
31. *Cars and Defense Work in the Same Plant,* Detroit, MI, Chrysler Corporation, © 12 June 1951, Cover.
32. Kimes, p 1241-1242.
33. Bradley, George, *Reeves and the Automobile,* Cleveland, OH, Reliance Electric Company, © 1967, part 1.
34. Bradley, part 2.
35. Bradley, part 3.
36. Bradley, part 4.
37. Huffman, Wallace S., *ReVere: America's Incomparable Car,* Horseless Carriage Gazette, January-February 1964, p 10.
38. Huffman, p 11.
39. Huffman, p 12.
40. Hudson, William W., *Pioneers of the Electric Automobile Industry,* American Motorist, April 1913, p 306.
41. Hudson, p 306.
42. Hudson, p 306.
43. *Silent Waverley Electrics,* Indianapolis, IN, The Waverley Company, © 1914.

Waverly electric vehicles were displayed at the 1899 New York Electrical Show.
NAHC

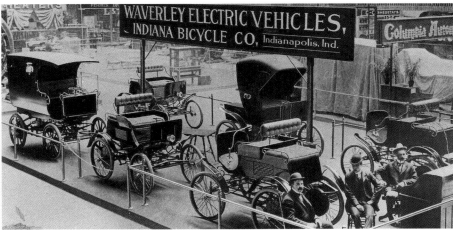

ReVere placed this ad in a January 1921 issue of *Motor Age.* Later that month, creditors forced ReVere into bankruptcy.
TAC

Pope Waverley was one of the four names under which Waverleys were produced. This ad appeared in 1905.
TAC

These renderings show two Indiana manufacturers at the height of production. Pictured above is the Stutz factory in Indianapolis. Below is the Waverley facility also located in Indianapolis.
TSC and HAS&SM

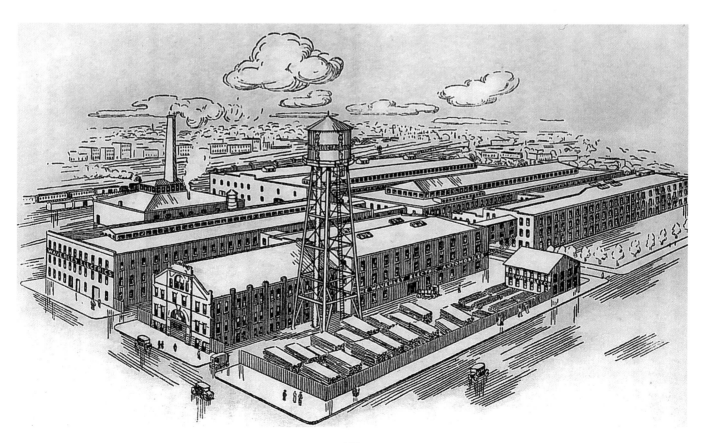

Note of Interest: Indiana's Highways and Byways

The intersecting of the country's railways gave Indiana its nickname as the "Crossroads of the Country." The state also enjoys the unique distinction of being at the crossroads of some of the nation's first highways.

National Road

This highway thread started with the National Road, which was the first major U.S. road built with federal funds. The road was also the most important route linking the Midwest with the Atlantic seaboard in the early nineteenth century. The highway was proposed by George Washington and Albert Gallatin in 1784. Financing was finally approved by Congress in 1805. Construction of the Indiana route from Richmond to West Terre Haute took place between 1827 and 1839. It was the road that led wagons and coaches westward.

By the early 1900s, the National Road was in the same poor shape as other routes that serviced wagons and coaches. Motorists demanded paved and wider roads. So, The National Old Trails Association was formed in 1913 to mark the route for autos and promote improvement. In 1926, the Old National Route became the new U.S. 40. The road once again gained importance as a major east-west route through the east and Midwest.

Completion of Interstate 70 in the 1960s changed the importance of U.S. 40. Motorists soon grew to prefer the fast-pace offered by interstate travel, and the National Road lost much of its importance. Yet, the National Road is still remembered for its contribution to Indiana's transportation history.

The Lincoln Highway

In 1912, Indianapolis industrialist Carl G. Fisher was the first individual to determine a feasible plan to finance America's first transcontinental highway from New York, New York, to San Francisco, California. He sought and found contributors motivated by the advantage of decent roads. They rightly believed that if roads were improved, people would travel more and product demand for automobiles would increase. Within 30 days, Fisher had $1 million in pledges and publicity nationwide. A few months later, Fisher received a letter from Henry B. Joy,

Packard Motor Company president, suggesting that the road be named for Abraham Lincoln.

On July 1, 1913, the Lincoln Highway Association was created and the route was designed to run through or touch 12 states. The Lincoln Highway was designated with red-white-and-blue striped markers with a large blue "L" in the center. In Indiana, the highway stretched from Fort Wayne to Dyer.

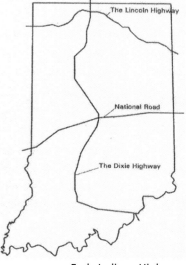
Early Indiana Highways

Changes to the highway came as early as 1925 when the federal highway numbering system was enacted. Indiana replaced the route with highways U.S. 30, U.S. 33, U.S. 20, and S.R. 2. The name "Lincoln Highway" was nearly wiped out, although some communities have chosen to mark this historical route as one of their city streets. Plus, advocates have placed historical markers for the Lincoln Highway and Ideal Section along U.S. 30 near Dyer. Remnants of the original highway can be found in eastern Allen county.

The Dixie Highway

While the Lincoln Highway provided for the public traveling east and west, there was little available for traveling north and south. Carl Fisher decided that a route from Chicago, Illinois, to Miami, Florida, should be developed. That route became known as the Dixie Highway. In April 1915, The Dixie Highway Association was formed. The Indiana segment of the route would pass through such cities as South Bend, Indianapolis, Paoli, and New Albany. In September 1916, Fisher and Indiana Governor Samuel Ralston attended a celebration in Martinsville opening the Indiana section of the roadway. Sometime after 1925, the southern route was straightened out from Indianapolis to Jeffersonville and remarked as U.S. 31. Portions of the highway in Indiana are still known as Dixie Highway or Dixie Way.

Note of Interest:
More on the Lincoln Highway

The skeleton of a national network of highways started to emerge within two years after Congress provided funding through the 1921 Federal Highway Act.

To help illustrate how highways should be constructed, the organizers of the transcontinental Lincoln Highway built the Ideal Section between Schererville and Dyer near the Illinois-Indiana border. This section of the Lincoln Highway was one-and-a-half miles long with 10-inch thick, steel-reinforced, concrete paving. It was also 40 feet wide to allow four lanes of traffic. The Section was designed for an average speed of 35 miles per hour. The plan included a 110-foot right of way, landscaping, and an adjacent footpath. Extensive lighting provided for night driving. These were considered innovations at the time.

United States Rubber Company provided $130,000 of the $167,000 to the Lincoln Highway Association for construction. The remainder came from state and county funds. When completed in December 1922, this exemplary piece of road was hailed as the "finest section of road in the world." The association accomplished its goal of serving as an ideal section of highway for engineers and road builders across the country.

Traveling the Lincoln Highway today

Remnants of the Lincoln Highway are still around today. To travel the Lincoln Highway as closely as possible today, follow these directions:

From the Ohio state line, take U.S. 30. A few yards on the right is the original route, unmarked. On the corner is a Hoosier Homestead Farm. The road goes through the towns of Townley and Zulu. At Howe Road, merge onto U.S. 30 and go west into Fort Wayne on Maumee Street. Proceed west on Washington Boulevard. Turn right on Harrison to Goshen Avenue. Follow Goshen Avenue out of Fort Wayne, and go north on U.S. 33. Towns on U.S. 33 include Churubusco, Wolf Lake, and Ligonier. In Ligonier, go north on Lincoln Way. Turn left on Lincoln Way West, which becomes U.S. 33 again through Benton. Enter Goshen on Lincoln Way. Turn right on Main Street to Pike and follow Pike to Lincoln Way West which turns into U.S. 33. Follow U.S. 33 to Elkhart, and enter the town on Lincoln Way.

Leave U.S. 33 and proceed on Main Street. Follow Main Street to Jackson and turn left. Make another left on Vistula Street, which angles right onto Franklin Street, which rejoins U.S. 33 on the west side of Elkhart.

Go through Mishawaka, and enter South Bend on Lincoln Way East. (The route may vary because of one-way streets.) Turn left on Jefferson Boulevard. Turn right on Main Street, then left on LaSalle. Turn right onto Lincoln Way West, which turns into U.S. 20.

Take U.S. 20 west to near Rolling Prairie where it merges with S.R. 2. Follow S.R. 2 to Laporte. Enter on Main Street, turn left on J Street, and turn right on Fourth to Lincoln Way West. This turns back into S.R. 2, which leads to Valparaiso.

Enter on Lincoln Way. Turn right on Garfield Street, left on Main Street, and right on Railroad Street. Turn left on Joliet Road/Lincoln Way West. Pick up U.S. 30 again on the west side of Valparaiso and take U.S. 30 through Deep River, Merrillville, Schereville and Dyer.

NOTE OF INTEREST

At the beginning of the century, highway signs were almost non-existent. In order to help participants in road tours, local American Automobile Associations would send out a pilot car to mark the route with confetti.

However, pandemonium erupted during one road rally when the pilot car ran out of confetti midway between South Bend and Chicago, Illinois. For a substitute, the driver bought a supply of corn and beans from a nearby farm. His corn-and-bean trail, however, drew hundreds of chickens into the path of surprised motorists.

"I followed the clearest trail that I have found since leaving home," said the tour's chairman, "and it wasn't corn and beans either. It was chicken feathers."

Note of Interest on Community Support

Throughout the last century, many Indiana communities have seen the economic value of having auto manufacturers within their city limits. In fact, some communities actively pursued companies early in automotive history. From 1907 to 1909, for example, five Indiana communities—Anderson, Connersville, Decatur, Muncie, and North Manchester—encouraged automakers to move there to boost their cities' economics. Following is a short history of these communities' early encouragement of auto manufacturing.

Anderson

Anderson, in an effort to encourage outside industry to relocate there, initiated a booster movement. The movement raised over $300,000 to offer lower taxes and favorable rent payments as incentives. As a result, The DeTamble Motor Company moved from Indianapolis and operated until 1912. Plus, The Rider Lewis Motor Company moved from Muncie and was sold to another auto firm in 1911. While these businesses do not exist today, they helped Anderson on its way to gaining a reputation as a leading producer of vehicular lighting and automotive bumper systems.

Connersville

Several industrialists in Connersville were concerned that too many of their companies were tied up in buggy and carriage building. They could see this field giving way to the automobile. They encouraged a group of investors to purchase the Lexington Motor Company and relocate it to the McFarlan industrial park on the north side of town. Lexington was one of a number of automotive firms in the park and enjoyed success for several years.

Rider-Lewis was located in both Muncie and Decatur at different times.
HAS&SM

In 1928, E.L. Cord purchased the Lexington Motor Company, Ansted Engine Company, and the Central Manufacturing Company buildings to expand the production of his Auburn Automobile Company. Automotive production continued in these buildings until 1948. Today automotive component production still exists in or near the McFarlan industrial park.

Decatur

In late 1907, the Decatur Commercial Club lured the Coppock Motor Company from Marion with an offer of monetary support. The firm was reorganized as the Decatur Motor Car Company. When its Decatur factory proved inadequate to meet the demand of its truck production, the company accepted an offer of $100,000 from Grand Rapids, Michigan, to move its plant to that town. Nevertheless, Decatur has developed into an area known for motor home production and van conversion.

Muncie

Large-scale automobile manufacturing started in Muncie in 1908 thanks to the efforts of the Commercial Club of Muncie (forerunner of the Chamber of Commerce). A group spearheaded by the five Ball brothers—George A., Frank C., William C., Edmund F. and Dr. Lucius L.—along with J.M. Marling and Tom Hart formed the Inter-State Motor Company. The Inter-State put Muncie on the automaker's map. The company stayed in production until 1918. William C. Durant, past president and founder of General Motors, took over the facility in 1921 to form Durant Motors, Inc., which closed in 1928. Nevertheless, Muncie is now known for auto transmissions produced at the New Venture Gear and Warner Gear facilities.

North Manchester

In 1908, community leaders in North Manchester developed a campaign to attract an auto factory. The North Manchester Industrial Association agreed to provide a lot valued at $600 and provide $1,500 to Vigil L. DeWitt. The first DeWitt rolled out of the new factory in April 1909. A little over a year later, the DeWitt factory burned to the ground and provided the end to the company. Auto-related manufacturing, however, is alive in the area. Now automotive wiring is produced at the United Technologies' North Manchester plant.

The 1910 Model 32 pictured above was specifically designed for the Marmon race team before Marmon started to produce trucks commercially from 1913-1915.
HAS&SM

Indiana's truck production parallels that of the country's. At the close of the 19th century, electric delivery vehicles were starting to stir in the major commercial centers across the country. Indiana saw its first self-propelled trucks—Waverley electric delivery vans—built in 1899. Several other Indiana automobile manufacturers—such as Lambert, Marion, McIntyre, Overland, Premier, and Studebaker—offered delivery bodies on a stock passenger car chassis in the 1900s. Many of these light truck offerings were marketed for a short time.

In the 1900s, Indiana truck manufacturers introduced the Coppock, Decatur, and Lindsley. Two of these three had one- and three-year life spans. Automotive offerings faired better. Marion and Premier's models lasted one and two years, respectively, while Studebaker offerings would last many decades. At the dawn of the 1910s, Decatur, Lambert, McIntyre, Studebaker, and Waverley were the Indiana firms manufacturing trucks.

Standardization of truck design and engineering began in the early 1910s. Sliding-gear transmissions replaced planetary transmissions. Molded solid

tires on steel wheels gradually substituted for inferior tires on heavy-duty trucks. In 1915, the American truck building industry got a boost by supplying the British and French war departments with trucks and tractors for their war efforts. The demand was so great for trucks that models in stock were depleted, requiring many plants to double their work shifts. This demand gave birth to manufacturing specially designed units for converting car chassis into 1-ton trucks. The Graham brothers of southern Indiana went on to leverage their conversion expertise into heavy trucks and automobiles.

American involvement in the war in 1917 led to the standardization of designs for two- and five-ton trucks. The war effort also created problems in shipping materials for railroad car construction to American seaports. A shortage of rail cars created an opportunity for the trucking industry to step in and fill the country's long haul freight needs. As a result, the industry developed the pneumatic truck tire to cushion the freight and increase speed. Semi-trailers were also developed. By merely dropping off the trailer instead of unloading freight before driving on, semi-truckers got quicker turnaround.

In the 1910s, 32 new makes of Indiana trucks entered the market. This decade marked the high point. Like the previous decade, Indiana automakers offered light commercial delivery versions of their passenger cars. The Auburn Motor Chassis, Inter-State, Marmon, Nyberg, and Pathfinder offerings were available for no more than three years. In mid-decade, cyclecar companies Comet, W.H. McIntyre, and Merz built light-delivery van versions that had the same market span. The tally shows 17 companies entering the market for a brief life span during the decade. Among them were Durable, Fort Wayne, Ideal, Mais, Rodefeld, South Bend, and Van Auken Electric. Four manufacturers from the previous two decades exited the industry. Eight remained to enter the 1920s: Gary, Graham Brothers, Huffman, Indiana, Mutual, Noble, Service, and Studebaker.

At the beginning of the 1920s, the U.S. government offered surplus army trucks to state and local agencies for road maintenance. This, plus an oversupply of trucks on the market, spelled trouble for the post-war truck industry. Eight new makes of Indiana trucks entered the market in the 1920s. Six companies entered the market for a brief life span during the decade. They were Alena Steam, Barrows, Betz, Red Ball, Relay, and Valley. Five manufacturers from the previous decades exited the industry. Five remained to enter the 1930s: Dodge, Indiana, International Harvester, Noble, and Studebaker.

In 1931, Marmon-Herrington incorporated to build all-wheel-drive vehicles for civilian and military applications. Cummins Engine Company of Columbus introduced the automotive-type diesel engine in 1932, and it was not long before diesel engines began replacing gas engines in over-the-road applications. Pak-Age-Car introduced the multi-stop delivery vehicle to replace house-to-house milk and bakery wagons in the early 1930s. Three new makes of Indiana trucks entered the market in the 1930s. Rockne offered a light commercial version from 1932 to 1933. Three manufacturers from the previous decades exited the industry. Marmon-Herrington, Pak-Age-Car, International, and Studebaker remained to enter the 1940s.

Crosley Motors, Inc., joined the light-duty truck market in 1940. America's preparation for World War II again called for standardized production of trucks across the line. International Harvester and Studebaker led the way for Indiana

in producing 2½-ton 6x6 trucks from 1941 to 1945. Marmon-Herrington built a large number of all-wheel-drive and track-laying vehicles for the allies. These four firms were the state's only truck producers to reach the 1950s. Crosley ceased production in 1953. Marmon-Herrington and Studebaker both closed their Indiana operations in 1963. International Harvester was the longest remaining Hoosier survivor and lasted for 60 years building trucks in Indiana until 1983.[1]

With America's growing interest in light-duty trucks and the boom of the sport utility market in the late 1980s, Indiana has experienced a resurgence in truck manufacturing. The GM Truck Group plant in Fort Wayne builds the Chevrolet and GMC full-size pick-up trucks. Subaru Isuzu Automotive, Inc., in Lafayette manufactures the Honda Passport, Isuzu Trooper, and the Subaru Legacy. In 1998, Toyota Motor Manufacturing in Princeton began producing the Tundra pick-up truck. In 2000, the plant started assembling the popular Sequoia sport utility vehicle as well as models.

Crosley, 1940-1941, and 1947-1953

Before embarking on building an automobile in 1939 in Richmond, industrialist Powel Crosley, Jr., was known for building radios, kitchen appliances, and broadcasting. His initial automobile was an air-cooled, two-cylinder, mini-car on an 80-inch wheelbase. Parkway Delivery Truck and Commercial Station Wagon variations on the Crosley theme appeared for the 1940 model year with a $325 price. A Pick-Up, Panel Delivery, and the Covered Wagon were added in 1941.

Critics remarked that little trucks were inappropriate for cargo-carrying duties. Crosley, the consummate promoter, employed novel approaches to selling his light trucks. The Covered Wagon was introduced at Macy's department store in New York. Renowned race car driver Cannonball Baker drove one on a cross-country endurance run.

Crosley attempted to compete for the U.S. Army contract for the ¼-ton reconnaissance car that later became known as the Jeep. During World War II, car and truck production at Crosley plants converted over to war goods. One of Crosley's outputs

The Graham Brothers "G-Boy" Stake Truck was advertised specifically for the farmer.
MEK

After a number of successful years in the glass business and farming in southwestern Indiana, the Graham brothers —Joseph B., Robert C., and Ray A.—decided to enter the truck conversion business based on Ray's engineering acumen. The brothers set up shop as Graham Brothers, Inc., in a three-story building at Fourth and Main in Evansville in 1916. Their first model was a unit to convert the ubiquitous Ford Model T automobile to a one-ton truck. Ray chose the Model T because of the availability of Ford parts and service at most every town or crossroads. The Graham truck unit had a 125-inch wheelbase and was driven by a dual chain drive. The unit was priced at $350 with a choice between two bodies. Sales of these initial units surpassed anything the Grahams expected. Within a year, 11 different styles of conversion units were available.

In 1917 the conversion units were made available for almost any type of automobile chassis. Through the use of heavier cars, Graham Brothers offered 1½-, 2-, 2½-, and 3-ton conversion units by the end of 1917. At this time, Graham was the world's largest manufacturer of complete truck attachments. By the end of World War I, truck units were available for over 50 makes of automobiles and three- and five-ton units for Ford, Dodge, and several makes.

In late 1919, the Grahams announced that they would build a new plant for Graham Brothers Speed Trucks. Plus, they offered a new 1½-ton truck on a 130-inch wheelbase with mechanical components from major independent manufacturers. Indiana-built engines Rutember and Weidley were used in addition to ones by Ford, Dodge, and Continental. Pneumatic cord tires were offered as the ultimate in truck economy. The chassis sold for $2,295, with the choice of four optional body styles for $200.

was a new single-overhead-camshaft, four-cylinder engine of brazed copper and stamped metal construction for the Navy. It was used in refrigeration, air conditioning, and aircraft applications.

Crosley postwar auto production began in 1946 adding trucks the following year at a Marion-based facility. The diminutive truck was offered in two versions, Pick-Up and Panel, starting at $800. Crosley trucks were rated at ¼-ton and weighed about one-third as much as their competition. This weight-saving advantage was offset by its cargo box length restriction. This limited the size of load they could carry. Crosley also offered two variations for conversion to other uses, the cab-and-chassis and the chassis with cowl. The Crosley truck appealed to a niche commercial market. It was promoted for use by department stores, repairmen, and flower shops. The restyled 1949 trucks sold for under $900, about $300 less than Ford and Chevrolet offerings.

A new Crosley creation debuted for 1950, the Farm-O-Road, priced at $835. It was designed for farm or road use with a 63-inch wheelbase, two-passenger utility body and fold-down windshield. Pick-Up and Dump models had dual-rear wheels and could be ordered with a full set of attachments including a hydraulic drawbar and front or rear power-take-off. A plow and a cultivator were also available. Crosley auto and truck operations were sold to General Tire in mid-1952. The remaining 32 trucks were titled as 1953 models.[2]

Graham Brothers

offer you all this

FOR

$350⁰⁰

all ready to attach to Ford chassis—
an extra value and saving of $75 to
$125 in body equipment.

Cab

Unit

Choice of either Stake
or Express Body

Express Body

This is the Stake body type
Graham Brothers one-ton unit attached to a Ford

Unit includ-
ing choice of
either Express
or Stake body
with cab

$350 f. o. b.
Evansville, Ind.

Graham Brothers
Evansville, Indiana

Lowest priced high grade unit offered

This advertisement emphasizes a low price and adaptability for the Graham Brothers one-ton unit.
MEK

115

Initially, the Grahams used a large number of the components for the Speed Truck from the Dodge Brothers because of their reputation. In April 1921, the Graham Brothers, Inc. contracted for sales and service through Dodge's worldwide system. The standard Graham chassis weighed 4,245 pounds and was powered by a 212 c.i.d., four-cylinder Dodge engine. Lockheed hydraulic brakes were available on Graham trucks in 1921.

Soon, another plant was needed to serve the increasing needs of the Graham Brothers operations. A 13,000 sq. ft. building in Detroit was selected for final assembly needs. The Evansville plant worked overtime to produce bodies and most components for the Detroit assembly operation. By year end, 1,086 Graham Brothers trucks were sold.

Over a 300 percent sales increase was realized in 1922. Also in 1922, the Grahams purchased a plant on Conant Avenue in Detroit. By the next year, further additions were needed there to keep up with demand. In 1924 Graham plants produced nearly 11,000 trucks. The Grahams purchased a plant on Lynch Road in Detroit in 1924. In June 1925, production commenced at the new Stockton, California, plant. Graham Brothers became an international producer by expanding operations to Toronto, Ontario, in 1925. The company also

became the world's largest independent producer of trucks in 1926, with almost 37,500 units sold.

In October 1924, Frederick J. Haynes, president of Dodge Brothers, decided that the Graham Brothers operations should officially become part of the automotive firm. A deal was struck to purchase 49 percent of the stock and make Graham Brothers a division of Dodge Brothers, Inc. The remaining 51 percent of Graham Brothers stock was purchased in late 1925 by Dillion, Read & Company, the investment firm that now controlled Dodge Brothers, Inc. Dodge continued to build the trucks as the Graham Brothers Division. In April 1926, the Grahams resigned their positions at Dodge Brothers, Inc. and began to liquidate their holdings as a result of their concern for the short-sighted business practices of the investment firm.

In the spring of 1928, Chrysler Corporation purchased Dodge Brothers, Inc., from Dillion, Read & Company. On January 2, 1929, the Chrysler Corporation issued a press release announcing that the Graham name was being dropped from truck production. From that point on, Graham trucks would be known as Dodge Brothers Trucks. In 1935, Chrysler converted the Evansville Dodge truck plant for assembly of the Plymouth. Plymouths were produced there until 1959, ending Evansville's link to automobile production.[3]

The Graham brothers resurfaced as the new owners of the Paige-Detroit Motor Car Company in May 1927. In 1929 Evansville's citizenry was excited by the prospects of the new 273,600 sq. ft. Graham-Paige body plant on East Columbia Street. Graham-Paige leased this plant to Briggs Indiana Corporation at the end of 1936. Briggs Indiana dedicated the plant to production of Plymouth auto bodies for the nearby Evansville assembly plant.

Indiana Truck, 1911-1933

In 1911, the newly named Harwood-Barley Manufacturing Company began production of Indiana trucks in Marion after successfully launching the Marion Chronicle truck in 1910. By 1913 the

The five-ton "Class B" Liberty truck by Indiana is pictured below. HAS&SM

company was doing business across the country. That year, it published a booklet to convince the public that trucks were a wiser purchase than horses and wagons.

In 1915 the firm's name changed to Indiana Truck Company. Indiana Truck increased production and expanded business during World War I by producing 475 5-ton "Class B" Liberty trucks. The 1918 catalog showed four models, including the Model T 1-ton Worm Drive—"heavy steel frame that will carry the load over the roughest roads with sureness"—Model D 2-ton Worm Drive—"America's Greatest Truck Value," and Model L 5-ton Worm Drive—"a big truck to carry big loads."

In 1925 the company had 14 depots across the country, with many in southern states. The 1927 line-up had 16 models. By the next year, the company offered 14 different trucks, including three of the Road Builder models with built-in dump bodies. Indiana claimed to be "one of the most successful manufacturers of high-grade Motor Trucks in the country." The company reported that the end of 1920s was one of the most productive times in the company's history. In 1932 Indiana became a subsidiary of White Motor Company, and the name was changed to Indiana Motors Corporation. White announced the move of production from Marion to Cleveland, Ohio, in December 1932, with production ceasing at the Marion location in 1933.

International Harvester, 1923-1983

In 1923, International Harvester built a new truck plant in Fort Wayne. During its first year of operation, the company built 433 trucks. Fifty years later in 1973, 68,000 trucks were produced there, earning Fort Wayne the distinction of being the "Heavy-Duty Truck Capital of the World."

IHC opened a new motor truck engineering lab at the plant in 1951. In 1960, a new master motor parts depot—totaling 625,000 square feet—opened in Fort Wayne. The Fort Wayne Works was expanded and improved in 1963. In 1973, the manufacturing plant had more than 7,000 workers involved in the assembly of heavy-duty trucks defined as having a gross vehicle weight of 26,000 pounds or more, and the Scout II, a light-duty, four-wheel-drive truck.

Annually, the plant put more than $200 million into the economy in northeastern Indiana in the form of wages, taxes, payment for utilities, and purchases. In 1980, the company decided to concentrate on heavy-duty truck production and then closed the plant in 1983 after the 1,527,299th truck rolled out.

The Scout, introduced in 1961, was the predecessor of today's sport utility vehicle. A 1965 survey showed that nearly 75 percent of all Scouts were purchased primarily for non-business use. Eighty-two percent of Scout sales were 4x4s. Station wagons and sports cars made up more than one-third of the trade-ins on new Scouts. Over 99 percent of all Scouts had four-wheel-drive running gear in 1979. Scouts were purchased by the same types of people who buy SUVs today. Unfortunately, IHC was ahead of the curve and never fully capitalized on this niche market.

The Scout's success surprised almost everyone. Initially Scout production was planned for 50 units per day, but within one month the rate was increased to 100 units per day. In the next month, there was another 33 percent bump in production. IHC purchased a nearby plant as the site for Scout production. In the first calendar year of production, more than 35,000 units were sold. In 1968, its seventh year of production, the 200,000th Scout was built in Fort Wayne. When production of the Scout stopped in October 1980, more than 500,000 units had been built.[4]

NOTE OF INTEREST

Keck Motor Company in Mount Vernon, Indiana, claims the honor of being the oldest continuously operating Ford dealership in Indiana and among about the 20 oldest in the United States. It started when local businessman John Keck bought an automobile in 1903. He was so excited by it that he started an automobile division of Keck Gonnerman in 1907. In its early history, Keck handled many car lines such as Oakland, General, Packard, Studebaker, and Cadillac, adding Ford in 1912. Keck started representing Ford exclusively in 1916. Today the business is located on Highway 62 West.

Wouldn't you rather play hooky today...

and take your SCOUT on a holiday?

You bought our compact SCOUT for a second car, to drive to work. Smart buy.

Its tough 4-cyl. engine gives you about 20 miles per gallon—regular gas only. Short length makes it easy to wheel through rush-hour traffic...and lets you park it almost anywhere.

But you'd rather keep right on going with the SCOUT — for the sheer carefree, outdoor fun of it.

Go ahead. Take off the top and you'll have a jaunty convertible. With bucket seats you may even feel like you're driving a sports car. But there isn't a sports car around that can take you to so many fishing or hunting places beyond the end of the roads.

In case you haven't yet checked out this great work-and-pleasure vehicle, with two-wheel drive or all-wheel drive, prices start at just $1690.85*.

Play an hour's-worth of hooky today and test drive it at your INTERNATIONAL Dealer or Branch — listed in the Yellow Pages. International Harvester Co., 180 North Michigan Avenue, Chicago 1, Illinois.

The Scout® by International® IH®

*Manufacturer's list price, f.o.b. factory, exclusive of state and local taxes, destination and handling charges

The Scout was the predecessor of today's sport utility vehicles.
TAC

Marmon Truck, 1913-1915

The Indianapolis-based Nordyke & Marmon Company entered the commercial vehicle market in September 1912 after *The Motor Truck* printed "Well Known Manufacturer of Pleasure Cars adds Light Delivery Wagon to its Line." The product was a light delivery version of Marmon's Model 32 automobile, with a carrying capacity of 1,200-1,500 pounds.

Two standard bodies were offered—a delivery van and an open box. Drive train components were strengthened throughout. Engine displacement was decreased from 318 to 251 cubic inches and fitted with a speed governor set at 20 m.p.h. The Model 48 trans-axle unit was incorporated for its strength. The truck chassis had reinforcing gussets and heavier gage cross members. Suspension spring arch and stiffness as well as wheels and tires were upgraded to commercial specifications.

Of particular interest is the Marmon Truck introduction of the dual pneumatic rear tires to the industry. This advance in truck design came from engineers who viewed the components of the vehicle as a "total system." This was the practice of Marmon's automotive side of the company for over a decade. Solid rubber rear tires were available as optional equipment.

The delivery van was furnished with dash, front seat, and floor boards. An outside body builder completed the vehicle to the customer's specifications. Standard equipment included a spare tire rim and lighting equipment. The Marmon Truck line closed at the end of the 1915 model year.[5]

Marmon-Herrington, 1931-1963

The Indianapolis company's first civilian application—a prototype truck for oil field operations—was demonstrated in August 1932. As certified by the AAA, the truck hauled 40 tons at an average speed of 25 m.p.h. for 100 miles. After a week of Syrian Desert operation, the Iraq Petroleum Company ordered three TH-300-6 Series six-wheel-drive trucks at $35,000 each.[6]

Walter Marmon oversaw the first conversion of a Ford 1½-ton V-8 powered truck to all-wheel-drive in 1935. Conversion of commercial units made sense for Marmon because a large part of the expense of these trucks was in the chassis and sheet metal. The resulting Marmon-Herrington (M-H) Ford conversion provided an all-wheel-drive vehicle at an attractive price. An additional advantage was the worldwide supply of parts and service from authorized Ford outlets. Marmon ads stated, "Two-fold Leadership Gives You the Greatest All-Wheel-Drive Truck Value in History." List prices for the conversion in 1937 began under $1,400.[7]

In 1936, M-H offered its first conversion of a 1/2-ton Ford pick-up truck to all-wheel-drive (AWD). This unit anticipated the development of a lightweight, all-terrain military vehicle known as the Jeep by four years. In fact, A.W. Herrington was one of the co-developers of the prototype Jeep for American Bantam Car Company demonstrated in March 1940.[8] In 1937 M-H offered AWD conversions of Ford passenger cars beginning with the "woody" station wagon. By 1938 a full Ford line was available with M-H conversions. This was accomplished when the Ford dealer delivered a standard Ford vehicle to M-H for conversion. The list price for a standard conversion was $895, with all work completed at the M-H factory. By mid-1938, M-H began offering AWD conversions for

Marmon's 1,500-pound delivery wagon with open express body was introduced in 1912.
TMH

One of Marmon-Herrington's first offerings was the Model TH-300-4, a four-wheel drive truck, which is pictured above. Below is the company's 1961 Highway Tractor, Model HDT.
TMH

Marmon-Herrington advertised the Ranger as the world's most versatile car. The vehicle was an all-wheel drive vehicle. TMH

the Ford 1-ton chassis. Ninety percent of the parts in the M-H conversion were listed as standard Ford items stocked by dealers. This level of readily available parts did a great deal to foster confidence among dealers about the ease of M-H conversion service.[9]

In 1944, A.W. Herrington noticed that a number of after-market suppliers were adding windows and two additional seats to the Ford panel delivery truck, creating a commercial station wagon. He forecasted that an off-road passenger version of this vehicle would be perfect. Subsequently, they marketed the Marmon-Herrington Ranger as their AWD conversion. The M-H Ranger preceded the International Scout of the 1960s and the sport utility vehicles of the 1990s by many decades.[10]

Post-war civilian transportation production began in late 1944 at a rate of 20 AWD trucks per day. A new V-8 AWD conversion came online in 1948. M-H Ford AWD conversions were updated in 1952 and 1956. In 1952 M-H announced a completely new AWD truck product line rated from 24,000 to 33,000 G.V.W.[11]

The company announced the Marmon-Herrington Highway Tractor in the July 1961 issue of *Automotive Topics*. The HDT-1 weighed 14,000 pounds and was rated at 43,000 G.V.W. as a truck and up to 72,000 G.C.W. as a tractor-trailer. It featured Caterpillar Diesel power..."Tailor-made to fit ALL Trucking needs." In July 1963, the M-H Truck Division was sold to Adrian H. Roop, and production moved to Denton, Texas.[12]

In 1962, control of the Marmon-Herrington Company transferred to outside interests, ending 31 years under the founding interests. After sales of the truck division in 1963, operations at the Indianapolis plant were shut down.[13]

Service Motor Truck, 1911-1926

The Service Motor Car Company started in Wabash in April 1911. Since the company specialized in manufacturing trucks, the "Car" of the name was changed to "Truck" in August 1918, to more accurately described its operations. The first trucks were high wheelers with solid tires. Production ran at a few trucks per week. The December 16, 1915 issue of *Motor Age* magazine printed that Service was making the transition from chain-drive to worm-drive trucks. Their trucks were rated at 1-, 1½-, 2-, 3½-, and 5-ton capacity. The Service Model 220 used a 159 c.i.d. Buda four-cylinder engine, with a Stromberg carburetor, Timken-Detroit worm gear drive, and Ross steering gear. The model also had a 137-inch wheelbase weighing 3,470 pounds and was priced at $2,415. The Model 101 sold for $5,275 and weighed 8,760 pounds. Its standard wheelbase was 171½ inches, while the long wheelbase was 190½ inches.

When the United States declared war on Germany in April 1917, Service's production was up to 64 vehicles per month. Upon U.S. troops deployment in Europe, the government selected Service to build 5-ton "Class B" Liberty trucks. Production soon rose over 450 percent to 300 vehicles per month. Commercial truck production continued at a slower pace on a line adjacent to the Liberty trucks.

Service Motor Truck was caught in the down-draft of the postwar recession that claimed a high number of automobile and truck manufacturers across the land. The company entered receivership in July 1925, and its assets were sold at a receiver's sale at the end of 1926.[14]

Service Motor Truck Company placed this advertisement in mid-1920.
HAS&SM

Use the *Correct* Truck for the Job

To be profitable, a motor truck must be exactly suited to the work it handles. The nature of the load carried, the road conditions encountered, the distances traveled—influence the kind and size of truck you need.

There are eighty combinations of power, speed and capacity in Service Motor Trucks. One of these combinations precisely conforms to your specific requirements. It is practically "made to measure" for your particular work.

Service Motor Trucks have been carefully adapted to trucking work in practically every field of industry. They have consistently rendered uninterrupted service at low ton-mile cost for the last ten years.

Their outstanding performance causes present Service users to increase their equipment to the extent of buying sixty-five per cent. of all the Service Motor Trucks that are now made.

The long experience of our Transportation Engineers in selecting the correct truck for the specific work to be done, is available to help *you* select the best truck to build *your* business.

Service MOTOR TRUCKS
Builders of Business

SERVICE MOTOR TRUCK COMPANY · WABASH, INDIANA, U. S. A.
NEW YORK—87-89 West End Avenue   CHICAGO—2617-2625 South Wabash Avenue

Studebaker, 1908-1963

The Studebaker Brothers Manufacturing company in South Bend made its first electric automobile in 1902. The company formally entered the light-duty truck market in 1914 with the 1/2-ton Delivery Car. This model was available as a Panel Side Delivery or Express Body Delivery, each priced at $1,150. At the outset of World War I in 1917, these models were priced at $925 and $875, respectively. Studebaker discontinued commercial vehicle production in 1918 to shift to war goods.

Studebaker heavy-duty truck production commenced in 1925, with light-duty commercial production resuming in 1927. A wide range of open and closed delivery vehicles were built on Studebaker's automotive chassis through 1931, when the company again abandoned the light-duty market.

In 1937 Studebaker reentered the light-duty market until the Indiana plant closed in December 1963. This offering was based on the pickup truck that was widely accepted in the market. The first offering was the 1/2-ton Coupe-Express pickup truck based on the Dictator series 5A, six-cylinder passenger car. Other variations included the Suburban, a woody station wagon, and a chassis without the pickup box. Heavy-duty trucks used the same cab as the Coupe Express. Included in this standard series were a 1½-ton Express pickup and a panel van. The 1938 light-truck line was based on the new Champion Series 7A passenger car, and in 1939 the offerings were based on the President passenger car.

Studebaker introduced an all-new light-duty series in 1941 designed from the ground up as a commercial vehicle. Some pieces carried over from the passenger car line. The Series M truck was produced in nearly the same way from 1941 through 1948. The Coupe Express was available with or without the pickup box. A Deluxe trim package included stainless steel grille bar overlays, a hood ornament, bright metal side moldings, chrome driver-side exterior rear view mirror, dome light, and body color fenders. A 1-ton Standard Express with an eight-foot pickup box was also available.

During World War II, Studebaker produced over 197,000 Model US6 2½-ton, 6x6 and 6x4 military trucks. These military trucks used a slightly modified M Series truck cab and Hercules power.

In 1949 Studebaker's postwar Series 2R debuted. Like Studebaker's 1947 automobiles, the styling was all-new, lower, and featured an absence of running boards. This model was designed by Robert Bourke, chief of Raymond Loewy's styling studio in South Bend. It shared virtually no components with its contemporary automobiles. The model range consisted of the 2R5 1/2-ton pickup with 6½-foot box, 2R10 3/4-ton pickup, and the 2R15 1-ton pickup both with eight-foot boxes. A 2-ton truck was also available. An ivory color highlighted the grille and the painted bumper. Models could be ordered without the pickup box or with a stake bed. Special applications included chassis only, cowl and chassis, or windshield cowl and chassis. The Series 2R was mechanically similar to the predecessor Series M. The series remained basically the same from 1949 to 1953. Studebaker's best light-duty truck production year was recorded in 1952 with 58,873 units built.

For 1954 the Series 2R received a minor facelift and the new designation of Series 3R. The facelift consisted of a new grille and one-piece curved windshield. A V-8 engine was introduced for the heavy-duty trucks. The model designation changed to Series E with scant styling changes and introduction of a V-8 engine for 1955. Studebaker's optional automatic transmission was available on 1/2- and 3/4-ton models.

Starting in 1957, Studebaker wanted the extra lift in sales that annual styling might introduce. The basic 1949 body was unchanged, but the grille, bumper, and body trim molding were tweaked to add an air of freshness. Optional four-wheel-drive for 1/2-, 3/4-, and 1-ton models with V-8 engines was introduced in 1958. Also new for 1958 was the Scotsman Model 3E1 stripped-down 1/2-ton truck. This model name was patterned after the successful basic Studebaker passenger car of the same name. This economical truck was available for $1,595. In 1959 Studebaker offered a Lark Panel Wagon based on the passenger car of the same name.

After 10 years with the same basic body structure, the 1/2- and 3/4-ton models finally got new styling in 1960. Studebaker took the Lark car body and converted it to a truck front end and cab. This model used a truck chassis instead of a car chassis plus the preceding pickup box. These models were called the Series 5E Champ. The last Studebaker truck was produced in December 1963.[15]

Mighty Allied armies mass in India and Studebaker trucks help transport them!

FOR months, the United Nations have been getting ready in India for the big push to defeat Japan.

From the Burma border to the Khyber Pass, correspondents report tremendous activity—with even public parks in big cities serving as armed camps.

Effective mobilization in a land of India's size requires adequate military transport. And many an American boy stationed there could tell you how much dependence is being placed on big multiple-drive Studebaker military trucks.

Those Studebaker trucks in India are counterparts of the powerful, dependable Studebakers that have been doing such a superb transport job for the conquering Soviet armies. And, in addition to trucks, the five great Studebaker factories continue to build huge quantities of mighty Wright Cyclone engines for the famous Boeing Flying Fortress as well as other vital war matériel.

AND THEY'RE BOTH BUYING BONDS!
They're doing it in millions of American families—where sons are fighting and fathers are working on war production . . . they're all buying Bonds . . . to help speed Victory now—and keep our Nation sound.

During World War II, Studebaker produced over 197,000 heavy-duty trucks.
TAC

124

Stutz Fire Engine Company, 1919-1929

New Stutz Fire Engine Company, 1929-1941

In January 1919, Harry C. Stutz and Alfred C. Mecklenburg began work on the first Stutz fire engine in downtown Indianapolis. The Stutz Fire Engine Company was incorporated on May 29, 1919. In June, Stutz and Mecklenburg demonstrated their new 500 gallon-per-minute (g.p.m.) pumper in a 12-hour test at the International Fire Chief's Convention in Kansas City, Kansas. The Stutz unit was the only one of eight contestants to earn a perfect score during the test.

As a result of the 12-hour test, six cities placed orders for three different sized pumpers. During the second half of the year, the company constructed a new two-story building at 1411 N. Capitol Avenue.

In June 1920, Stutz demonstrated a new 750 g.p.m., triple-combination pumper at the International Fire Chief's Convention in Toronto, Ontario. With this model, Stutz earned another perfect score in the official test—a unique accomplishment among fire apparatus manufacturers. The company leveraged this showing into additional orders from cities like Chicago, Illinois, which ordered two Stutz units.

Stutz produced the first diesel-powered fire engine in the United States for the fire department in Columbus. The engine was manufactured by the Columbus-based Cummins Engine Company.
TSC

On November 8, 1920, The Indianapolis City Council approved a bond issue for motorized fire apparatus. The city contracted with Stutz for seven 750 g.p.m, triple-combination pumpers; 18 triple-combination pumpers with 600 g.p.m; and 10 city service ladder trucks. Indianapolis paid $7,785 for each city service truck, $9,265 for each 600 g.p.m. pumper, and $11,023 for each 750 g.p.m. pumper.

In what appears to be standard Stutz practice from his automotive days, the 600 g.p.m. pumpers and city service trucks were powered with four-cylinder, Wisconsin T-head engines. The 750 g.p.m. pumpers used six-cylinder, Wisconsin T-head engines. Plus, several other items were furnished by a number of Indianapolis suppliers: Pioneer Brass cast the bells, suction strainers and couplings; Metal Auto Parts formed the hoods, splash and dust shields, fenders, and gas tank; Insley built the hose body; and Jim Brown manufactured the headlights.

Stutz records indicate 16 pumpers, two chemical engines and one chemical engine with turret were delivered in 1920 to various buyers. Eight of the 16 pumpers were part of the Indianapolis contract.

Stutz's biggest year for deliveries was in 1921, with 76 units. Sixty-two pumpers, three chemical and hose cars, and 11 city service ladder trucks left the Stutz factory. Ten city service trucks and 17 pumpers completed the 1919 Indianapolis Fire Department order. In 1922 Stutz sold 50 units, including 12 Model K pumpers, 18 Model C 750 g.p.m. pumpers, and 20 other units. The number increased to 57 units in 1923.

Stutz also added one important innovation for fire apparatus in 1923: the company was the first manufacturer to offer four-wheel brakes on its fire apparatus.

In 1924 Harry C. Stutz decided to concentrate on his H.C.S. Cab Manufacturing Company and left the Stutz Fire Engine Company. With this change, H.C.S. taxicabs were built in the fire engine plant. Fire engine operations moved to

1101 East 22nd Street in Indianapolis, the former location of the National Automobile Company. This version of the Stutz Fire Engine Company produced 64 units in 1924. The firm totaled 30 units in 1925, and only six units were delivered in 1926.

Stutz built an unrecorded number of units from 1927 to 1929. The last report filed by the company with the Indiana Secretary of State was dated August 18, 1927. In 1929 a bankruptcy court sold off the company's assets.

The Stutz Fire Engine Company manufactured about 300 units by the time it ceased operations.

Late in 1929, a successor arose—the New Stutz Fire Apparatus Company. Walt J. Holtz and Alfred C. Mecklenburg briefly set up shop for the new company at two different Indianapolis locations near the original plant.

By July 1931, Mecklenburg relocated operations to Hartford City, Indiana, after soliciting favorable investors in this new locale. The company offered New Stutz fire apparatus on a variety of commercial and light-duty chassis made by such companies as Ford, GMC, and Dodge. The first New Stutz was built on a 1931 Chevrolet chassis. New Stutzs were also built on one Indiana Truck chassis and two Stutz auto chassis.

In 1937 Stutz produced the first diesel-powered fire engine in the United States for the fire department in Columbus, Indiana. The 1,000 g.p.m. pumper had a 175 h.p. Cummins HR-6 engine. This purchase was authorized after a 24-hour continuous pumping test.

With World War II brewing in Europe, the New Stutz Company turned its attention to subcontracting machine work for the war effort and shipped its last fire apparatus in 1941.[16]

Waverley, 1899-1916

Among the commercial vehicles that the Waverley Company of Indianapolis built were many open and closed light delivery wagons, and

trucks with 1-ton, 1½-ton, 2-ton, and 3-ton ratings. In 1906 Waverley built 16 1½-ton trucks for the Anheuser Busch Brewing Company in St. Louis, Missouri. These trucks were still rendering successful service in 1913. Some were reported as giving 45 miles on a charge.

Endnotes

1. Bailey, L. Scott, *The American Car Since 1775,* New York, NY, Automoblie Quarterly, Inc., © 1971, p 376 - 404.
2. Gunnell, John A., *Standard Catalog of American Light Duty Trucks,* Iola, WI, Krause Publications, © 1987, p 134 - 140.
3. Keller, Michael E., *The Graham Legacy: Graham-Paige to 1932,* Paducah, KY, Turner Publishing Company, © 1998, p 31 -59.
4. Starkey, John H., *Hoosiers Put Big Rigs On Road,* Indianapolis, IN, Indianapolis Star, © 1974, March 24, 1974 issue.
5. Hanley, George Philip, *The Marmon Heritage,* Rochester, MI, Doyle Hyk Publishing Co., © 1985, p 89 - 92.
6. Hanley, p 502.
7. Hanley, p 517 - 520.
8. Hanley, p 530.
9. Hanley, p 522.
10. Hanley, p 522 - 523.
11. Hanley, p 553 - 556.
12. Hanley, p 573 - 576.
13. Hanley, p 594.
14. Huffman, Wallace S., *Service Motor Truck Company,* Hershey, PA, Antique Automobile Club of America, Vol. 34, No. 6, © 1970, p 39 - 42.
15. Gunnell, p 630 - 654.
16. Katzell, Raymond A., *The Splendid Stutz: The Cars, Companies, People and Races,* Indianapolis, IN, The Stutz Club, © 1996, p 337 - 349.

Indianapolis-based pharmaceutical company Eli Lilly & Company once used a Waverley screenside delivery van. ELCA

A List of Indiana-Built Trucks

Name	Manufacturer	City	Dates
Alena Steam	Alena Steam Products, Co.	Indianapolis	1922-1923
American	American Motor Vehicle Co.	LaFayette	1918
Barrows	Barrows Motor Truck Co.	Indianapolis	1927-1929
Betz	Betz Motor Truck Co.	Hammond	1920
Brown	Brown Commercial Car Co.	Peru	1912-1914
Comet Delivery	Comet Cyclecar Co.	Indianapolis	1914
Coppock	Coppock Motor Car Co.	Decatur	1908-1909
Coppock	Coppock Motor Car Co.	Marion	1907
Crosley	Crosley Motors, Inc.	Marion	1947-1953
Crosley	Crosley Motors, Inc.	Richmond	1940-1941
Decatur	Decatur Motor Car Co.	Decatur	1909-1912
Dodge Truck	Chrysler Corporation	Evansville	1928-1938
Durable	Durable Motor Truck Co.	Hammond	1917-1918
Fort Wayne	Fort Wayne Auto. Mfg. Co. Inc.	Fort Wayne	1910-1913
Gary	Gary Motor Truck Co.	Gary	1916-1927
Graham Brothers Truck	Graham Brothers Inc.	Evansville	1916-1927
Handy Wagon	Auburn Motor Chassis Co.	Auburn	1912-1913
Hoosier Limited	Decatur Motor Car Co.	Decatur	1911
Huffman	Huffman Bros. Motor Co.	Elkhart	1919-1927
Ideal	Ideal Auto Co.	Fort Wayne	1910-1915
Imp Closed Delivery	W.H. McIntyre Co.	Auburn	1913-1915
Indiana	Harwood-Barley Mfg. Co.	Marion	1911-1939
Inter-State	Inter-State Motor Co.	Muncie	1916-1917
International	International Harvester Co.	Fort Wayne	1923-1983
Jonz	American Automobile Mfg. Co.	New Albany	1911-1913
Lambert	Buckeye Mfg. Co.	Anderson	1901-1918
Lindsley	J.V. Lindsley & Co.	Indianapolis	1908
Lowell	Lowell Motor Truck Co.	Lowell	1918-1919
Mais	Mais Motor Truck Co.	Peru	1911-1917
Mais	Mais Motor Truck Co.	Indianapolis	1911-1917
Marion	Marion Motor Car Co.	Indianapolis	1905
Marmon Truck	Nordyke & Marmon Co.	Indianapolis	1913-1915
Marmon-Herrington	Marmon-Herrington	Indianapolis	1931-1963
McIntyre	W.H. McIntyre Co.	Auburn	1909-1915
Merz Delivery Van	Merz Cyclecar Co.	Indianapolis	1913-1915
Mutual	Mutual Truck Co.	Sullivan	1919-1921
Noble	Noble Motor Truck Co.	Kendallville	1917-1931
Nyberg	Nyberg Automobile Works	Anderson	1912-1913
Overland	Overland Automobile Co.	Indianapolis	1908-1911
Pak-Age-Car	Auburn Automobile Co.	Connersville	1938-1941
Pak-Age-Car	Stutz Motor Car Co.	Indianapolis	1930-1938
Pathfinder Light Van	Motor Car Mfg. Co.	Indianapolis	1912-1914
Premier	Premier Motor Mfg. Co.	Indianapolis	1905-1906
Real Van	H. Paul Prigg Co.	Anderson	1914
Red Ball	Red Ball Motor Truck Corp.	Frankfort	1924-1927
Relay	Relay Motors Corp.	Wabash	1927

A List of Indiana-Built Trucks (continued)

Name	Manufacturer	City	Dates
Rockne	Studebaker Corp.	South Bend	1932-1933
Rodefeld	Rodefeld Mfg. Co.	Richmond	1915-1917
Service	Service Motor Car Co.	Wabash	1911-1926
South Bend	South Bend Motor Works	South Bend	1913-1916
Studebaker	Studebaker Corp.	South Bend	1908-1963
Tructor	Highway Tractor Co.	Indianapolis	1917-1918
Valley	Valley Motor Truck Co.	Elkhart	1927-1930
Van Auken	Van Auken Electric Car Co.	Connersville	1913-1915
Waverley Electric	The Waverley Co.	Indianapolis	1899-1916
Whitesides	Whitesides Commercial Car Co.	New Castle	1911-1912
White Steam	White Steam Wagon Co.	Indianapolis	1900-1903
Winkler	Winkler Bros. Mfg. Co.	South Bend	1910-1911
Zimmerman	Zimmerman Mfg. Co.	Auburn	1912-1916

The General Motors Fort Wayne Assembly Truck Plant covers 937 acres and has more than 2.5 million square feet enclosed. GM has produced trucks in Indiana since late 1986. Pictured below is the Chevrolet Silverado for 2003.
GMTG

128

Indiana-Built Military Vehicles

The American auto industry has been called the "Arsenal of Democracy" because of its tremendous contributions to the military during wartime. Part of the credit for the title has to be given Indiana's automakers. The state's automotive manufacturers have built more than 875,000 military vehicles. These vehicles range from the "Class B" 5-ton Liberty trucks built by Indiana Truck Co. and Service Motor Truck Co. during World War I through the M998 HMMWV produced by AM General today.

AM General, 1903-1909 and 1964 to Present

AM General's Indiana origins trace to 1903 when the Standard Wheel Company of Terre Haute expanded its wheel-building operations to include the Overland Automobile Department. Automotive operations moved to Indianapolis in 1905. During the national panic of 1907, John N. Willys saved the Overland Automobile Company from near bankruptcy and assumed control of the organization. In 1909 Willys took over the Pope automaking facilities in Toledo, Ohio, and consolidated his new Willys-Overland operations there.

In 1963 Willys Motors was renamed the Kaiser Jeep Corporation. Early in 1964, Kaiser purchased Studebaker Corporation's Chippewa Avenue manufacturing facilities in South Bend. Kaiser then assumed contracts for the production of the M39 5-ton military truck and the M44 2½-ton trucks. The Chippewa facility produced nearly 112,000 5-ton and 150,000 2½-ton trucks over the next 25 years. Kaiser also produced over 100,000 M151 1/4-ton trucks in South Bend. In 1965 the company designed and developed the M715 1¼-ton series truck. Delivery of over 33,000 vehicles began in 1967 and included the M715 cargo truck, M726 ambulance and the M726 maintenance truck.

On April 1, 1971, the division was incorporated as AM General Corporation, a wholly owned subsidiary of the American Motors Corporation. In the early 1970s, AM General designed the

---

AM General continues to produce both military and civilian versions of the High Mobility Multi-Purpose Wheeled Vehicle. AMG

M809 series 5-ton truck and produced over 92,000 vehicles. AM General developed and produced over 21,000 M939 series 5-ton trucks, beginning in 1982. In 1976 AM General developed the M915 truck series, which utilized a multi-purpose chassis and accommodated a variety of special purpose vehicles. These included Line Haul Tractors, a Bituminous Spreader, Dump Trucks and Concrete Transporters. Delivery of 7,300 vehicles was finished in 1984.

In March 1983, AM General won a contract to produce in Mishawaka the M998 Series High Mobility Multi-Purpose Wheeled Vehicle (HMMWV), a 1 1/4-ton truck intended to replace light tactical vehicles. The HMMWV soon became known as the Humvee. AM General delivered 55,000 HMMWVs in five basic models and 15 different configurations over a five-year period beginning in 1985. The total contract order of 70,000 HMMWVs was completed in December 1989.

In 1983 the LTV Corporation bought AM General from American Motors Corporation and established it as a wholly owned subsidiary of the LTV Aerospace and Defense Company. In August 1989, the U.S. Army awarded AM General a new multi-year contract for continued production of more then 33,000 HMMWVs. Deliveries under this new contract began in January 1990. AM General received an additional contract for 1,200 HMMWVs in 1994, and 8,800 in 1995 to be produced through the year 2000. This brought the total to over 150,000 vehicles built and delivered to the U.S. Armed Forces and more than 30 overseas nations.

In 1992, AM General began production of civilian versions of the HMMWV, called the HUMMER®. Known as "the world's most serious 4x4," the revolutionary vehicle found favor with users who appreciate the value of HUMMER's long life, performance, toughness, and mobility.[1]

Chrysler Corporation-Plymouth Assembly, 1942-1944

Although it didn't make new military vehicles, the Plymouth Assembly plant was known as the Evansville Ordinance Plant during World War II. Between late June 1942 and April 20, 1944, the Evansville location reconditioned 1,662 General Sherman tanks; rebuilt 4,000 Army trucks; delivered 800,000 tank grousers (track overshoes that made tanks more maneuverable on muddy terrain); produced more than three billion .45 caliber cartridges; and almost half a billion .30 caliber cartridges.[2]

International Harvester, 1923-1983

International Harvester Corporation (IHC) built the M-5H-6 2 1/2-ton 6x6 truck in Fort Wayne from 1941-1945. Almost exclusively, the Marine Corps and the Navy used this model. The locking differentials greatly improved traction, which helped in the poor soil conditions of beachhead landings. The truck used International's famous Red Diamond 318 c.i.d., six-cylinder, engines with Delco Remy electrical components. This 6x6 truck featured a soft cab with a convertible top that stowed behind the seat and a folding one-piece windshield. The doors had side curtains for severe weather. The rear cargo bodies were eight or 12 feet long.[3]

IHC also built the M5A high-speed tractor from 1942-1945.[4] From 1943 to 1944, the company built the M5 and the M9A1 half-tracks. The M5 was an improved version over its predecessor. Standardized components that carried over from previous models were the frame and most driveline items. The body armor was thicker, and the rear sides were one-piece instead of bolted assemblies. The six-cylinder engines were 450 c.i.d. with overhead valves. Most were sent overseas as part of the Lend Lease program. The M9 was similar to the M5 series with a few upgrades. Access to the stowage and radio cabinets was from the interior.[5]

In the early 1950s, IHC built the M75 armored personnel carrier. The M75 was designed with light armor to transport 10 men, excluding the crew, into combat zones. The unit was not fully amphibious, but it could ford water with some preparation. The armored body was a one-piece welded structure. Troops sat in rows of seats along each side facing each other. Two exit doors were in the rear. It used an 895 c.i.d., six-cylinder, horizontally opposed, Continental engine with overhead valves. General Motors Allison Division made the CD-500-4 cross-drive transmission with torque converter in Indianapolis.[6] From 1950 to the late 1970s, IHC built a series of M41, M54, and M55 5-ton cargo trucks, M51 dump trucks, M52 tractors, M139 cab and chassis units, and M62, M246, and M543 wreckers.[7]

Marmon-Herrington, 1931-1963

As a colonel in World War I, Arthur W. Herrington recognized the need for better vehicles to transport troops and supplies. This need led to his developing and patenting a driving mechanism for the front wheels of motor vehicles in 1930. By 1931, the U.S. Army Quartermaster Depot was prepared to award him an order for a fleet of all-wheel drive refueling trucks. But Herrington faced a dilemma. He had an order for trucks, but nowhere to build them. He then approached Fred E. Moskovics, an associate of the Marmon brothers from their early automotive days.[8]

In March 1931, Walter C. Marmon, chairman of the board of directors of Nordyke & Marmon, and Herrington organized a subsidiary firm,

Marmon-Herrington (M-H). The Indianapolis-based subsidiary would manufacture all-wheel drive military and off-road vehicles. In late 1931, Marmon-Herrington became an independent firm with Walter C. Marmon as chairman and A.W. Herrington as president and chief engineer.[9]

Together they completed the quartermaster's initial order of 33 unit military trucks on May 30, 1931. The new truck incorporated a "drop" frame that lowered the load and the vehicle's center of gravity. The front wheels were far forward in order to climb up and over obstructions.[10] Subsequent Quartermaster Depot orders included six wheel-drive trucks with various load ratings. By 1934 there were 26 models, with some rated as high as 35 tons.

In 1936 M-H offered its first conversion of a Ford pick-up truck to all-wheel drive (AWD). This unit anticipated the development of a lightweight, all-terrain military vehicle known as the Jeep by four years. In fact, A.W. Herrington was one of the co-developers of the prototype Jeep for American Bantam Car Company demonstrated in March 1940.[11]

M-H developed another military first in 1936— a half-track vehicle with powered front wheels. The chassis of the vehicle was a M-H AWD Ford conversion with rear tracks. M-H's pioneering

Marmon-Herrington converted a Ford pick-up truck to all-wheel drive in 1936. This served as a model for the Jeep. TMH

Marmon-Herrington also built the M-22 Locust 7-ton tank in 1942.
TMH

half-track work led the way for one of the most capable vehicles of World War II.[12]

Beginning in 1937, M-H began making prototypes for the full spectrum of U.S. military agencies. This conversion of the Ford 2½-ton 6x6 was the first to see Army service, and it developed the ensuing standards for military production. Various versions of this unit saw service in all the U.S. military services. Plus, many of the world's allied powers used M-H designed vehicles.

M-H also did prototype work on two amphibious vehicles: the amphibious Jeep, later produced by Ford Motor Company, and the famous "Duck" Model DUKW, subsequently produced by the GMC Truck and Coach Division.[13]

M-H revealed its first track-laying, armored vehicle—a Light Combat Tank or CTL—in June 1935. A civilian version called the Track Laying Tractor or TRL was first offered in 1936. This M-H unit used Goodrich rubber tracks for traction on wet pavement, packed snow, and ice.

In 1942, M-H produced two versions of medium tanks: a three-man Medium Tank (CTM) and a four-man Medium Heavy Tank (MTL). Both of these were of riveted-plate hull construction with 360° rotation turret. Another familiar M-H military vehicle was the M-22 7-ton, airborne Locust tank, equipped with both a 37 m.m. cannon and a 50 caliber machine gun. In Europe these glider transported tanks were noteworthy for their maneuverability in supporting infantry troops.[14]

Studebaker, 1902-1963

Studebaker in South Bend produced the US6, 2½-ton, 6x6 truck from 1941 to 1945. The company's offering used many of the standardized components on similar trucks. The main differences were in the transmission, engine, and cab. Studebaker used a Borg Warner transmission, Hercules engine, and its own Series M truck cab. The Series M cab had a two-piece windshield that was hinged at the top. Engines were Hercules JXD, 320 c.i.d. six-cylinder, L-head versions. The Borg Warner transmission featured overdrive and five forward speeds and one reverse. Studebaker produced the second largest total of 2½-ton trucks for the armed forces with 197,000 units built.[15]

Studebaker designed, developed, and built the M29 Weasel as a tracked light-cargo carrier with all-terrain and fully amphibious capabilities. Originally designed for use in snow, the Weasel quickly became popular for use as an all-terrain vehicle. Its 20-inch wide tracks made crossing mud, sand, and marsh effortless. The Weasel became known as a "Go anywhere" vehicle and gained renown when General Douglas MacArthur used it as his personal vehicle during World War II. The Weasel used a 170 c.i.d., six-cylinder Studebaker Champion engine that sat in front immediately to the right of the driver's seat. Steering and braking were accomplished by two levers with mechanical linkage to the rear differential. The one-piece, welded, steel hull had a series of drain plugs for use after amphibious operations. Cargo capacity was 1,200 pounds. The tracks and suspension were unique to this vehicle. Studebaker built 15,000 Weasels between 1942 and 1945.[16]

Endnotes

1. Editors, *Website: History of the AM General Corporation,* South Bend, IN, AM General Corporation, © 1999.

2. Stout, Wesley W., *Bullets by the Billion,* Detroit, MI, Chrysler Corporation, © 1946.

3. Berndt, Thomas, *Standard Catalog of U.S. Military Vehicles 1940-1965,* Iola, WI, Krause Publications, © 1993, p 259-261.

4. Berndt, p 87 - 90.

5. Berndt, p 144 - 154.

6. Berndt, p 169 - 171.

7. Berndt, p 109 - 113.

8. Hanley, George P. and Stacey P., *The Marmon Heritage,* Rochester, MI, Doyle Hyk Publishing Co., © 1985, p 488.

9. Hanley, p 491.

10. Hanley, p 497.

11. Hanley, p 530.

12. Hanley, p 532.

13. Hanley, p 545.

14. Hanley, p 545 - 551.

15. Berndt, p 90 - 91.

16. Berndt, p 219 - 221.

Studebaker made the US6 truck for military use from 1941 to 1945.
SNM

"Those engines sure have the power!"

THE brother of a waist gunner on a Boeing Flying Fortress wrote Studebaker quoting him as saying:

"Those Wright Cyclone engines that Studebaker builds are really dependable and sure have the power."

Comments like that are fully appreciated, of course. But Studebaker men and women know that what count most are the accomplishments of stout-hearted air crews and rugged ground crews of our country's warplanes and the achievements of our fighting forces everywhere.

Whatever satisfaction the Studebaker organization may derive from the extent and consequence of its war work is always tempered by the realization that Studebaker is only one unit in a vast American fighting and producing team on which everyone's effort is important.

UNSUNG HERO OF OUR NAVY
Aerial radio gunner in a Navy dive bomber! One of the toughest jobs of all! Let's show him we're for him and
★ **BUY MORE BONDS** ★

Awarded to Aviation Division of The Studebaker Corporation

Studebaker **BUILDS WRIGHT CYCLONE ENGINES FOR THE BOEING FLYING FORTRESS**

Studebaker supplied 64,000 Cyclone engines during World War II.
TAC

134

A List of Indiana-Built Military Vehicles

Name	Manufacturer	City	Dates
Class B 5-ton Liberty truck	Indiana Truck Co.	Marion	1917-1918
Class B 5-ton Liberty truck	Service Motor Truck Co.	Wabash	1917-1918
AWD refueling truck	Marmon-Herrington	Indianapolis	1931
US6 2½-ton truck	Studebaker Corp.	South Bend	1941-1945
M-5H-6 2½-ton truck	International Harvester Co.	Fort Wayne	1941-1945
M5A High-speed tractor	International Harvester Co.	Fort Wayne	1942-1945
M5 Half-track	International Harvester Co.	Fort Wayne	1943-1944
M9A1 Half-track	International Harvester Co.	Fort Wayne	1943-1944
M39 5-ton cargo truck	Studebaker Corp.	South Bend	1950s to 1963
M41 5-ton cargo truck	International Harvester Co.	Fort Wayne	1950s
M44 2½-ton truck	Kaiser Jeep Corp.	South Bend	1960s
M51 5-ton dump truck	International Harvester Co.	Fort Wayne	1950s
M52 5-ton tractor	International Harvester Co.	Fort Wayne	1950s
M54 5-ton cargo truck	International Harvester Co.	Fort Wayne	1950s
M55 5-ton cargo truck	International Harvester Co.	Fort Wayne	1950s
M62 5-ton wrecker	International Harvester Co.	Fort Wayne	1950s
M75 Armored Personnel	International Harvester Co.	Fort Wayne	1950s
M139 5-ton cab/chassis	International Harvester Co.	Fort Wayne	1950s
M151 1/4-ton truck	Kaiser Jeep Corp.	South Bend	1960s
M246 5-ton wrecker	International Harvester Co.	Fort Wayne	1970s
M543 5-ton wrecker	International Harvester Co.	Fort Wayne	1970s
M715 1¼-ton truck	Kaiser Jeep Corp.	South Bend	1960s
M809 5-ton cargo truck	AM General Corp.	South Bend	1970s
M915 Truck Series	AM General Corp.	South Bend	1970s
M939 5-ton cargo truck	AM General Corp.	South Bend	1980s
M998 HMMWV	AM General Corp.	South Bend	1985 to pres
M22 7-ton Locust Tank	Marmon-Herrington	Indianapolis	1942
M29 'Weasel'	Studebaker Corp.	South Bend	1942-1945
CTL Light Combat Tank	Marmon-Herrington	Indianapolis	1935
CTM Medium Tank	Marmon-Herrington	Indianapolis	1942
MTL Medium Heavy Tank	Marmon-Herrington	Indianapolis	1942

AM General's HMMWV, or Humvee, is designed to traverse all kinds of terrain, including the desert.
AMG

Indiana Body/Coachbuilders

Custom body/coachbuilding made the natural transition from the carriage trade to automobiles. When horseless carriages began to replace horse-drawn vehicles, the same clientele demanded the services of coach building artisans to provide fittings for their automobiles to equal or excel those of their glamorous carriages. Luxury cars were often built as a chassis only, leaving the purchaser free to select a coachbuilder to construct the body. This custom was common, and small carriage shops flourished across the country. A prospective auto owner only had to take his new chassis to his local coachbuilder for a motor car finished to his taste and exact specifications.

Studebaker is as an example of a carriage firm that entered the field by building automobile bodies as an extension of its wagon-building trade. This sideline eventually grew into a complete auto manufacturing enterprise. McFarlan is another example of a carriage builder that transitioned to building bodies before going on to building luxury automobiles. Union City Body Company (UCBC)—founded to build carriage bodies for the local market—grew into building bodies for a number of firms. UCBC exists today and has grown into an enterprise providing truck bodies across the nation.

Elaborate bodies, often incorporating the latest ideas in construction and styling, came from specialists. Some coachbuilders had their own design staff and builders who supplied several different makes. Plus, several luxury automakers employed internal design staffs that contracted with outside custom builders to make bodies to their specifications. Union City Body Company served these manufacturers as well. Some UCBC bodies were built under the La Grande nameplate for Duesenberg. The wake of the Great Depression and the advent of all-steel body construction in the 1930s hastened the demise of custom coachbuilding in the United States.

A.H. Walker made the body for the Duesenberg pictured below. In fact, it is one of the last grand cars made by Duesenberg. It was purchased by pharmaceutical baron J.K. Lilly in 1934. This streamlined coupe became one of the highest-priced cars sold by Duesenberg. The completed car, with coachwork by Walker, is said to have sold for $25,000. During World War II, the car saw duty overseas and, at one point, was used as a tow truck. Reports indicate that the car languished for years in a Long Island garage in New York until Tonight Show host Jay Leno discovered it. After years of negotiation, Leno bought the car in 1995 and had it restored to its nearly original condition by Duesenberg expert Randy Ema.
ACDM

A.H. Walker,
1934-1935

Albert H. Walker, a British designer, took over the Weymann American Body Company in 1934 and established the A.H. Walker Company in Indianapolis. One of the company's most unusual special orders designed by Duesenberg's J. Herbert Newport, was built for pharmaceutical baron J.K. Lilly. Lilly is said not to have set his eyes upon the car until after its completion after his check had been tendered at the front office. The car was a three-passenger Walker La Grande coupe. Following an uncompromising departure from classic Duesenberg design, this streamlined coupe became the highest-priced body bought by Duesenberg, Inc. The completed car is said to have sold for $25,000.[1]

Briggs Indiana,
1936-1959

Briggs Indiana Corporation took over the former Graham-Paige auto body factory on East Columbia Street in Evansville in 1936. Briggs built bodies for the nearby Chrysler Corporation's Plymouth assembly plant on Morgan Avenue. In 1953 Chrysler acquired the Briggs factory and continued manufacturing bodies at this location until 1959.[2]

Central Manufacturing,
1898-1948

Central Manufacturing Company was incorporated on April 7, 1898, to manufacture vehicle woodwork at 123 West Seventh in Connersville. In 1903 it began to manufacture rear entrance automobile bodies for Cadillac. A Central car was built here in 1905, but was lost when the plant burned in 1905. The company moved to a new building in the McFarlan industrial park (on 18th Street north of the intersection at Georgia Street) in 1906. Central bodies became standard units on Auburn, Apperson, Cole, Davis, Elcar, Empire, Gardner, Haynes, H.C.S., Lexington, Lincoln, Moon, National, Overland, Paige, Premier, Stutz, and Wescott automobiles.

In 1928 Errett Lobban Cord purchased the Central Manufacturing Company and added 110,000 square feet more manufacturing space to the existing Central facilities. In the fall of 1933, Cord moved the Limousine Body Company of Kalamazoo, Michigan, (builder of the Auburn open car bodies) into the Central Manufacturing facilities.

The non-automotive stamping business was profitable since its inception in the early thirties. Howard Darrin built his Packard Darrin in the factory during 1940 and 1941. On March 10, 1941, Willys-Overland awarded Auburn-Central (the new corporate name) a contract to build 1,600 Jeep bodies. This was the first of many contracts that lasted through 1948 for Willys and Ford. The total for Jeep bodies reached 445,000 over a 45-month period.[3]

Graham-Paige,
1929-1935

In 1929 Graham-Paige Corporation announced construction of a new 273,600 sq. ft. Graham-Paige body plant in Evansville. The plant built bodies for Graham-Paige operations in Detroit, Michigan. The company leased this plant to Briggs Indiana Corporation at the end of 1935.[4]

Hayes Body,
1928-1930

In mid-1928, Hayes Body Corporation of Grand Rapids, Michigan, assumed control of Marmon Motor Car Company Plant 3 in Indianapolis for production of the 1930 bodies. After one model year, it reverted to Marmon ownership. In 1930 Marmon once more began assembling bodies in their plant.[5]

Weymann provided the Versailles aluminum body for the 1931 Stutz DV-32.
TSC

McFarlan Motor Car, 1856-1928

In 1856 John B. McFarlan moved to Connersville and combined several small buggy companies to form the McFarlan Carriage Company. McFarlan built an imposing four-story carriage factory in one corner of his industrial park—the first one in the country—in 1886. McFarlan made the transition from carriage manufacturer to coachbuilder in 1902. In addition to building the McFarlan luxury automobile from 1910 to 1928, the firm also built custom bodies.

E.L. Cord bought the McFarlan plant, which was five blocks south of his existing plants, in 1929 and used it to store leather upholstery materials, small parts, and finished Auburn and Cord cars.

Murray, 1926-1928

In June 1926, Marmon Motor Car Company leased Plant 3 in Indianapolis to Murray Corporation of Detroit. For the next two model years, Murray operated Plant 3 and made automobile bodies for Marmon and other auto manufacturers, such as Hupp, Paige, and Jordan. Murray set up its assembly lines in much the same way that Marmon had. Production began on the fifth floor and ended on the first. Executives hoped that the plant could be made more profitable by manufacturing bodies for several brands of cars. Apparently, this arrangement did not work. In mid-1928, Hayes Body Corporation assumed the lease for one model year.[6]

Studebaker, 1852-1963

In the late 1890s, the Studebaker Brothers Manufacturing Company in South Bend did a flourishing business as a body builder for electric vehicle manufacturers. Studebaker leveraged the company's experience in building carriages and wagons into building their first electric automobile in 1902. *See the Studebaker chapter for the complete story.*

Union City Body, 1898 to Present

Union City businessmen C.C. Adelsperger, S.R. Bell, and J.W. Wogoman formed Union City Body Company (UCBC) to manufacture bodies for the horseless carriage in 1898. Early manufacturing was done primarily for customers located within a 100-mile radius. The company produced bodies for automotive pioneers, including Haynes, Apperson, Clark, Davis, H.C.S., Lexington, National, Premier, and Chandler. Later UCBC built bodies for some of the great names in America's automotive past such as Duesenberg, Cord, Essex, Pierce-Arrow, and Auburn. The company manufactured these bodies until the decline of the specialty automobile industry in the late 1920s.

In the 1930s, the company began the production of school bus bodies for various chassis manufacturers and truck cabs for Studebaker. During World War II, transit busses built on a Ford chassis were the sole products.

In the 1950s, truck bodies were produced for installation on Ford, Dodge, GMC, and Chevrolet chassis until 1957 when an exclusive agreement was signed with Chevrolet and GMC Truck & Coach Division.

Today, the company builds four delivery truck models with 64 different sizes and a medium duty van in 14 different body sizes. UCBC customers include Frito-Lay, UPS, U.S. Postal Service, and Federal Express. The company has manufactured more than a half million vehicles since its first walk-in van was introduced.[7]

The Workhorse Walk-in Truck represents the current work of Union City Body.
UCBC

Weymann American Body, 1926-1934

The Weymann-American Body Company was established in Indianapolis in late 1926 in one of the factory buildings of the former National Motor Car Co. on East 22nd Street. Weymann coachwork featured flexible, European-type, fabric-covered closed bodies for American chassis. Weymann was known for quiet, lightweight bodies. Later Weymann-American offered designs with metal panels as well. Stutz listed this option in the Monte Carlo style. Weymann made bodies for other manufacturers like Cord, Duesenberg, Packard, and Pierce-Arrow. They were most closely associated with Stutz, which had a plant nearby.[8]

Endnotes

1. Elbert, J.L., *Duesenberg: The Mightiest American Motor Car*, Arcadia, CA, Dan R. Post Publications, © 1951, p 38.
2. Editor, *Briggs Purchases Graham Brothers Factory Property*, Evansville, IN, Evansville Courier, © August, 4, 1936.
3. Walters, H. Max, *The Making of Connersville and Fayette County*, Baltimore, MD, Gateway Press, Inc. © 1988, p 221.
4. Keller, Michael E., *The Graham Legacy*, Paducah, KY, Turner Publishing Co., © 1998, p 135.
5. Hanley, George P. and Stacey P., *The Marmon Heritage*, Rochester, MI, Doyle Hyk Publishing Co., © 1985, p 430.
6. Hanley, p 433.
7. Historical material gathered from the Union City Body Company, © 2002.
8. Katzell, Raymond A., *The Splendid Stutz: The Cars, Companies, People, and Races,* Indianapolis, IN, The Stutz Club, Inc., © 1996, p 249.

NOTE OF INTEREST

Union City was home for a while to an early automotive pioneer, John W. Lambert. He formed the Union Automobile Company in 1902 with a goal to produce 10 cars a month. One source lists that over 300 Union cars were sold throughout the company's three-year life span.

A List of Indiana Body/Coachbuilders

Name	City	Date
A.H. Walker Co.	Indianapolis	1934-1935
Briggs Indiana Corp.	Evansville	1936-1959
Central Manufacturing Co.	Connersville	1898-1948
Graham-Paige Corp.	Evansville	1929-1935
Hale Kilburn & Co.	Indianapolis	1925-1933
Hayes Body Corp.	Indianapolis	1928-1930
Lehman-Peterson Co.	Indianapolis	1925-1971
McFarlan Motor Car Co.	Connersville	1856-1928
Millspaugh & Irish	Indianapolis	1915-1928
Murray Corp. of America	Indianapolis	1926-1928
Robbins Body Co.	Indianapolis	1921-1928
Studebaker Corp.	South Bend	1852-1963
Union City Body Co.	Union City	1898 to present
Weymann American Body Co.	Indianapolis	1926-1934
Martin and Parry	Indianapolis	1919-1929

Note of Interest:
On the Road with Premier

During the infancy of automotive history, consumers were skeptical of the reliability of automobiles. So to prove their products' capabilities on the road, many automakers sponsored coast-to-coast trips.

Premier Motor Manufacturing Company was one that followed this policy. In fact, 12 Premiers in 1911 became the first caravan of autos ever to cross the United States. They used a network of roads to travel from Atlantic City, New Jersey, to Venice Park, California.

The journey started with an idea formed by several wealthy Premier owners, mostly from Pennsylvania and New York. They wanted to show that previous sponsors of transcontinental races had overplayed their victories by describing the roads as more treacherous than they were.

So, 40 travelers out of the group set out from the Atlantic Ocean on June 26, 1911, and headed west to report their findings.

Premier supported the effort by supplying the caravan's 12th vehicle, a mechanic, and factory test driver to accompany the travelers. Nicknamed the "millionaire auto party," the caravan made headlines across the route.

Premier provided the 12th vehicle to carry baggage for the participants of the 1911 Ocean to Ocean tour.
NAHC

They stopped each night in the best hotels available in the location and traveled in relative luxury for the time. Each vehicle traveled about 4,617 miles with mechanical troubles amounting to only four broken springs. After 45 days, the group concluded their journey by dipping their wheels in the Pacific Ocean.

"There is a general feeling that the Pacific and Atlantic coasts have been brought closer together," according to *Motor Age*, "and transcontinental touring by pleasure parties is now expected to become common since the first tour of this kind has been such an unqualified success."

Indiana Automotive Pioneers

Many people have contributed to making Indiana's mark on automotive history. This chapter discusses only a few. Most of those listed are inductees in the Automotive Hall of Fame located in Dearborn, Michigan. They include

- Gordon M. Buehrig
- Louis Chevrolet
- Errett L. Cord
- Clessie L. Cummins
- Frederick S. Duesenberg
- Carl G. Fisher
- Anton "Tony" Hulman, Jr.
- Raymond Loewy
- Edward "Eddie" V. Rickenbacker
- Louis Schwitzer, Sr.
- Wilbur Shaw
- Harry C. Stutz
- Ralph R. Teetor.

The authors felt that the Hall of Fame's list served as an equitable way to make the distinction. Yet, like any list, it is an incomplete record of those who made significant contributions. In fact, the authors felt strongly that at least four other people should be added:

- Charles H. Black
- Elwood Haynes
- John W. Lambert
- Howard C. Marmon.

The following provides short biographical sketches for each of these individuals.

Charles H. Black
(1850-1918)

Working as an Indianapolis carriagebuilder, Charles H. Black helped to herald the entry of the self-propelled motor wagon into Indiana. It has even been speculated that he may have built Indiana's first automobile in 1891. Unfortunately, no contemporary newspaper accounts exist to corroborate this claim.

Black asserted in an article in the December 27, 1913 issue of the *Indianapolis News* that "In 1891, after making most of my parts in my blacksmith shop and having others made for me, I was ready with my first machine. I tried it out on the streets of Indianapolis, using the Circle and Delaware Street mostly as they were paved." The article listed 12 prominent Indianapolis businessmen who recalled seeing Black operating his auto in the spring of 1891.

Further complicating his claim of being the first is the fact that about the same time a German-made Benz owned by Sam Pierson was stored in Black's carriage factory. Black was documented as driving this car. The Benz may have provided some inspiration to Black, but the differences in the two autos are apparent. Most obvious is that the Benz used wire wheels, while the Black used Sarven wood wheels. Other differences could be noted on some of the engines mechanical features.

As a skilled blacksmith and carriagebuilder, Black had the expertise to make most anything he needed. He built his own spark coil after rejecting one made in Germany. He commissioned a local storage battery company to build a battery specifically for his purpose.

Black is also known for a few other notable firsts. For example, in June 1892, Chicago Mayor Carter Harrison issued Black a license (possibly the first in the country) to drive on the city streets. Black probably also paid the first damage claim for an automobile accident in 1892 when he gave $1 to an ash hauler for a broken harness when the horse was frightened by the noise of his auto. Plus in 1893, President Benjamin Harrison rode in his car in Indianapolis just after leaving the presidency.

The fact remains that Charles H. Black conducted automotive experiments in the early 1890s. Plus, the C.H. Black Manufacturing Co. is documented as commercially producing autos from 1896 to 1900. The 1896 date establishes the firm as one of the first auto manufacturers in the state. The company's printed catalog described five models from a lightweight two-passenger Business Wagon for $600 up to a 10-passenger Wagonette priced at $1,800. Black sold his designs and manufacturing rights in late 1899.[1]

Gordon M. Buehrig
(1904-1990)

Gordon Buehrig
ACDM

An instructor expelled Gordon Buehrig from class on one occasion because the student's notebook was full of automobile drawings. This early interest in auto design shaped the rest of his life.

Many regard Buehrig as one of the most important automotive designers. His career spanned nearly four decades while working at Dietrich Inc., Packard, General Motors, Stutz, Duesenberg, Auburn Automobile Company, the Budd Company, Raymond Loewy's Studebaker studio, and Ford Motor Company. His famous designs include the 1932 Duesenberg Model J Beverly, the 1934 Auburn 851 Boattail Speedster, and the 1936 Cord Model 810.

In late 1933, during his second stint with General Motors Art and Color Section, Buehrig designed an aerodynamic car with air intakes on each side of a wraparound hood. Sometime later, while back in E.L. Cord's employment, this design study became the genesis for the Cord Model 810. In 1951 the Museum of Modern Art in New York recognized the Cord 810 as "the outstanding American contribution to automobile design."[2]

Louis Chevrolet
(1878-1941)

Before achieving success in building automobiles, Louis Chevrolet gained fame as a racing driver. In his first race in 1905, he defeated Barney Oldfield. On June 19, 1909, Chevrolet drove a Buick to victory in the first 400-mile Cobe Cup race in Crown Point, Indiana. He then won the inaugural 10-mile race at the Indianapolis Motor Speedway on August 19, 1909.

In 1911, with the encouragement of William C. Durant of General Motors, Chevrolet developed the first automobile to bear his name—the Chevrolet Classic Six retailing for $2,150. By 1913 there was a growing rift between the two individuals over the type of car that should wear the Chevrolet name.

Louis Chevrolet at the wheel of the 1915 Cornelian car.
IMS

The man left the company, but General Motors retained the rights to the "Chevrolet" name.

Louis Chevrolet went on to design the lightweight Cornelian race car with four-wheel independent suspension and a monocoque chassis for the Indianapolis 500 in 1915. Both innovations proved to be successful about 50 years later. These innovations reappeared on the rear-engine cars used from the 1960s to the present.

In the late 1910s, Louis built a number of Frontenac racing cars that he and his brothers, Arthur and Gaston, drove to many victories. For the 1920 Indianapolis 500, William Small of Indianapolis contracted with Chevrolet to build four Monroe and three Frontenac race cars. Gaston Chevrolet won the race driving one of the Monroes and become the first driver in Indy history to go the full 500 miles without changing tires. Another Chevrolet-design Frontenac with Tommy Milton as the driver won the 1921 Indianapolis 500. With this victory, Chevrolet became the first car builder to win two Indianapolis 500 Mile Races. Additionally, he accomplished that feat with new four-cylinder and eight-cylinder engines of his own design.

Later, Louis and Arthur Chevrolet and Cornelius W. Van Ranst developed a new overhead valve cylinder head that would develop higher horsepower from a Ford Model T engine and make it competitive in races on dirt tracks. They also incorporated the Chevrolet Brothers Manufacturing Company in Indianapolis to produce "Fronty-Ford" cylinder heads in 1922. They produced over 10,000 units during the next five years that dominated dirt track racing across America.

Louis Chevrolet's motto was "Never Give Up." He never did.[3]

Errett L. Cord
(1894-1974)

Before graduating from high school, E.L. Cord demonstrated the spirit that led to his entrepreneurial success. He purchased a Model T Ford, modified its engine, hand-built a speedster body, and then sold it at a substantial profit. Later, he barnstormed for a time as a racing driver and mechanic, while continuing to sell modified Ford speedsters at an average $500 profit per vehicle. In the early 1920s,

E.L. Cord
ACDM

Cord became a successful salesman at the Moon Dealer in Chicago, Illinois.

In 1924 a group of investors enlisted Cord to salvage the faltering Auburn Automobile Company. He took over the general manager position at no salary with the provision to acquire a controlling interest in the company if his efforts were successful. Cord had the large stock of unsold cars repainted in bright, attractive colors. He also instituted new designs and models and offered them at attractive prices. Sales moved forward, and by 1926, E.L. Cord was president of the company. About the same time, he purchased Duesenberg Motors and instructed Fred Duesenberg to design the world's finest motorcar.

In 1929 he assembled a holding company called the Cord Corporation. The holdings included Auburn, Duesenberg, Central Manufacturing, Lycoming Engine, Limousine Body, and Columbia Axle. In the 1930s, he added Stinson Aircraft Co., Century Airlines, and New York Shipbuilding Corp.

Cord lured top designers, engineers and marketers to his companies and encouraged excellence. For example, Auburn became one of the first automakers to offer straight-eight power in a medium-priced car. He also introduced the

Cord L-29—America's first front-drive automobile—and the magnificent Duesenberg Model J—the most luxurious and best-engineered motorcar of the day.

Production at the automotive operations ceased in 1937. Later, Cord developed a career in broadcast ownership, real estate, ranching, and politics.[4]

Clessie L. Cummins
(1888-1968)

Clessie L. Cummins' automotive adventures started before finishing the eighth grade when he stated, "I want to be a machinist and make things." He started his journey of achievements when he served on the pit crew of the first winner of the Indianapolis 500 Mile Race in 1911. Ten years later, he had incorporated the Cummins Engine Company in Columbus and received two patents for fuel injection on diesel engines.

Cummins introduced the automotive diesel to the United States in January 1930 in a 792-mile trip from Indianapolis to the New York Automobile Show. The trip required 30 gallons of fuel at a total cost of $1.38. In August 1930, a Cummins diesel-powered truck set a coast-to-coast record of 97 hours and 20 minutes on $11.22 in fuel. Later in the year, the Cummins truck set a non-stop record around the Indianapolis Motor Speedway for 13,535 miles. In 1931, the number 8 Cummins Diesel started the Indianapolis 500 in the sixth row and finished the race nonstop. The diesel-powered car finished 13th with an average speed of 86.17 m.p.h.

In 1955 he launched Cummins Enterprises Company to develop his new ideas. He immediately patented

Clessie Cummins pictured above and below standing beside one of company-sponsored race cars.
DOCC and IMS

the diesel engine brake. He also introduced new fuel injection metering pumps in the late '50s.

Clessie Cummins worked on his mechanical dreams throughout his life. In a career spanning more than 56 years, his inventive genius garnered 33 U.S. patents and numerous honors for his pioneering achievements.[5]

Dave Evans, driver = Thane Houser, mech.
Cummins Diesel.
Indianapolis Motor Speedway—1931

Fred Duesenberg (at right) with his brother August.
ACDM

Frederick S. Duesenberg
(1877-1932)

In 1897 Fred Duesenberg, assisted by his brother August, built a rotary valve engine. This was the beginning of a grand era of automobile racing and the construction of what many have called America's greatest luxury car—the Duesenberg.

Fred Duesenberg built his first automobile in 1904. This auto served as a prototype for the Mason automobile that debuted two years later. The brothers established the Duesenberg Motor Company in 1913 to build their new four-cylinder "walking beam" engines. In 1916 a Duesenberg finished in second place in the Indianapolis 500.

The brothers also built the "walking beam" engine under a U. S. government contract for use in light training airplanes later in 1916. In 1918 they developed and shipped 40 V-16 aviation engines before World War I ended. This engine spawned Fred's desire to build America's first overhead camshaft, straight-eight automotive engine.

In 1920, Duesenberg racers finished the Indianapolis 500 in third, fourth, and sixth places. Later that year the brothers announced that the Duesenberg Model A automobile would be built about two miles from the Indianapolis Motor Speedway's main gate. In addition to an innovative engine, the auto premiered the first American use of four-wheel hydraulic brakes. The racecar version finished first in the 1921 French Grand Prix. This accomplished another first for an American manufacturer—winning a European Grand Prix. Duesenberg's racing fortunes multiplied in the mid-1920s with first place finishes at the Indianapolis 500 in 1924, 1925, and 1927.

In 1926 E.L. Cord assumed control of Duesenberg operations and commissioned Fred to build the mighty Duesenberg Model J. It nearly doubled the horsepower of its nearest rival. Many still tout the Model J as one of the finest production cars ever made.[6]

Carl G. Fisher
(1874-1939)

Carl G. Fisher is perhaps best known as one of the founders of the Indianapolis Motor Speedway in 1908. He is also credited with helping to establish the Lincoln Highway, America's first transcontinental highway; manufacturing some of the first gas headlights; and developing Miami Beach as a winter playground. Fisher has been called "The Hoosier Barnum," a "Practical Visionary," and a "Prime Mover."

His vision for grand ventures was first demonstrated when he and James Allison obtained the rights to manufacture and market compressed acetylene headlight systems for automobiles in 1904. They founded the prosperous Prest-O-Lite. In 1913 Union Carbide purchased the company for $9 million. Fisher and Allison would invest their new wealth in other ventures.

In 1908 after being a competitor and spectator at numerous auto races across the nation, Fisher was eager to build a proving ground "to establish American automobile supremacy." He optioned 320 acres for $72,000, brought in three partners, and created the Indianapolis Motor Speedway. The first auto races were in August 1909, with the first Indianapolis 500 on Memorial Day, 1911. Fisher sold his interest in the Speedway to Eddie Rickenbacker in 1927.

Fisher next funneled his promotional skills on a problem that had plagued travelers for decades—

bad roads. His appeal led to the founding of the Lincoln Highway Association in 1913.

He used proceeds from the sale of Prest-O-Lite to build his "winter play land for himself and his friends." Development of land and facilities in Miami Beach took place over more than a decade by the shrewd marketing and promotional activities of Fisher and other like-minded individuals.

As revenues from his Miami Beach ventures began to mount in the mid-1920s, Fisher began to develop his dream of "The Miami Beach of the North" at Montauk, New York, on Long Island's eastern tip.[7]

During his life, he made and lost fortunes developing his ideas.

Elwood Haynes (1857-1925)

Ideas for one of America's first automobiles formulated in Elwood Haynes' mind as early as 1888, while he traveled Jay County's rutted sandy roads in a horse and buggy. He was concerned about the horse's lack of performance and endurance.

Haynes' thoughts stemmed from his formal training at the Worcester Polytechnic Institute in Massachusetts. He was one of the first automotive pioneers with formal training in engineering and technology. His technical training would serve him well in the automotive and metallurgical industries.

Elwood Haynes demonstrated his first automobile on July 4, 1894, in Kokomo. Haynes and the Apperson brothers formed an informal partnership to build a new car for America's first automobile race, the Chicago Times-Herald race in 1895. This auto drew on Haynes' metallurgical experiments and used an aluminum alloy in the two-cylinder engine. This alloy is the first recorded use of aluminum in an automotive engine. He was also the first to introduce a nickel-steel alloy in automotive use in 1896.

The Haynes-Apperson Company was incorporated in 1898 to manufacture motor carriages, gasoline motors, and gearing for motor vehicles. The 1903 Haynes-Apperson models featured new patented carburetors, one for each cylinder.

Carl G. Fisher
IMS

Elwood Haynes
EHM

In addition to being president of the automotive firm, Haynes continued his metallurgical and mechanical experiments. In 1905 he relinquished direct control of the automobile company to V.E. Minich and devoted his attention to metallurgy. In 1907, while he was researching a suitable material for use in the distributor, he discovered the alloy that he patented under the name of Stellite. This alloy proved to be harder than steel and resistant to wear and corrosion even at high temperatures. In 1912 the U.S. Patent and Trademark Office approved Stellite as a tool metal alloy. Stellite had a strategic importance during World War I in machining aircraft cylinder forgings and turning metal shell casings. Stellite is still in use today in space exploration and other highly corrosive environments.

Haynes improved his iron and steel alloys by adding chromium, thus developing one of the first types of stainless steel also in 1912. Stainless steel became popular for cutting utensils and other corrosive applications.

In 1913 he supported road improvements across the country and participated in the Indiana Automobile Manufacturers Association continental tour from Indianapolis to San Francisco, California.[8]

Haynes passed away in April 1925, a couple of months after the assets from the company bearing his name were sold at a receiver's sale.

Although the company eventually failed, Haynes' legacy to the U.S. industry lives on. His contributions to industry definitely place him among the high achievers in automotive history.

Anton J. "Tony" Hulman, Jr.
(1901-1977)

The Indianapolis Motor Speedway has served not just as the home for spectacular entertainment, but also as a proving ground for automotive advances. Yet, it was once in peril of extinction.

Tony Hulman is best remembered for saving the Indianapolis Motor Speedway from destruction and for making the annual race the "Greatest Spectacle in Racing."

With a degree from Yale University's Scientific School in 1924, Hulman returned to Terre Haute and joined the family's grocery business, Hulman & Company. Here he built a fortune.

Hulman's interest in the Speedway occurred after World War II. At the time, the track was rapidly deteriorating. He was persuaded by Wilbur Shaw, a three-time Indianapolis 500 winner, to save the track. Hulman purchased the Speedway in November 1945 and made numerous improvements to the track. The first postwar running of the Indianapolis 500 took place on May 30, 1946.

Throughout the years, Hulman spent millions of dollars on improvements and innovations at the track. He became famous for his traditional starting announcement, "Gentleman, start your engines!" He also established the Indianapolis Speedway's Hall of Fame Museum to display classic race cars and racing memorabilia. Thanks to Tony Hulman, the Indianapolis 500 became known as the largest one-day sporting event in the world.[9]

Tony Hulman
IMS

John W. Lambert
(1860-1952)

A 1960 article in *Antique Automobile* and an entry in the *Encyclopedia Britannica* credited former Indiana resident John W. Lambert with building America's first successful automobile in January 1891. At the time, Lambert was a resident of Ohio City, Ohio, which is just across the state line.

This event predated both Duryea's and Haynes' claims of being first. Lambert may not have pressed his claim because he felt that although extremely successful mechanically, it was a financial failure. He was unable to generate sufficient sales for more.

The 1891 Lambert was a three-wheel vehicle with a one-cylinder gas engine, a carburetor, and a drive system of his own design. By 1892 Lambert improved his one-cylinder engine. He then joined his father and brother in Union City, Ohio, to manufacture stationary gas engines.

In 1894 Lambert moved to Anderson to oversee their expanded operations of the newly named Buckeye Manufacturing Company. After attending a race in 1895, he returned home with a renewed desire to manufacture an automobile. By 1898 he fitted the Buckeye engine to a four-wheel buggy and operated it with success. That year also saw another Lambert innovation—the friction-drive transmission.

In 1902 Lambert formed the Union Auto Company in Union City to produce a rear-engine automobile with gearless, friction-drive. In 1905 Lambert closed this firm and formed the Lambert Automobile Company in Anderson. For the next 12 years, the company manufactured automobiles, trucks, fire engines, and farm tractors. All used the friction-drive pioneered by Lambert.

At the end of World War I, John correctly prophesied that a medium-sized, independent manufacturer would have to expand tremendously or merge with one of the large companies capable of mass production. The Lamberts chose instead to go into associated fields of automobile manufacturing.

By the end of his career, John W. Lambert had over 600 patents in the automobile, gasoline engine, and other mechanical fields.[10]

Raymond Loewy
(1893-1986)

Many recognize Raymond Loewy as one of the founding fathers of industrial design as a basic element in the development and marketing of consumer products.

Raymond Loewy with a 1953 Starliner Coupe. SNM

Loewy had always enjoyed drawing automobiles, and in 1932 he restyled the Hupmobile line. His most popular automotive design consultancy was with Studebaker, where his firm designed the 1939 Champion, 1947 Starlight Coupe, 1950 Champion, 1953 Starliner Coupe, and the 1963 Avanti.

Loewy and his company had a hand in designing everything from refrigerators and streamlined railroad locomotives to Coca-Cola's classic bottle.[11]

Howard C. Marmon
(1876-1943)

Howard C. Marmon's first prototype car for Nordyke and Marmon Company was remarkably progressive for 1902. It featured an overhead valve, air-cooled, two-cylinder, 90-degree V configuration engine with pressure lubrication. Marmon's design was the earliest automotive application of a system that became universal to the internal combustion piston engine.

Early on, Marmon recognized that weight was the enemy in car design. His early automobiles featured cast aluminum bodies, which weighed substantially less than other makes.

The effectiveness of a lighter body was proven in 1911 with a six-cylinder racing model named the Marmon Wasp. This car, driven by Ray Harroun, won the first Indianapolis 500 Mile Race.

The most recognizable of Marmon's creations was the Marmon Sixteen with its magnificent 491 c.i.d., 200 h.p., V-16 engine. The Marmon Sixteen was the largest American passenger car engine of its era. In February 1931, before production started on the Sixteen, the Society of Automotive Engineers honored Marmon's huge and gleaming V-16 engine design as "the most notable engineering achievement of 1930." The society was especially impressed by the extensive use of lightweight aluminum, generally a difficult metal to work and maintain in automobile power plants.

At the very end, Howard Marmon built, at his own expense, the HCM Special, a prototype auto with a 150 h.p. V12 engine, independent front-suspension, DeDion rear axle and tubular back-bone frame. Independent suspension and tubular backbone chassis—with some engineering

Howard Marmon
TMH

refinements—would resurface in about 30 years in exotic car applications.

Howard Marmon's products may have been ahead of their time for the general public, but the engineering community recognized them upon their introduction.[12]

Edward V. "Eddie" Rickenbacker
(1890-1973)

Eddie Rickenbacker's automotive adventures started when he was a riding mechanic for Lee A. Frayer in the 1906 Vanderbilt Cup race. In the summer of 1910, Rickenbacker began his racing career. At one two-day event, he won nine out of the 10 scheduled races. Rickenbacker was also a relief driver for Frayer in the first Indianapolis 500.

By 1913 he was team manager for the Duesenberg brothers and the team enjoyed success campaigning across the country. He drove his number 10 Duesenberg racer to a tenth place finish in the 1914 Indianapolis 500. In 1916 Rickenbacker assumed captain duties for the Maxwell team and continued winning.

In 1916 Glenn Martin gave Rickenbacker his first airplane ride in a two-seat biplane. This event and America's entry into World War I changed Rickenbacker's life forever. He flew his first combat mission as part of the Hat-in-the-Ring Squadron in April 1918. By the end of October, he earned his 26th victory and finished the war with the title "American Ace of Aces."

During quiet days on the European front, Rickenbacker dreamed about building an automobile under his name. He accomplished his dream when the first Rickenbacker cars debuted at the New York Automobile Show in January 1922. His new car featured a high-speed engine, low-slung body, and the first medium-priced American application of four-wheel brakes. Unfortunately, the country entered a recession in 1925, and his company declared bankruptcy in 1927.

In November 1927, Rickenbacker purchased the Indianapolis Motor Speedway from Carl G. Fisher and James A. Allison and immediately set out to improve it. Most of the track was resurfaced with asphalt. The retaining walls were reinforced with steel, and an 18-hole golf course was installed. The race was first broadcast by radio in 1928.

Eddie Rickenbacker pictured above and below at the Indianapolis Motor Speedway.
IMS

The Speedway provided the venue for many innovations during his ownership. For example, new oils were tested, and the fuel-injection system perfected at the Speedway became standard equipment on all World War II piston aircraft engines. Following the 1941 race, racing ceased for the duration of World War II.

After Allison's death in 1928, Rickenbacker purchased the Allison Engineering Company in Speedway. During his time of ownership, he contracted with the Navy to build the prototype of a 12-cylinder, water-cooled aviation engine with 750 to 800 h.p. In less than a year, he sold the company to the Fisher Brothers Investment Trust of Detroit. They sold it to General Motors in 1929. Over 80,000 Allison engines powered American fighter planes in World War II.

In June 1929, Rickenbacker joined General Motors as vice-president of sales for its Fokker Aircraft division. In April 1938, he purchased Eastern Air Lines from the corporation. Rickenbacker retired from active management of Eastern in December 1963. During his 25-year stewardship, Eastern always showed a profit, paid stockholders reasonable dividends, and never took a nickel of the taxpayer's money in subsidy.[13]

He eventually sold the Speedway to Tony Hulman.

Louis Schwitzer, Sr.
(1880-1967)

The winner of the first 10-mile race at the Indianapolis Motor Speedway in August 1909 was Louis Schwitzer, an automotive engineer. He drove a stripped-down, five-cylinder Stoddard Dayton touring car at an average speed of 57.4 m.p.h. for five miles on the macadam track.

Schwitzer's work in the automobile industry began as an engineer for Pierce-Arrow where he worked on one of the first six-cylinder engines made in America.

Schwitzer also designed the six-cylinder engine that powered the Marmon Wasp race car driven by Ray Harroun to win the first 500 Mile Race at the Speedway in 1911.

In 1912 Schwitzer joined the Indianapolis Motor Speedway Technical Committee and served as its chairman from 1919 through 1945. Also in 1912, Schwitzer was hired by the Empire Motor Car Company, leaving in 1914 to join the United States Army Motor Transport Corps. He was deeply involved in the design of class "B" military trucks.

After World War I, he started his own business to manufacture automotive cooling fans and develop cartridge-type packing gland seals. These seals opened new markets in industrial equipment, food processing, and the chemical industries. During the 1920s, his experience in gear production for the oil pump business was easily transferred to "positive displacement" rotary lobe type superchargers. Schwitzer is credited with building the first high-production supercharger for gasoline and diesel engines in America.

Following World War II, Schwitzer designed the low-cost, efficient "turbocharger." Schwitzer's turbocharger debuted on the Cummins diesel race car that won the pole position for the 1952 Indianapolis 500. Today, turbochargers are considered standard equipment on almost all diesel engines. Schwitzer also contributed to the development of crankshaft dampers, which are used on heavy-duty engines.[14]

Wilbur Shaw
(1902-1954)

Wilbur Shaw is probably best known as a three-time winner of the Indianapolis 500 in 1937, 1939, and 1940. He was also the first to win consecutive races.

Yet that is only part of his story. Another notable achievement in his career was his leadership in restoring the Indianapolis Motor Speedway following World War II.

Shaw's racing career began in 1921. He raced his own car built from used parts. By 1924 he was assigned the famed old Red Special and became the National Light Car Champion.

As a rookie driver, he finished fourth in his first Indianapolis 500 in 1927. He finished second in 1933 and 1935. In 1936 he returned to Indianapolis as a majority owner of the Gilmore Special and finished in seventh place. Driving the same auto, he finally won the 500 in 1937. After a second place

Wilbur Shaw pictured above as a Speedway executive and below as the 1939 winner of the 500 Mile Race
IMS

the Boyle car. He was well on his way to becoming the first four-time winner of the Indy 500 in 1941 when his right rear wheel collapsed, and his Maserati crashed into the wall.

During World War II, Shaw organized and directed Firestone Tire and Rubber Company's aviation division. He developed Firestone's Channel Tread tire and the self-sealing fuel tank.

Following World War II, Shaw was back at the Indy track. This time he drove a 500-mile test run at Firestone's request to test the durability of a new automobile tire made from synthetic rubber. He was the first to drive the track after the war.

He found the famous Speedway in deplorable shape. Weather had almost stripped the paint from the wooden stands, and hundreds of cracks marred the track surface in all four turns. As soon as possible, Shaw visited Speedway owner Eddie Rickenbacker to ascertain his plans for the track. Shaw developed a prospectus for potential investors and finally interested Anton Hulman, Jr., in saving the once-grand racing facility in the fall of 1945.

Wilbur Shaw served in the dual role of president and general manager of the Speedway until his untimely death in an airplane accident in 1954.[15]

finish in the Shaw Special the following year, he charged back in 1939 to win in one of the most famous cars in Speedway history—the Boyle Maserati. In 1940 it was another win for Shaw in

Harry C. Stutz
TSC

Harry C. Stutz
(1876-1930)

Harry C. Stutz is the quintessential automotive pioneer. During his career, Stutz had a hand in developing and designing many cars, such as the American, Marion, Empire, and Ideal. The one bearing his own name, the Stutz, is the most well known.

One of his early innovations developed in 1908 was the transaxle, a device that combined the transmission and rear differential. In 1909 he organized The Stutz Auto Parts Company to manufacture and sell his patented transaxle.

In 1911 Stutz formulated his dream of a quality sports car built from assembled, high-quality components manufactured by outside suppliers at a price below $2,000. The first Stutz was built in just five weeks and garnered an eleventh place finish in the inaugural Indianapolis 500. The Ideal Motor Car Company was organized to manufacture duplicates of the Indy race car for passenger use. The famous Stutz Bearcat sports car appeared in 1912 for a run of ten years. The Ideal Motor Car Company was reorganized as the Stutz Motor Car

Company, with Harry Stutz as president in June 1913.

In 1919 Harry Stutz founded two new ventures, the Stutz Fire Engine Company and the H.C.S. Motor Car Company. His creative spirit continued on through the late 1920s when he developed a revolutionary, horizontally opposed, four-cylinder aircraft engine. However, he died in June 1930 before this Stutz-Bellanca engine could be commercialized.[16]

Ralph R. Teetor
(1890-1982)

Ralph R. Teetor is most well known as the inventor of cruise control and president of Perfect Circle Corporation in Hagerstown. Throughout his career, he displayed an astonishing competence with machinery and confidence with people and places even though he had been blind from the age of five. Teetor developed unusual coping mechanisms and lived his life as if he could see. Many who came into contact with him never realized he was blind.

Ralph Teetor
OMV

His interest in automobiles developed early on. When he was 12 years old, Teetor and his second cousin built an automobile during the summer of 1902. Mechanical engineering became his career choice, and he graduated from the University of Pennsylvania in 1912 with a degree in this field.

In 1918 while working on a contract for the Navy at the New York Shipbuilding Corporation in Camden, New Jersey, Teetor developed a process to dynamically balance steam turbine rotors. He succeeded where many other engineers had failed. The new process was used through World War II.

In May of 1924 Teetor invented and patented a fluid-actuated automatic gear shift. The Bendix Company bought the patent and produced an automatic gearshift for Hudson. After World War II, popularity of the automatic transmission grew dramatically. For the next 40 years, most of the automatic transmissions on automobiles were based on the principles of his invention.

In 1936 Teetor was inspired to invent cruise control while riding with his patent lawyer one day. The lawyer would slow down while talking and speed up while listening. The rocking motion so annoyed Teetor that he was determined to invent a speed control device. He filed for the first patent on his device in the spring of 1945. Obstacles developed in production and delayed the debut of cruise control until 1958 on the Chrysler Imperial, New Yorker and Windsor models. Teetor's persistence paid off again in the commercialization of a device that is now standard equipment on many automobiles.

In 1946 Teetor became president of Perfect Circle Corporation, where he had worked in various engineering capacities for the previous 32 years.[17]

NOTE OF INTEREST

The monuments of many Indiana automobile pioneers are in Crown Hill Cemetery in Indianapolis. The list includes Black, the Duesenberg brothers, Fisher, Marmon and Stutz.

For help in locating gravestones, contact the Crown Hill office, Monday through Friday, 8:30 a.m. to 5 p.m., and Saturday, 8:30 a.m. to 2 p.m. On Sunday, you can find information at the community mausoleum, 9 a.m. to 5 p.m.

Endnotes

1. "America's First Automobile," *Indianapolis News,* December 27, 1913.
2. Georgano, Nick, *Art of the American Automobile: The Great Stylists and Their Work,* New York, NY, Smithmark Publishers, © 1995, p 201 - 211.
3. Editors, *The Louis Chevrolet Memorial: Indianapolis Motor Speedway,* Indianapolis, IN, The Louis Chevrolet Memorial Committee, © 1976.
4. Borgeson, Griffith, *Errett Lobban Cord His Empire, His Motor Cars: Auburn, Cord and Duesenberg,* Princeton, NJ, Automobile Quarterly Publications, © 1984.
5. Cummins, Lyle, *The Diesel Odyssey of Clessie Cummins,* Wilsonville, OR, Carnot Press, © 1998.
6. Steinwedel, Louis W., *The Duesenberg: The Story of America's Premier Car,* Philadelphia, PA, Chilton Book Company, © 1970.
7. Fisher, Jerry M., *The Pacesetter: The Untold Story of Carl G. Fisher,* Fort Bragg, CA, Lost Coast Press, © 1998.
8. Gray, Ralph D., *Alloys and Automobiles: The life of Elwood Haynes,* Indianapolis, IN, Indiana Historical Society, © 1979.
9. Bloemker, Al, *500 Miles to Go: The History of the Indianapolis Speedway,* New York, NY, Coward-McCann, Inc., © 1961.
10. Bailey, L. Scott, "1891 Lambert: A new claim for America's first gasoline Automobile," *Antique Automobile,* October 1960, p 341 - 345.
11. Georgano, p 189 - 199.
12. Hanley, George P. and Stacey P., *The Marmon Heritage,* Rochester, MI, Doyle Hyk Publishing Co., © 1985.
13. Rickenbacker, Edward V., *Rickenbacker,* Englewood Cliffs, NJ, Prentice-Hall, Inc, © 1967.
14. Kollins, Michael J., *A Guy Named Louie,* Detroit, MI, National Automotive History Collection, © 1998 Wheels Winter/Spring.
15. Bloemker, Al.
16. Katzell, Raymond A., *The Splendid Stutz: The Cars, Companies, People and Races,* Indianapolis, IN, The Stutz Club, © 1996, p 7 - 17.
17. Meyer, Marjorie Teetor, *One Man's Vision: The Life of Automotive Pioneer Ralph R. Teetor,* Indianapolis, IN, Guild Press of Indiana, © 1995.
18. This material was excerpted from the Souvenir Cards, Dearborn, MI, Automotive Hall of Fame, © 1997.

Notable Slogans

"Built to Stay Young"—Lexington

"In Union, there is strength"—Union

"No Dirt, No Odor, No Grease, No Bother"—Waverley Electric

"The Easiest Riding Car in the World"—Marmon

"The Always Ready Automobile"—Pope Waverly

"First by far with a postwar car"—Studebaker

"America's First Car"—Haynes

Personality Traits of Indiana Automotive Pioneers

Many of the automotive pioneers discussed on previous pages share some personality traits. In other words, they are naturally inclined to have and use certain characteristics. The following describes those traits most commonly shared among these pioneers.

Creative Spirit

Creative Spirits are risk takers who love adventure. They are rarely afraid of making mistakes. Creative Spirits tend to look at mistakes in a positive way. Instead of seeing a mistake as something wrong, Creative Spirits often see a mistake as a brand new way of doing something right.

Innovator

An Innovator is someone who believes that there are new and better ways of doing things. Sometimes Innovators invent brand new things, but most of the time they improve things that have already been invented. They find ways of overcoming obstacles. Innovators love challenges and usually never stop until they achieve their goals.

Prime Mover

Prime Movers plan and organize ways of achieving goals. They share their ideas with others and then look for the best way of getting where they want to go. Prime Movers know that not everyone will agree with them all the time. They use their leadership skills to overcome problems like this in order to get the job done.

Problem Solvers

Problem Solvers are good at understanding how things should work. They look at difficult situations as challenges. When something isn't working right, Problem Solvers are good at figuring out what's wrong and how to fix it.

Visionaries

Visionaries love to think about the future. They say things like, "I wonder what would happen if..." Visionaries also enjoy making their dreams into realities. They rarely enjoy doing the same things over and over again.

Each of us has these personalities within us to varying degrees, but one trait tends to dominate our personality. All of these traits are necessary to get the work of an organization done. It's all a matter of balancing the traits in a way that allows the organization to dream the dream and still get it accomplished.[18]

Individual	Creative	Innovate	Prime	Problem	Vision
Charles H. Black		X		X	X
Gordon M. Buehrig	X				X
Louis Chevrolet		X	X		
Errett L. Cord			X		X
Clessie L. Cummins		X			X
Frederick S. Duesenberg	X	X			X
Carl G. Fisher			X		
Elwood Haynes		X		X	X
Anton "Tony" Hulman Jr.			X		
Raymond Loewy	X		X		
Howard C. Marmon		X		X	
Edward V. "Eddie" Rickenbacker	X		X		
Louis Schwitzer Sr.		X			
Wilbur Shaw			X	X	
Harry C. Stutz					X
Ralph R. Teetor		X		X	

A Battery and a Service for Every Car

PREST-O-LITE is the universal battery, designed and built to give greater vitality, endurance and durability to every electric system. Back of it is a great, country-wide Prest-O-Lite System of Service waiting to furnish courteous, intelligent attention to every car owner.

Prest-O-Lite Batteries are used as standard equipment by leading manufacturers on hundreds of thousands of cars. And wherever you find a car with a Prest-O-Lite Battery you'll find an electric system with greater reserve power and capacity — quicker, surer starts — more real battery value.

Tour where you please, from coast to coast

—you will find Prest-O-Lite Direct Factory Branches backed up by Prest-O-Lite Battery Service Stations, carrying stocks of new batteries and battery parts — ready to serve you.

No matter what battery you use, Prest-O-Lite Service — including expert inspection, tests, repairs and recharging — is always ready to give cheerful, painstaking care to your battery requirements.

The Prest-O-Lite Co., Inc.

U. S. Main Office and Factory: Indianapolis, Indiana
Canadian General Office and Factory: Toronto, Ontario
Factory Branches in Principal Cities
Special Service Stations Everywhere

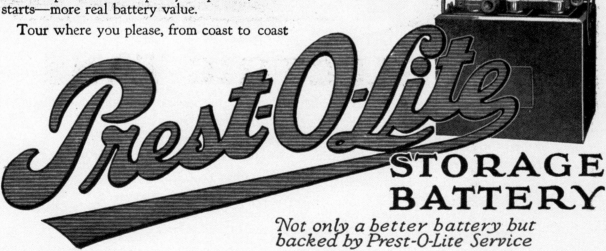

Not only a better battery but backed by Prest-O-Lite Service

In addition to cofounding the Indianapolis Motor Speedway, Carl Fisher coestablished Prest-O-Lite in Indianapolis.
TAC

Appendixes

Appendix 1

Inflation Calculator
(compares value of $1,000 through the decades)

1913	1923	1933	1943	1953	1963	1973	1983	1993	2002
									$1,000
								$1,000	$1,244
							$1,000		$1,805
						$1,000			$4,050
					$1,000				$5,875
				$1,000					$6,734
			$1,000						$10,393
	$1,000								$10,515
		$1,000							$13,831
$1,000									$18,161

Source: Bureau of Labor Statistics — Consumer Price Index calculator July 2002
Legend: $1,000 in 1913 has the same buying power as $18,161 in 2002,
or a $1,000 auto in 1913 would cost $18,161 in 2002.

Milestones in Indiana Automotive History

Early 19th century National Road, U.S. highway built. Begun in 1815 and completed in 1833, it was the most ambitious U.S. road-building project undertaken up to that time. When completed, it extended from Cumberland, Maryland, to St. Louis, Missouri, and was the great highway of western migration. The present U.S. Highway 40 follows its route closely.

1885 The world's first gas pump is invented by Sylvanus F. Bowser of Fort Wayne.

1891 Charles H. Black of Indianapolis garners the dubious distinction of having Indiana's first auto accident when he ran a German-manufactured Benz automobile into downtown store windows.

1894 Elwood Haynes demonstrates one of the earliest American automobiles along Pumpkinvine Pike on the outskirts of Kokomo.

1895 Elwood Haynes introduces the first use of aluminum alloy in an automobile in the Haynes-Apperson crankcase.

1896 The corrugated metal pipe culvert is invented by two Crawfordsville men; Stanley Simpson, the town engineer; and James H. Watson, a sheet metal worker. Their patented pipe culvert has now become a common sight on highway construction projects around the world.

1900 Tom and Harry Warner, Abbott and J.C. Johnson, Col. William Hitchcock, and Thomas Morgan found Warner Gear Company of Muncie. Warner Gear's first major contribution to the industry was the differential.

1902 The Marmon motor car, designed by Indianapolis automaker Howard C. Marmon, has an air-cooled overhead valve V-twin engine and a revolutionary lubrication system that uses a drilled crankshaft to keep its engine bearings lubricated with oil-fed under pressure by a gear pump. This is the earliest automotive application of a system that has long since become universal to internal combustion piston engine design.

1902 The first Studebaker motor car, introduced in South Bend, is an electric car. Studebaker Bros. had produced more than 750,000 wagons, buggies, and carriages since 1852.

1903 The Overland has its engine in the front, and rear-seat entrances are through the sides rather than the rear.

1903 The Auburn motorcar, introduced by Auburn Automobile Co. of Auburn, is a single-cylinder runabout with solid tires and a steering tiller. Charles, Frank and Morris Eckhart of Eckhart Carriage Co. started the firm with $7,500 in capital.

1903 The Haynes-Apperson is designed with a tilting steering column to allow low, easy access for the driver or passenger upon entering or leaving the vehicle.

1903 Premier claims that the oak leaf on its radiator badge is the first use of an emblem as an automobile trademark.

1905 The Haynes Model L has a semi-automatic transmission.

1906 American Motors Company of Indianapolis develops the American Underslung car, one of the first examples of low-center-of-gravity engineering.

1906 Maxwell-Briscoe, (predecessor of Chrysler Corporation), builds its plant in New Castle. It is the largest automobile plant in the nation.

1906 National Motor Vehicle Company introduces a six-cylinder model, one of the first in America.

1907 Willys-Overland Motors is established by auto dealer John North Willys, who takes over control of Overland Automobile of Indianapolis and moves it in 1909 to the old Pope-Toledo plant in Toledo, Ohio.

1909 Carl G. Fisher, James A. Allison, Arthur C. Newby, and Frank H. Wheeler pool $250,000 in capital to form the Indianapolis Motor Speedway Company and transform an Indianapolis west side farm into a two-and-a-half-mile oval that becomes synonymous with automobile racing. The Speedway is designed as an automotive testing ground for U.S. manufactured automobiles to establish American auto supremacy. After the August motorcycle and auto races, the macadam track is repaved with 3,200,000 ten-pound bricks.

1911 The first Indianapolis 500 Mile Race is held May 30. A Marmon Wasp averages 75 m.p.h. to win. The Wasp employs streamlining via elongated front and rear sections and adds the innovation of a rearview mirror.

1911 Haynes Automobile Company is the first to equip an open car with a top, a windshield, headlamps and a speedometer as standard equipment.

1912 Stutz Motor Car Company is founded by Harry C. Stutz, who merges his Stutz Auto Parts with Ideal Motor Car.

1912 The Davis car is the first to have a center-control gearshift and the Bendix self-starter.

1912 The Stutz Bearcat is introduced with a design patterned on the White Squadron racing cars that won victories in 1913. Stutz also produces family cars, while the Bearcat provides lively competition for the Mercer made at Trenton, New Jersey.

1913 On July 1, the Lincoln Highway Association is created with Henry B. Joy (president, Packard Motor Company) as president and Carl G. Fisher as vice president. The Lincoln Highway is conceived as America's first transcontinental highway.

1913 Premier and Studebaker concurrently introduce a six-cylinder engine featuring mono bloc engine casting.

1914 The Haynes is one of the first autos to offer the Vulcan Electric Gear Shift as standard equipment.

1916 The Marmon 34 priced at $2,700 and up is introduced with a "scientific lightweight" engine of aluminum. Its only cast-iron engine components are its cylinder sleeves and one-piece "firing head." Body, fenders, hood, transmission case, differential housing, clutch cone wheel, and radiator shell are all of aluminum.

1918 The Cole Aero-Eight introduces the use of balloon tires.

1919 Westcott Motor Car Company introduces front and rear bumpers as standard equipment.

1920 The Duesenberg brothers (Fred S. and August S.) set up shop at Indianapolis to make motor cars.

1921 The Lafayette introduces thermostatically controlled radiator shutters.

1922 The Model A Duesenberg, introduced by Duesenberg Motor Distributing Co. of Indianapolis, is the first U.S. production motor car with hydraulic brakes, the first with an overhead camshaft, and the first U.S. straight eight engine. Ninety-two of the luxury cars are sold, a number that will rise to 140 in 1923.

1924 Chicago executive E. L. (Erret Lobban) Cord, age 30, joins Auburn Automobile, gives its unsold inventory of 700 cars some cosmetic touch-ups, and nets $500,000. He also breathes new life into the company that is now owned by Chicago financiers including William Wrigley, Jr., but producing only six cars per day. Cord will double sales in 1925, introduce a new model, outperform and undersell the competition, and become president of Auburn in 1926.

1926 Safety-glass windshields are installed as standard equipment on high-priced Stutz motor car models.

1926 E. L. Cord's Auburn Automobile Co. acquires Duesenberg Automobile and Motor Co.

1926 Warner Gear Company of Muncie develops the standardized transmission. It could be mass-produced at half the cost of specialty transmissions and is suitable for use in most automobiles.

1928 Studebaker sets 160 endurance or speed records.

1929 Auburn comes out with an eight-cylinder, 115 h.p. model advertised with a picture of 115 stampeding horses. Its boattailed speedster travels at 108.6 m.p.h. at Daytona, Florida, in March and later in the year averages 84.7 m.p.h. for 25 hours at Atlantic City, New Jersey.

1929 The first motor car (Cord L-29) with front-wheel drive is introduced by E. L. Cord's Auburn Automobile Company.

1929 The Model J Duesenberg introduced by E. L. Cord's Duesenberg, Inc., is a "real Duesy." The costly 265 h.p. luxury car can go up to 116 m.p.h. and will be built until 1937.

1929 Marmon warrants a listing in the Guinness Book of Records for its factory-installed radio.

1930 The Roosevelt has the distinction of being the first eight-cylinder car in the world to sell for less than $1,000.

1931 The Society of Automotive Engineers honored Colonel Howard Marmon for "the most notable engineering achievement of 1930," his huge and gleaming V-16 engine design. The society was especially impressed by his extensive use of lightweight aluminum, generally a difficult metal to work and maintain in automobile power plants.

1931 Studebaker introduces free-wheeling.

1931 Stutz introduces drop-side bodies, an American production first. These bodies had doors that dropped to the running boards and covered the frame rails completely. Within a few years, all American cars followed Stutz's lead.

1932 Auburn motor car sales soar to 34,228, and profits equal those of 1929 after a depressing 1930 sales year. E. L. Cord signs up 1,000 new dealers as his car climbs from 23rd place in retail sales to 13th on the strength of the new Auburn 8-98. The new Auburn is the first rear-drive motor car with a frame braced by an X-cross member and the first moderately priced car with L.G.S. Free Wheeling.

1932 The first gasoline pump that could measure dispensed gas and give the price in dollars and cents is introduced in Fort Wayne.

1932 The Duesenberg SJ is the first stock automobile to be equipped with a centrifugal type supercharger, although some previously had Roots type blowers.

1932 The Stutz DV32 is one of the few American cars equipped with a four-speed transmission.

1932 William B. Barnes invents overdrive, a device that would increase the life of the engine, yet improve fuel efficiency. Muncie's Warner Gear backs the development.

1936 The Cord 810 introduced by Auburn Automobile Company is a sleek modern motor car with advanced features that include disappearing headlights, concealed door hinges, rheostat-controlled instrument lights, variable speed windshield wipers, Bendix Electric Hand (steering column-mounted electric gear pre-selection unit), and is the first automobile in this country to adopt unit body construction in its full sense. (Chrysler-Airflow and Lincoln-Zepher used modified forms.)

1937 Studebaker is the first American car to offer windshield washers.

1947 Guide Lamp introduces plastic taillight lenses.

1958 Ralph Teetor, Perfect Circle Corporation president, invents cruise control, introduced on the Chrysler Imperial, New Yorker, and Windsor models.

1984 AM General of Mishawaka introduces the High Mobility Multi-Purpose Wheeled Vehicle (Humvee).

1989 The first joint venture between Japanese-owned Fuji Heavy Industries and Isuzu Motors Unlimited rolls out its first vehicles — a Subaru Legacy sedan and an Isuzu pickup truck.

1998 Toyota Motor Corporation produces its first vehicles from Indiana — a Tundra pickup truck and Sequoia full-size sport utility vehicle.

A Word About Lists

Compiling lists about the automotive genesis is an imprecise art. There is no single source of information for the American automobiles' progression. Some reference works are fairly complete regarding makes, manufacturers, cities and dates. These same works may miss some instances where a manufacturer's model is built in a plant other than that company's main places of business.

The work is further compounded by list compilers who chose to include instances where only one car was made by an individual whether or not they planned to proceed to manufacture it in quantity. In Indiana's case, for every one vehicle achieving production about two announcements of intent to manufacture or build a prototype were proclaimed.

Early lists about the actual number of automobiles made in the United States started at 1,500 and then progressed to about 5,000. More recent lists approach around 3,000. Early Indiana lists started at 160 makes made in more than 30 cities and have progressed to over 520 vehicles manufactured or assembled in more than 80 cities.

Only those vehicles built with the intent of marketing to the public are included in this book's lists. In cases where no actual numbers are given, we counted the auto if a prototype was produced. Defined thus, our list shows 414 autos produced in 76 cities.

Indiana Cars Listed by Name

Name	Manufacturer	City	Dates
Ade	Brook Motor Car Co.	Brook	1909
Adrem	Adrem Motor Co.	New Castle	1909
Albany	Albany Automobile Co.	Albany	1907-08
Alena Steam	Alena Steam Products Co.	Indianapolis	1922
Allied	Allied Cab Mfg. Co.	Elkhart	1932-34
American	American Motors Co.	Indianapolis	1906-14
American Junior	American Motor Vehicle Co.	Lafayette	1916-20
American Scout	American Motors Co.	Indianapolis	1912-13
American Simplex	Simplex Motor Car Co.	Mishawaka	1906-10
American Tourist	American Motors Co.	Indianapolis	1907-12
American Traveler	American Motors Co.	Indianapolis	1909-13
American Underslung	American Motors Co.	Indianapolis	1906-14
Amplex	Simplex Motor Car Co.	Mishawaka	1910-13
Anahuac	Frontenac Motor Co.	Indianapolis	1922
Anderson	Anderson Carriage Mfg. Co.	Anderson	1907-10
Anderson Highwheeler	Anderson Machine Co.	Bedford	1906
Anderson Steam	Anderson Steam Carriage Co.	Anderson	1901-02
Anghein	M. J. Anghein	Bourbon	1899
Ansted	Lexington Motor Car Co.	Connersville	1921, 1926
Apperson	Apperson Bros. Automobile Co.	Kokomo	1902-26
Atlas Motor Buggy	Atlas Engine Works	Indianapolis	1909
Attica	Attica Automobile Co.	Attica	1909
Auburn	Auburn Automobile Co.	Auburn	1900-36
Auburn	Auburn Automobile Co.	Connersville	1929-36
Auburn Motor Chassis	Auburn Motor Chassis Co.	Auburn	1912-15
Auburn-Cummins	Auburn Automobile Co.	Auburn	1935
Auto Red Bug	American Motor Vehicle Co.	Lafayette	1916-20
Automotive Syndicate	Automotive Syndicate	Indianapolis	1928
Avanti	Studebaker Corp.	South Bend	1962-63
Avanti II	Avanti Motor Corp.	South Bend	1965-85
Bailey-Klapp	Elwood Iron Works	Elwood	1915
Barth-Keith	Barth-Keith Motor Car Co.	Indianapolis	1919
Beetle Flyer	Fodrea-Malott Mfg. Co.	Noblesville	1909
Bell	Carl Bell	Greencastle	1901
Bendix	Bendix Co.	Logansport	1908-09
Benninghof	Benninghof-Nolan Co.	Evansville	1904
Best	Best Automobile Co.	Indianapolis	1908-10
Birch	Crow-Elkhart Motor Car Co.	Elkhart	1916-23
Black	C.H. Black Mfg. Co.	Indianapolis	1896-1900
Black Crow	Crow Motor Car Co.	Elkhart	1909-11
Blackhawk	Stutz Motor Car Co.	Indianapolis	1929-30
Bour-Davis	Shadburne Bros. Co.	Frankfort	1918
Brazil	Brazil Motors Co.	Brazil	1917
Brook	Brook Motor Car Co.	Brook	1909
Brook	Spacke Machine & Tool Co.	Indianapolis	1920-21

Brown	Brown Motor Co.	Washington	1910
Bryan Steamer	Bryan Boiler Co.	Peru	1918-23
Buckeye	J.W. Lambert-Buckeye Mfg. Co.	Anderson	1895
Bush	Crow-Elkhart Motor Car Co.	Elkhart	1916-25
Butler High Wheel	Butler Co.	Butler	1908
Caesar	Alonzo R. Marsh	Anderson	1914
Capital	Capital Auto Co.	Indianapolis	1906
Carey	Carey Motor Car Co.	Fairmount	1905
Casady	W.S. Casady Mfg. Co.	South Bend	1905
Central	Central Motor Car Co.	Indianapolis	1903
Central	Central Manufacturing Co.	Connersville	1905
Champion	Famous Manufacturing Co.	East Chicago	1909
Champion	Champion Auto Equipment Co.	Wabash	1916
Chevrolet Silverado	GM Truck Group	Fort Wayne	1988-present
Clark	Clark Motor Car Co.	Shelbyville	1910-12
Clark Special	J.D. Clark Auto Co.	Anderson	1908
Co-Auto	Co-Auto Motor Co.	Indianapolis	1910
Coats Steamer	Coats Steamers Inc.	Indianapolis	1921-22
Cole	Cole Motor Car Co.	Indianapolis	1909-25
Cole Solid Tire Auto.	Cole Carriage Co.	Indianapolis	1908-09
Coliseum	Coliseum Machine & Garage Co.	South Bend	1914
Colonial Six	Colonial Automobile Co.	Indianapolis	1917
Columbia	Columbia Machine Works	Fort Wayne	1902
Columbia Electric	The Columbia Electric Co.	McCordsville	1905-06
Comet	Comet Cyclecar Co.	Indianapolis	1914
Comet Racer	Marion Motor Car Co.	Indianapolis	1904
Connersville	Connersville Motor Vehicle Co.	Connersville	1906
Connersville	Connersville Buggy Co.	Connersville	1914
Continental	Indian Motor & Mfg. Co.	Franklin	1910-13
Coppock	Coppock Motor Car Co.	Marion	1906-07
Cord	Cord Corp.	Auburn	1929-32
Cord	Cord Corp.	Connersville	1936-37
Cory	The Cory Automobile Co.	Albany	1907
Coyote	Union Automobile Co. of Albany	Albany	1909
Craig-Hunt	Craig-Hunt Motor Co.	Indianapolis	1920
Cramer	Claude Cramer	Garrett	1901
Craven	Craven Sectional Tire Co.	Albany	1905
Crimmell & Hailman	Crimmell & Hailman	Hartford City	1903
Crosley	Crosley Motors Inc.	Richmond	1939-42
Crosley	Crosley Motors Inc.	Marion	1946-52
Cross	Harry E. Cross	Indianapolis	1924
Crow	Crow Motor Car Co.	Elkhart	1911
Crow-Elkhart	Crow-Elkhart Motor Car Co.	Elkhart	1911-23
Cummins	Cummins Engine Co.	Columbus	1929
Custer	Custer Mfg. Co.	Marion	1909
Cyclop	L. Porter Smith & Bros.	Indianapolis	1910
Cyclops	Cyclops Cyclecar Co.	Indianapolis	1914
Dart	Dart Mfg. Co.	Anderson	1910
DaVinci	James Scripps-Booth	Indianapolis	1925
Davis	George W. Davis Motor Car Co.	Richmond	1908-29
De Freet	Thomas M. De Freet	Indianapolis	1895
De Kalb	De Kalb Mfg. Co.	Fort Wayne	1915
De Soto	Zimmerman Mfg. Co.	Auburn	1913-14
De Tamble	De Tamble Motor Co.	Anderson	1908-13
Dearborn	J & M Motor Car Co.	Lawrenceburg	1911
Decatur	Decatur Motor Car Co.	Decatur	1908-11

Derrickson	Derrickson Mfg. Co.	Muncie	1903
DeWitt	DeWitt Motor Vehicle Co.	North Manchester	1909-10
Diamond	Diamond Automobile Co.	South Bend	1910
Diehnart	Diehnart & Smith	Lafayette	1901
Dixie	Dixie Mfg. Co.	Vincennes	1916
Dolly Madison	Madison Motor Co.	Anderson	1915
Dovetail	Dovetail Carriage Co.	Crawfordsville	1900
Duesenberg	Duesenberg Motors Corp.	Indianapolis	1920-37
Duesenberg II	Duesenberg Corp.	Indianapolis	1966
Durant	Durant Motors, Inc.	Muncie	1922-28
E.I.M.	Eastern Indiana Motor Car Co.	Richmond	1915
Eclipse	Eclipse Buggy Co.	Fort Wayne	1902
Economy	Economy Motor Buggy Co.	Fort Wayne	1908-09
Eichstaedt	Roman Eichstaedt	Michigan City	1898-1902
El-Fay	Elkhart Motor Co.	Elkhart	1931-35
Elcar	Elkhart Motor Co.	Elkhart	1916-31
Elcar Electric	Elcar Corp.	Elkhart	1974
Electro	Electro Lighting Co.	Indianapolis	1911
Electrobile	National Vehicle Co.	Indianapolis	1901-06
Elgin	Elgin Motors Inc.	Indianapolis	1923-24
Elmer	Elmer Auto Corp.	Elkhart	1911
Elwood	Elwood Iron Works	Elwood	1915
Empire	Empire Motor Car Co.	Indianapolis	1909-19
Empire	Empire Motor Car Co.	Connersville	1912-15
Erie	Erie Cycle & Motor Carriage Co.	Anderson	1899-1902
Erskine	Studebaker Corp.	South Bend	1927-30
Evansville	Evansville Automobile Co.	Evansville	1907-09
Excellent Six	Rider-Lewis Motor Car Co.	Anderson	1908-11
Famous	Famous Manufacturing Co.	East Chicago	1908
Farm O Road	Crosley Motors Inc.	Marion	1951
Fauber	Cyclecar Engineering Co.	Indianapolis	1914
Federal	Industrial Automobile Co.	Elkhart	1909
Feeny	Feeny Mfg. Co.	Muncie	1914
Fellwock	Fellwock Automobile Mfg. Co.	Evansville	1907-08
Fisher	Fisher Automobile Co.	Mooresville	1903
Flandermobile	Flandermobile Co.	Anderson	1901
Ford	Ford Motor Co.	Indianapolis	1914-32
Fort Wayne	Fort Wayne Automobile Co.	Fort Wayne	1903
Fort Wayne-Commercial	Fort Wayne Automobile Mfg. Co.	Fort Wayne	1911-13
Fowler	Fowler Manufacturing Co.	Alexandria	1910
Frankfort	Frankfort Motor Co.	Frankfort	1917
Frazier-Elkhart	O. Z. Frazier	Elkhart	1915
Frontenac	Frontenac Motor Co.	Indianapolis	1921-25
Gale Four	Garde Gale	Indianapolis	1920
Garrett	Garrett Machine Works	Garrett	1909
Gary Six	Gary Automobile Mfg. Co.	Gary	1914
Geiger	Ray Geiger	Covington	1919
Geneva	Geneva Auto Specialty & Repair	Geneva	1914
Gillette	Gillette Motor Co.	Mishawaka	1916
Glascar	Robert Tucker	Richmond	1956
GMC Sierra	GM Truck Group	Fort Wayne	1988-present
Goabout	Standard Mfg. Co.	Kokomo	1901-02
Goshen	Goshen Motor Werks	Goshen	1905-07
Great Western	Great Western Mfg. Co.	LaPorte	1902-05

Great Western	Great Western Automobile Co.	Peru	1909-14
H.C.S.	H.C.S. Motor Co.	Indianapolis	1920-25
H.C.S. Cab	H.C.S. Cab Mfg. Co.	Indianapolis	1924-27
Hamiltonian	Harry Hamilton	Greensburg	1909
Handy Wagon	Auburn Motor Chassis Co.	Auburn	1912-15
Harper	Harper Buggy Co.	Columbia City	1907-08
Hassler	Hassler Motor Co.	Indianapolis	1917
Hassler Motor Buggy	Robert H. Hassler	Indianapolis	1898
Hayn	R.B. Hayn	Mishawaka	1901
Haynes Pioneer	Elwood Haynes	Kokomo	1893-94
Haynes	Haynes Automobile Co.	Kokomo	1904-25
Haynes-Apperson	Haynes-Apperson Automobile Co.	Kokomo	1898-1904
Henderson	Henderson Motor Car Co.	Indianapolis	1912-14
Hercules	Hercules Motor Car Co.	New Albany	1914-15
Hercules Electric	Hercules Corp.	Evansville	1919
Herff-Brooks	Herff-Brooks Corp.	Indianapolis	1915-16
Herrmann	Charles Herrmann	Tell City	1905
HMMWV	AM General	Mishawaka	1985-present
Honda Passport	Subaru Isuzu Automotive, Inc.	Lafayette	1994-present
Hoosier Scout	Warren Electric & Machine Co.	Indianapolis	1914
Howard	Lexington-Howard Co.	Connersville	1913-14
Huffman	Huffman Bros. Motor Co.	Elkhart	1920-25
Hummer	AM General	Mishawaka	1992-present
Hummer H2	AM General	Mishawaka	2002
Hunter	Riley & Scott, Inc.	Indianapolis	1994
Hunter-Hammond	Hunter-Hammond Auto Co.	Indianapolis	1912
Huntingburg	Huntingburg Wagon Works	Huntingburg	1902-03
Ideal	Ideal Automobile Mfg. Co.	New Castle	1902
Ideal	Ideal Motor Co.	Indianapolis	1911-12
Ideal-Commercial	Ideal Auto Co.	Fort Wayne	1910-14
Imp	W. H. McIntyre Co.	Auburn	1913-14
Indiana	Indiana Motor & Vehicle Co.	Indianapolis	1901
Indianapolis	C. H. Black Mfg. Co.	Indianapolis	1897-00
Industrial	Industrial Automobile Co.	Elkhart	1909
Inter-State	Inter-State Automobile Co.	Muncie	1909-19
Isuzu Amigo	Subaru Isuzu Automotive, Inc.	Lafayette	1998-present
Isuzu Axiom	Subaru Isuzu Automotive, Inc.	Lafayette	2001-present
Isuzu Rodeo	Subaru Isuzu Automotive, Inc.	Lafayette	1990-present
Isuzu Trooper	Subaru Isuzu Automotive, Inc.	Lafayette	1989-present
Izzer	Great Western Automobile Co.	Peru	1911
Jack Rabbit	Apperson Bros. Automobile Co.	Kokomo	1911-13
James	J & M Motor Car Co.	Lawrenceburg	1909-11
Jonz	American Automobile Mfg. Co.	New Albany	1910-12
Keller	J.M. Keller	Goshen	1901
Kendallville	Kendallville Buggy Co.	Kendallville	1910
Kenworthy	Kenworthy Motors Corp.	Mishawaka	1920-21
Kernodle-McDaniel	Kernodle-McDaniel Mfg. Co.	Frankfort	1912
Kiblinger	W. H. Kiblinger Co.	Auburn	1907-08
Kindall	A. J. Kindall	Bluffton	1903
King	King Motor Vehicle Co.	Auburn	1908
Kirsch	Peter Kirsch	Decatur	1905-16
Knightstown	Knightstown Buggy Co.	Knightstown	1900
Kokomo	Shortridge, Sellers & Irvin	Kokomo	1901
Komet	Elkhart Motor Car Co.	Elkhart	1911

L.C.S.	L.C.S. Motor Co.	Fort Wayne	1910
Lafayette	Lafayette Motors Co.	Indianapolis	1921-22
Lambert	Buckeye Mfg. Co.	Anderson	1906-17
LaPorte	LaPorte Carriage Co.	LaPorte	1895
Laurel	Laurel Motor Car Co.	Richmond	1916-17
Laurel	Laurel Motors Corp.	Anderson	1917-20
Lawter	Safety Shredder Co.	New Castle	1909
Leader	Leader Mfg. Co.	McCordsville	1905-07
Leader	Leader Mfg. Co.	Knightstown	1907-12
Leist	Leist Automobile Mfg. Co.	Michigan City	1911
Lever	Lever Motors Corp.	Elkhart	1930
Lexington	Lexington Motor Co.	Connersville	1910-27
Lindsay	T.J. Lindsay Automobile Parts Co.	Indianapolis	1902-03
Liquid Air	Liquid Air Co.	Indianapolis	1900
Lohr	Elmer Auto Corp.	Elkhart	1911
Lorraine	Lorraine Car Co.	Richmond	1920-21
Losure	Zan Losure	Van Buren	1906
Lyons-Knight	Lyons-Atlas Co.	Indianapolis	1913-15
M.C.M	The M.C.M. Motor Co.	Bedford	1914
Madison	Madison Motors Corp.	Anderson	1915-19
Marathon	Herff-Brooks Corp.	Indianapolis	1915-16
Marion	Marion Motor Car Co.	Indianapolis	1904-14
Marion Flyer	Marion Automobile & Mfg. Co.	Marion	1910
Marmon	Nordyke & Marmon Co.	Indianapolis	1902-33
Martel	Elkhart Motor Co.	Elkhart	1925-27
Martindale & Millikan	Indian Motor & Mfg. Co.	Franklin	1914
Maxwell	Maxwell-Briscoe Motor Co.	New Castle	1906-16
McCurdy	Hercules Corp.	Evansville	1922
McFarlan	McFarlan Motor Car Co.	Connersville	1910-28
McGill	McGee Mfg. Co.	Indianapolis	1917-28
McGowan	W.H. McGowan	Vincennes	1913
McIntyre	W. H. McIntyre Co.	Auburn	1909-15
McIntyre Special	W. H. McIntyre Co.	Auburn	1911-15
McLellen	McLellen Auto Shop	Indianapolis	1912
Menges	Sterling-Hudson Whip Co.	Elkhart	1907
Mercer	Elcar Motor Co.	Elkhart	1931
Merz	Merz Cyclecar Co.	Indianapolis	1914
Mier	Mier Carriage & Buggy Co.	Ligonier	1908-09
Million	Robert J. Million	Monticello	1896
Mills Electric	Mills Electric Co.	Lafayette	1917
Model	Model Gas Engine Works	Auburn	1903-06
Model	Model Automobile Co.	Peru	1906-09
Mohawk	Mohawk Cycle & Automobile Co.	Indianapolis	1903-05
Mollenhour	A.T. Mollenhour	Mentone	1908
Monroe	William Small Co.	Indianapolis	1918-23
Morriss-London	Century Motors Co.	Elkhart	1919-25
Motor Buggy	Motor Buggy Co.	Fort Wayne	1909
Muncie	Muncie Wheel & Jobbing Co.	Muncie	1903
Munson	Munson Co.	LaPorte	1896-1900
Muntz Jet	Muntz Car Co.	Evansville	1950-51
Murillo	Murillo Mfg. Co.	Marion	1906
National	National Motor Vehicle Co.	Indianapolis	1904-24
National Electric	National Automobile & Electric Co.	Indianapolis	1900-04
Nesom	Nesom Motors Co.	Indianapolis	1912

New Parry	Parry Auto Co.	Indianapolis	1911-12
New York Six	Automotive Corp. of America	Richmond	1927-28
Niagara Four	Crow Motor Car Co.	Elkhart	1915-16
Nyberg	Nyberg Automobile Works	Anderson	1911-13
Octoauto	Reeves Pulley Co.	Columbus	1911-12
Ogden	Dore Ogden	Columbus	1902
Ohio Falls	Ohio Falls Motor Car Co.	New Albany	1913-14
Oliver	Oliver Trackless Car Co.	South Bend	1905
Olson	C.J. Olson Buggy & Carriage Mfg.	Pittsboro	1908
Otis	Otis Motor Car Co.	South Bend	1912
Overland	Standard Wheel Works	Terre Haute	1903-05
Overland	Standard Wheel Works	Indianapolis	1905-06
Overland	Overland Auto Co.	Indianapolis	1906-08
Overland	Willys-Overland Co.	Indianapolis	1908-11
Packard	Studebaker-Packard Corp.	South Bend	1954-58
Packard Darrin	Packard Motor Car Co.	Connersville	1940-41
Pak-Age-Car	Stutz Motor Co.	Indianapolis	1930-38
Pak-Age-Car	Auburn Central Co.	Connersville	1938-41
Pan	Pan Motor Co.	Indianapolis	1919-21
Paragon Cab	Elcar Motor Co.	Elkhart	1930
Parkison	Parkison Gear Co.	Brook	1909
Parrish	William N. Parrish & Son	Richmond	1915
Parry	Parry Auto Co.	Indianapolis	1910
Pathfinder	Motor Car Mfg. Co.	Indianapolis	1912-17
Perfection	Perfection Automobile Works	South Bend	1907-08
Peters	Spacke Machine & Tool Co.	Indianapolis	1921
Pilgrim	Ohio Falls Motor Car Co.	New Albany	1913-14
Pilot	Pilot Motor Car Co.	Richmond	1909-24
Plymouth	Chrysler Corp.	Evansville	1935-56
Pope-Waverley	Pope Motor Car Co.	Indianapolis	1904-08
Postal	Postal Automobile & Engineering Co	Bedford	1906-08
Pratt	Pratt Motor Car Co.	Elkhart	1911-15
Pratt-Elkhart	Elkhart Carriage & Harness Mfg. Co	Elkhart	1909-11
Premier	Premier Motor Mfg. Co.	Indianapolis	1903-26
Premier Taxicab	Premier Motor Car Co.	Indianapolis	1923-26
Princeton	Durant Motors, Inc.	Muncie	1923-24
Prosperity	Allied Cab Mfg. Co.	Elkhart	1933
Prowler Prototype	Riley & Scott, Inc.	Indianapolis	1994
Pullman Flyer	Model Automobile Co.	Peru	1907-08
R.A.C.	Ricketts Automobile Co.	South Bend	1910-11
Raber-Lang	Raber-Lang Co.	South Bend	1909
Rayfield	Great Western Automobile Co.	Peru	1915
Rea	Rea Machine Co.	Rushville	1901-02
Real Cyclecar	Real Cyclecar Co.	Anderson	1914
Real Light Car	Real Light Car Co.	Converse	1914-15
Red Ball-Taxi	Red Ball Transit Co.	Frankfort	1924
Reeves	Reeves Pulley Co.	Columbus	1896-1910
ReVere	Revere Motor Car Corp.	Logansport	1918-26
Rex	Rex Motor Car Co.	Indianapolis	1908
Richmond	Wayne Works	Richmond	1904-17
Richmond Steam	Richmond Automobile Co.	Richmond	1902-03
Richter	H. Richter	Brazil	1902
Ricketts	Ricketts Automobile Co.	South Bend	1909-11
Rider-Lewis	Rider-Lewis Motor Car Co.	Muncie	1908

Rider-Lewis	Rider-Lewis Motor Car Co.	Anderson	1908-11
Roach & Albanus	Roach & Albanus	Fort Wayne	1899-1900
Rockne	Studebaker Corp.	South Bend	1932-33
Rodefeld	Rodefeld Co.	Richmond	1909-17
Roosevelt	Marmon Motor Car Co.	Indianapolis	1929-30
Rose City	Rose City Auto Co.	New Castle	1912
Royal	Royal Motor Co.	Elkhart	1913
Royal Martel	Elkhart Motor Co.	Elkhart	1925-27
Rubber Bill	Rubber Bill Co.	LaPorte	1919
Rupp	Kendallville Buggy Co.	Kendallville	1910
Rutenber	Rutenber Mfg. Co.	Logansport	1902
Ruth	Ruth Automobile Co.	North Webster	1907
Saf-T-Cab	Auburn Automobile Co.	Auburn	1926-28
Schebler	Wheeler & Schebler Carburetor Co.	Indianapolis	1908-09
Scout	International Harvester Co.	Fort Wayne	1961-80
Sears Motor Buggy	Hercules Buggy Co.	Evansville	1908-09
Sears Steam	Sears Bros.	Indianapolis	1901
Sedgwick Steam	Isham H. Sedgwick	Richmond	1901
Seidel	Seidel Buggy Co.	Richmond	1908-09
Senator	Victor Automobile Co.	Ridgeville	1907-10
Sextoauto	Reeves Pulley Co.	Columbus	1912
Shad-Wyck	Shadburne Bros Co.	Frankfort	1917-18
Sheridan	Sheridan Motor Car Co.	Muncie	1920-21
Shimer	Shimer & Co.	Anderson	1901
Shoemaker	Shoemaker Automobile Co.	Elkhart	1907-08
Siefker Steam	William Siefker	Seymour	1880
Signor	A. J. Signor	Elkhart	1901
Simplicity	Ira J. Hollensbee	Greensburg	1902
Simplicity	Evansville Automobile Co.	Evansville	1907-11
Single-Center	Single-Center Buggy Co.	Evansville	1906-08
Six & Vance	Don Six & Claire Vance	Logansport	1914
Slattery Electric	M.M.M. Slattery	Fort Wayne	1899
Smart	Smart Auto & Mfg. Co.	Indianapolis	1912
Soudan	Soudan Mfg. Co.	Elkhart	1900-01
South Bend	South Bend Motor Car Works	South Bend	1913-16
Spacke	Spacke Machine & Tool Co.	Indianapolis	1919
St. Joe	St. Joe Motor Car Co.	Elkhart	1908
Standard Six	Standard Automobile Co. of America	Wabash	1910-11
Stanley	Stanley Automobile Co.	Mooreland	1907-08
Stanley	Stanley Motor Co.	Liberty	1913
Star	Model Automobile Co.	Peru	1908
Star	Star Motor Car Co.	Indianapolis	1909-11
Star	Durant Motors, Inc.	Muncie	1923
Sterling	Elkhart Motor Car Co.	Elkhart	1909-11
Strattan	Strattan Motors Corp.	Indianapolis	1923
Stratton	Stratton Carriage Co.	Muncie	1909
Streamline	Streamline Motor Car Co.	Indianapolis	1923
Studebaker	Studebaker Corp.	South Bend	1904-63
Studebaker Electric	Studebaker Bros. Mfg. Co.	South Bend	1902-12
Stutz	Stutz Motor Car Co.	Indianapolis	1912-35
Subaru Legacy	Subaru Isuzu Automotive, Inc.	Lafayette	1989-present
Subaru Outback	Subaru Isuzu Automotive, Inc.	Lafayette	1999-present
Sun	Sun Motor Car Co.	Elkhart	1916-17
Super Allied	Allied Cab Mfg. Co.	Elkhart	1935

T.J.K. Special	T.J. Kehoe	Fort Wayne	1909
Teetor-Hartley	Teetor-Hartley Motor Co.	Hagerstown	1916
Terre Haute	Terre Haute Carriage & Buggy Co.	Terre Haute	1899
Tincher	Tincher Motor Car Co.	South Bend	1907-09
Tone	Tone Car Corp.	Indianapolis	1913
Toyota Sequoia	Toyota Motor Manufacturing Indiana	Princeton	2000-present
Toyota Sienna	Toyota Motor Manufacturing Indiana	Princeton	2003
Toyota Tundra	Toyota Motor Manufacturing Indiana	Princeton	1998-present
Traveler	Traveler Automobile Co.	Evansville	1910-11
Tricolet	H. Pokorney & Richards Auto. & Gas	Indianapolis	1904-06
Tritt	Tritt Electric Co.	South Bend	1905
Troy	Troy Mfg. Co.	Mooreland	1911
Turner	George Turner	Indianapolis	1910
Ultimotor	Frank Martindale	Franklin	1915
Union	Union Automobile Co.	Union City	1902-04
Union	Buckeye Mfg. Co.	Anderson	1905
Union	Union Automobile Co.	Auburn	1916
Union City Six	Union City Carriage Mfg. Co.	Union City	1916
United	United Engineering Co.	Greensburg	1919-20
Universal	Universal Motor Co.	New Castle	1910
Upton	Upton Automobile Co.	Bristol	1914
Van Auken Electric	Connersville Buggy Co.	Connersville	1913
Vanderbilt	Union Steel Mfg. Co.	Brazil	1921
Vanell Steam	Frank Vanell	Vincennes	1895
Vaughn	Marion E. Vaughn	Indianapolis	1912
Vincennes	Vincennes Motor Mfg. Co.	Vincennes	1910
Vixen	Vixen Motor Co.	Indianapolis	1912
W.A.C.	Woodburn Auto Co.	Woodburn	1905-12
Walker Steamer	Earl C. Walker	New Albany	1901
Warner	Muncie Wheel & Jobbing Co.	Muncie	1903-06
Washington	Washington Motor Car Co.	Washington	1906
Waverley	Waverley Co.	Indianapolis	1909-16
Waverley Electric	Indiana Bicycle Co.	Indianapolis	1898-1903
Westcott	Westcott Motor Car Co.	Richmond	1909-16
Williams	W.S. Casady Mfg. Co.	South Bend	1905
Windsor	Windsor Automobile Co.	Evansville	1906
Wizard	Wizard Motor Co.	Indianapolis	1914
Woodburn	Woodburn Auto Co.	Woodburn	1905-12
Worth	Worth Motor Car Mfg. Co.	Evansville	1906-07
Wyman	W.A. Wyman	Scottsburg	1901
Yarlott	Yarlott Bros. Motor & Car Co.	Fort Wayne	1919-20
Zentmobile	Schuyler W. Zent	Evansville	1903
Zimmerman	Zimmerman Mfg. Co.	Auburn	1908-15

Indiana Cars Listed by Date

Dates	Name	Manufacturer	City
1880	Siefker Steam	William Siefker	Seymour
1893-94	Haynes Pioneer	Elwood Haynes	Kokomo
1895	Buckeye	J.W. Lambert-Buckeye Mfg. Co.	Anderson
1895	De Freet	Thomas M. De Freet	Indianapolis
1895	LaPorte	LaPorte Carriage Co.	LaPorte
1895	Vanell Steam	Frank Vanell	Vincennes
1896	Million	Robert J. Million	Monticello
1896-1900	Black	C.H. Black Mfg. Co.	Indianapolis
1896-1900	Munson	Munson Co.	LaPorte
1896-1910	Reeves	Reeves Pulley Co.	Columbus
1897-00	Indianapolis	C. H. Black Mfg. Co.	Indianapolis
1898	Hassler Motor Buggy	Robert H. Hassler	Indianapolis
1898-1902	Eichstaedt	Roman Eichstaedt	Michigan City
1898-1903	Waverley Electric	Indiana Bicycle Co.	Indianapolis
1898-1904	Haynes-Apperson	Haynes-Apperson Automobile Co.	Kokomo
1899	Anghein	M. J. Anghein	Bourbon
1899	Slattery Electric	M.M.M. Slattery	Fort Wayne
1899	Terre Haute	Terre Haute Carriage & Buggy Co.	Terre Haute
1899-1900	Roach & Albanus	Roach & Albanus	Fort Wayne
1899-1902	Erie	Erie Cycle & Motor Carriage Co.	Anderson
1900	Dovetail	Dovetail Carriage Co.	Crawfordsville
1900	Knightstown	Knightstown Buggy Co.	Knightstown
1900	Liquid Air	Liquid Air Co.	Indianapolis
1900-01	Soudan	Soudan Mfg. Co.	Elkhart
1900-04	National Electric	National Automobile & Electric Co.	Indianapolis
1900-36	Auburn	Auburn Automobile Co.	Auburn
1901	Bell	Carl Bell	Greencastle
1901	Cramer	Claude Cramer	Garrett
1901	Diehnart	Diehnart & Smith	Lafayette
1901	Flandermobile	Flandermobile Co.	Anderson
1901	Hayn	R.B. Hayn	Mishawaka
1901	Keller	J.M. Keller	Goshen
1901	Kokomo	Shortridge, Sellers & Irvin	Kokomo
1901	Indiana	Indiana Motor & Vehicle Co.	Indianapolis
1901	Sears Steam	Sears Bros.	Indianapolis
1901	Sedgwick Steam	Isham H. Sedgwick	Richmond
1901	Shimer	Shimer & Co.	Anderson
1901	Signor	A. J. Signor	Elkhart
1901	Walker Steamer	Earl C. Walker	New Albany
1901	Wyman	W.A. Wyman	Scottsburg
1901-02	Anderson Steam	Anderson Steam Carriage Co.	Anderson
1901-02	Goabout	Standard Mfg. Co.	Kokomo
1901-02	Rea	Rea Machine Co.	Rushville
1901-06	Electrobile	National Vehicle Co.	Indianapolis
1902	Columbia	Columbia Machine Works	Fort Wayne

1902	Eclipse	Eclipse Buggy Co.	Fort Wayne
1902	Ideal	Ideal Automobile Mfg. Co.	New Castle
1902	Ogden	Dore Ogden	Columbus
1902	Richter	H. Richter	Brazil
1902	Rutenber	Rutenber Mfg. Co.	Logansport
1902	Simplicity	Ira J. Hollensbee	Greensburg
1902-03	Huntingburg	Huntingburg Wagon Works	Huntingburg
1902-03	Lindsay	T.J. Lindsay Automobile Parts Co.	Indianapolis
1902-03	Richmond Steam	Richmond Automobile Co.	Richmond
1902-04	Union	Union Automobile Co.	Union City
1902-05	Great Western	Great Western Mfg. Co.	LaPorte
1902-12	Studebaker Electric	Studebaker Bros. Mfg. Co.	South Bend
1902-26	Apperson	Apperson Bros. Automobile Co.	Kokomo
1902-33	Marmon	Nordyke & Marmon Co.	Indianapolis
1903	Central	Central Motor Car Co.	Indianapolis
1903	Crimmell & Hailman	Crimmell & Hailman	Hartford City
1903	Derrickson	Derrickson Mfg. Co.	Muncie
1903	Fisher	Fisher Automobile Co.	Mooresville
1903	Fort Wayne	Fort Wayne Automobile Co.	Fort Wayne
1903	Kindall	A. J. Kindall	Bluffton
1903	Muncie	Muncie Wheel & Jobbing Co.	Muncie
1903	Zentmobile	Schuyler W. Zent	Evansville
1903-05	Mohawk	Mohawk Cycle & Automobile Co.	Indianapolis
1903-05	Overland	Standard Wheel Works	Terre Haute
1903-06	Model	Model Gas Engine Works	Auburn
1903-06	Warner	Muncie Wheel & Jobbing Co.	Muncie
1903-26	Premier	Premier Motor Mfg. Co.	Indianapolis
1904	Benninghof	Benninghof-Nolan Co.	Evansville
1904	Comet Racer	Marion Motor Car Co.	Indianapolis
1904-06	Tricolet	H. Pokorney & Richards Auto. & Gas	Indianapolis
1904-08	Pope-Waverley	Pope Motor Car Co.	Indianapolis
1904-14	Marion	Marion Motor Car Co.	Indianapolis
1904-17	Richmond	Wayne Works	Richmond
1904-24	National	National Motor Vehicle Co.	Indianapolis
1904-25	Haynes	Haynes Automobile Co.	Kokomo
1904-63	Studebaker	Studebaker Corp.	South Bend
1905	Carey	Carey Motor Car Co.	Fairmount
1905	Casady	W.S. Casady Mfg. Co.	South Bend
1905	Central	Central Manufacturing Co.	Connersville
1905	Craven	Craven Sectional Tire Co.	Albany
1905	Herrmann	Charles Herrmann	Tell City
1905	Oliver	Oliver Trackless Car Co.	South Bend
1905	Tritt	Tritt Electric Co.	South Bend
1905	Union	Buckeye Mfg. Co.	Anderson
1905	Williams	W.S. Casady Mfg. Co.	South Bend
1905-06	Columbia Electric	The Columbia Electric Co.	McCordsville
1905-06	Overland	Standard Wheel Works	Indianapolis
1905-07	Goshen	Goshen Motor Werks	Goshen
1905-07	Leader	Leader Mfg. Co.	McCordsville
1905-12	W.A.C.	Woodburn Auto Co.	Woodburn
1905-12	Woodburn	Woodburn Auto Co.	Woodburn
1905-16	Kirsch	Peter Kirsch	Decatur
1906	Anderson Highwheeler	Anderson Machine Co.	Bedford
1906	Capital	Capital Auto Co.	Indianapolis
1906	Connersville	Connersville Motor Vehicle Co.	Connersville
1906	Losure	Zan Losure	Van Buren

1906	Murillo	Murillo Mfg. Co.	Marion
1906	Washington	Washington Motor Car Co.	Washington
1906	Windsor	Windsor Automobile Co.	Evansville
1906-07	Coppock	Coppock Motor Car Co.	Marion
1906-07	Worth	Worth Motor Car Mfg. Co.	Evansville
1906-08	Overland	Overland Auto Co.	Indianapolis
1906-08	Postal	Postal Automobile & Engineering Co	Bedford
1906-08	Single-Center	Single-Center Buggy Co.	Evansville
1906-09	Model	Model Automobile Co.	Peru
1906-10	American Simplex	Simplex Motor Car Co.	Mishawaka
1906-14	American	American Motors Co.	Indianapolis
1906-14	American Underslung	American Motors Co.	Indianapolis
1906-16	Maxwell	Maxwell-Briscoe Motor Co.	New Castle
1906-17	Lambert	Buckeye Mfg. Co.	Anderson
1907	Cory	The Cory Automobile Co.	Albany
1907	Menges	Sterling-Hudson Whip Co.	Elkhart
1907	Ruth	Ruth Automobile Co.	North Webster
1907-08	Albany	Albany Automobile Co.	Albany
1907-08	Fellwock	Fellwock Automobile Mfg. Co.	Evansville
1907-08	Harper	Harper Buggy Co.	Columbia City
1907-08	Kiblinger	W. H. Kiblinger Co.	Auburn
1907-08	Perfection	Perfection Automobile Works	South Bend
1907-08	Pullman Flyer	Model Automobile Co.	Peru
1907-08	Shoemaker	Shoemaker Automobile Co.	Elkhart
1907-08	Stanley	Stanley Automobile Co.	Mooreland
1907-09	Evansville	Evansville Automobile Co.	Evansville
1907-09	Tincher	Tincher Motor Car Co.	South Bend
1907-10	Anderson	Anderson Carriage Mfg. Co.	Anderson
1907-10	Senator	Victor Automobile Co.	Ridgeville
1907-11	Simplicity	Evansville Automobile Co.	Evansville
1907-12	American Tourist	American Motors Co.	Indianapolis
1907-12	Leader	Leader Mfg. Co.	Knightstown
1908	Butler High Wheel	Butler Co.	Butler
1908	Clark Special	J.D. Clark Auto Co.	Anderson
1908	Famous	Famous Manufacturing Co.	East Chicago
1908	King	King Motor Vehicle Co.	Auburn
1908	Mollenhour	A.T. Mollenhour	Mentone
1908	Olson	C.J. Olson Buggy & Carriage Mfg.	Pittsboro
1908	Rex	Rex Motor Car Co.	Indianapolis
1908	Rider-Lewis	Rider-Lewis Motor Car Co.	Muncie
1908	St. Joe	St. Joe Motor Car Co.	Elkhart
1908	Star	Model Automobile Co.	Peru
1908-09	Bendix	Bendix Co.	Logansport
1908-09	Cole Solid Tire Auto.	Cole Carriage Co.	Indianapolis
1908-09	Economy	Economy Motor Buggy Co.	Fort Wayne
1908-09	Mier	Mier Carriage & Buggy Co.	Ligonier
1908-09	Schebler	Wheeler & Schebler Carburetor Co.	Indianapolis
1908-09	Sears Motor Buggy	Hercules Buggy Co.	Evansville
1908-09	Seidel	Seidel Buggy Co.	Richmond
1908-10	Best	Best Automobile Co.	Indianapolis
1908-11	Decatur	Decatur Motor Car Co.	Decatur
1908-11	Excellent Six	Rider-Lewis Motor Car Co.	Anderson
1908-11	Overland	Willys-Overland Co.	Indianapolis
1908-11	Rider-Lewis	Rider-Lewis Motor Car Co.	Anderson
1908-13	De Tamble	De Tamble Motor Co.	Anderson

1908-15	Zimmerman	Zimmerman Mfg. Co.	Auburn
1908-29	Davis	George W. Davis Motor Car Co.	Richmond
1909	Ade	Brook Motor Car Co.	Brook
1909	Adrem	Adrem Motor Co.	New Castle
1909	Atlas Motor Buggy	Atlas Engine Works	Indianapolis
1909	Attica	Attica Automobile Co.	Attica
1909	Beetle Flyer	Fodrea-Malott Mfg. Co.	Noblesville
1909	Brook	Brook Motor Car Co.	Brook
1909	Champion	Famous Manufacturing Co.	East Chicago
1909	Coyote	Union Automobile Co. of Albany	Albany
1909	Custer	Custer Mfg. Co.	Marion
1909	Federal	Industrial Automobile Co.	Elkhart
1909	Garrett	Garrett Machine Works	Garrett
1909	Hamiltonian	Harry Hamilton	Greensburg
1909	Industrial	Industrial Automobile Co.	Elkhart
1909	Lawter	Safety Shredder Co.	New Castle
1909	Motor Buggy	Motor Buggy Co.	Fort Wayne
1909	Parkison	Parkison Gear Co.	Brook
1909	Raber-Lang	Raber-Lang Co.	South Bend
1909	Stratton	Stratton Carriage Co.	Muncie
1909	T.J.K. Special	T.J. Kehoe	Fort Wayne
1909-10	DeWitt	DeWitt Motor Vehicle Co.	North Manchester
1909-11	Black Crow	Crow Motor Car Co.	Elkhart
1909-11	James	J & M Motor Car Co.	Lawrenceburg
1909-11	Pratt-Elkhart	Elkhart Carriage & Harness Mfg. Co	Elkhart
1909-11	Ricketts	Ricketts Automobile Co.	South Bend
1909-11	Star	Star Motor Car Co.	Indianapolis
1909-11	Sterling	Elkhart Motor Car Co.	Elkhart
1909-13	American Traveler	American Motors Co.	Indianapolis
1909-14	Great Western	Great Western Automobile Co.	Peru
1909-15	McIntyre	W. H. McIntyre Co.	Auburn
1909-16	Waverley	Waverley Co.	Indianapolis
1909-16	Westcott	Westcott Motor Car Co.	Richmond
1909-17	Rodefeld	Rodefeld Co.	Richmond
1909-19	Empire	Empire Motor Car Co.	Indianapolis
1909-19	Inter-State	Inter-State Automobile Co.	Muncie
1909-24	Pilot	Pilot Motor Car Co.	Richmond
1909-25	Cole	Cole Motor Car Co.	Indianapolis
1910	Brown	Brown Motor Co.	Washington
1910	Co-Auto	Co-Auto Motor Co.	Indianapolis
1910	Cyclop	L. Porter Smith & Bros.	Indianapolis
1910	Dart	Dart Mfg. Co.	Anderson
1910	Diamond	Diamond Automobile Co.	South Bend
1910	Fowler	Fowler Manufacturing Co.	Alexandria
1910	Kendallville	Kendallville Buggy Co.	Kendallville
1910	L.C.S.	L.C.S. Motor Co.	Fort Wayne
1910	Marion Flyer	Marion Automobile & Mfg. Co.	Marion
1910	Parry	Parry Auto Co.	Indianapolis
1910	Rupp	Kendallville Buggy Co.	Kendallville
1910	Turner	George Turner	Indianapolis
1910	Universal	Universal Motor Co.	New Castle
1910	Vincennes	Vincennes Motor Mfg. Co.	Vincennes
1910-11	R.A.C.	Ricketts Automobile Co.	South Bend

1910-11	Standard Six	Standard Automobile Co. of America	Wabash
1910-11	Traveler	Traveler Automobile Co.	Evansville
1910-12	Clark	Clark Motor Car Co.	Shelbyville
1910-12	Jonz	American Automobile Mfg. Co.	New Albany
1910-13	Amplex	Simplex Motor Car Co.	Mishawaka
1910-13	Continental	Indian Motor & Mfg. Co.	Franklin
1910-14	Ideal-Commercial	Ideal Auto Co.	Fort Wayne
1910-27	Lexington	Lexington Motor Co.	Connersville
1910-28	McFarlan	McFarlan Motor Car Co.	Connersville
1911	Crow	Crow Motor Car Co.	Elkhart
1911	Electro	Electro Lighting Co.	Indianapolis
1911	Elmer	Elmer Auto Corp.	Elkhart
1911	Dearborn	J & M Motor Car Co.	Lawrenceburg
1911	Izzer	Great Western Automobile Co.	Peru
1911	Komet	Elkhart Motor Car Co.	Elkhart
1911	Leist	Leist Automobile Mfg. Co.	Michigan City
1911	Lohr	Elmer Auto Corp.	Elkhart
1911	Troy	Troy Mfg. Co.	Mooreland
1911-12	Ideal	Ideal Motor Co.	Indianapolis
1911-12	New Parry	Parry Auto Co.	Indianapolis
1911-12	Octoauto	Reeves Pulley Co.	Columbus
1911-13	Fort Wayne-Commercial	Fort Wayne Automobile Mfg. Co.	Fort Wayne
1911-13	Jack Rabbit	Apperson Bros. Automobile Co.	Kokomo
1911-13	Nyberg	Nyberg Automobile Works	Anderson
1911-15	McIntyre Special	W. H. McIntyre Co.	Auburn
1911-15	Pratt	Pratt Motor Car Co.	Elkhart
1911-23	Crow-Elkhart	Crow-Elkhart Motor Car Co.	Elkhart
1912	Hunter-Hammond	Hunter-Hammond Auto Co.	Indianapolis
1912	Kernodle-McDaniel	Kernodle-McDaniel Mfg. Co.	Frankfort
1912	McLellen	McLellen Auto Shop	Indianapolis
1912	Nesom	Nesom Motors Co.	Indianapolis
1912	Otis	Otis Motor Car Co.	South Bend
1912	Rose City	Rose City Auto Co.	New Castle
1912	Sextoauto	Reeves Pulley Co.	Columbus
1912	Smart	Smart Auto & Mfg. Co.	Indianapolis
1912	Vaughn	Marion E. Vaughn	Indianapolis
1912	Vixen	Vixen Motor Co.	Indianapolis
1912-13	American Scout	American Motors Co.	Indianapolis
1912-14	Henderson	Henderson Motor Car Co.	Indianapolis
1912-15	Auburn Motor Chassis	Auburn Motor Chassis Co.	Auburn
1912-15	Empire	Empire Motor Car Co.	Connersville
1912-15	Handy Wagon	Auburn Motor Chassis Co.	Auburn
1912-17	Pathfinder	Motor Car Mfg. Co.	Indianapolis
1912-35	Stutz	Stutz Motor Car Co.	Indianapolis
1913	McGowan	W.H. McGowan	Vincennes
1913	Royal	Royal Motor Co.	Elkhart
1913	Stanley	Stanley Motor Co.	Liberty
1913	Tone	Tone Car Corp.	Indianapolis
1913	Van Auken Electric	Connersville Buggy Co.	Connersville
1913-14	De Soto	Zimmerman Mfg. Co.	Auburn
1913-14	Howard	Lexington-Howard Co.	Connersville
1913-14	Imp	W. H. McIntyre Co.	Auburn
1913-14	Ohio Falls	Ohio Falls Motor Car Co.	New Albany
1913-14	Pilgrim	Ohio Falls Motor Car Co.	New Albany

1913-15	Lyons-Knight	Lyons-Atlas Co.	Indianapolis
1913-16	South Bend	South Bend Motor Car Works	South Bend
1914	Caesar	Alonzo R. Marsh	Anderson
1914	Coliseum	Coliseum Machine & Garage Co.	South Bend
1914	Comet	Comet Cyclecar Co.	Indianapolis
1914	Connersville	Connersville Buggy Co.	Connersville
1914	Cyclops	Cyclops Cyclecar Co.	Indianapolis
1914	Fauber	Cyclecar Engineering Co.	Indianapolis
1914	Feeny	Feeny Mfg. Co.	Muncie
1914	Gary Six	Gary Automobile Mfg. Co.	Gary
1914	Geneva	Geneva Auto Specialty & Repair	Geneva
1914	Hoosier Scout	Warren Electric & Machine Co.	Indianapolis
1914	M.C.M.	The M.C.M. Motor Co.	Bedford
1914	Martindale & Millikan	Indian Motor & Mfg. Co.	Franklin
1914	Merz	Merz Cyclecar Co.	Indianapolis
1914	Real Cyclecar	Real Cyclecar Co.	Anderson
1914	Six & Vance	Don Six & Claire Vance	Logansport
1914	Upton	Upton Automobile Co.	Bristol
1914	Wizard	Wizard Motor Co.	Indianapolis
1914-15	Hercules	Hercules Motor Car Co.	New Albany
1914-15	Real Light Car	Real Light Car Co.	Converse
1914-32	Ford	Ford Motor Co.	Indianapolis
1915	Bailey-Klapp	Elwood Iron Works	Elwood
1915	De Kalb	De Kalb Mfg. Co.	Fort Wayne
1915	Dolly Madison	Madison Motor Co.	Anderson
1915	E.I.M.	Eastern Indiana Motor Car Co.	Richmond
1915	Elwood	Elwood Iron Works	Elwood
1915	Frazier-Elkhart	O. Z. Frazier	Elkhart
1915	Parrish	William N. Parrish & Son	Richmond
1915	Rayfield	Great Western Automobile Co.	Peru
1915	Ultimotor	Frank Martindale	Franklin
1915-16	Herff-Brooks	Herff-Brooks Corp.	Indianapolis
1915-16	Marathon	Herff-Brooks Corp.	Indianapolis
1915-16	Niagara Four	Crow Motor Car Co.	Elkhart
1915-19	Madison	Madison Motors Corp.	Anderson
1916	Champion	Champion Auto Equipment Co.	Wabash
1916	Dixie	Dixie Mfg. Co.	Vincennes
1916	Gillette	Gillette Motor Co.	Mishawaka
1916	Teetor-Hartley	Teetor-Hartley Motor Co.	Hagerstown
1916	Union	Union Automobile Co.	Auburn
1916	Union City Six	Union City Carriage Mfg. Co.	Union City
1916-17	Laurel	Laurel Motor Car Co.	Richmond
1916-17	Sun	Sun Motor Car Co.	Elkhart
1916-20	American Junior	American Motor Vehicle Co.	Lafayette
1916-20	Auto Red Bug	American Motor Vehicle Co.	Lafayette
1916-23	Birch	Crow-Elkhart Motor Car Co.	Elkhart
1916-25	Bush	Crow-Elkhart Motor Car Co.	Elkhart
1916-31	Elcar	Elkhart Motor Co.	Elkhart
1917	Brazil	Brazil Motors Co.	Brazil
1917	Colonial Six	Colonial Automobile Co.	Indianapolis
1917	Frankfort	Frankfort Motor Co.	Frankfort
1917	Hassler	Hassler Motor Co.	Indianapolis
1917	Mills Electric	Mills Electric Co.	Lafayette
1917-18	Shad-Wyck	Shadburne Bros Co.	Frankfort

1917-20	Laurel	Laurel Motors Corp.	Anderson
1917-28	McGill	McGee Mfg. Co.	Indianapolis
1918	Bour-Davis	Shadburne Bros. Co.	Frankfort
1918-23	Monroe	William Small Co.	Indianapolis
1918-23	Bryan Steamer	Bryan Boiler Co.	Peru
1918-26	ReVere	Revere Motor Car Corp.	Logansport
1919	Barth-Keith	Barth-Keith Motor Car Co.	Indianapolis
1919	Geiger	Ray Geiger	Covington
1919	Hercules Electric	Hercules Corp.	Evansville
1919	Rubber Bill	Rubber Bill Co.	LaPorte
1919	Spacke	Spacke Machine & Tool Co.	Indianapolis
1919-20	United	United Engineering Co.	Greensburg
1919-20	Yarlott	Yarlott Bros. Motor & Car Co.	Fort Wayne
1919-21	Pan	Pan Motor Co.	Indianapolis
1919-25	Morriss-London	Century Motors Co.	Elkhart
1920	Craig-Hunt	Craig-Hunt Motor Co.	Indianapolis
1920	Gale Four	Garde Gale	Indianapolis
1920-21	Brook	Spacke Machine & Tool Co.	Indianapolis
1920-21	Kenworthy	Kenworthy Motors Corp.	Mishawaka
1920-21	Lorraine	Lorraine Car Co.	Richmond
1920-21	Sheridan	Sheridan Motor Car Co.	Muncie
1920-25	H.C.S.	H.C.S. Motor Co.	Indianapolis
1920-25	Huffman	Huffman Bros. Motor Co.	Elkhart
1920-37	Duesenberg	Duesenberg Motors Corp.	Indianapolis
1921, 1926	Ansted	Lexington Motor Car Co.	Connersville
1921	Peters	Spacke Machine & Tool Co.	Indianapolis
1921	Vanderbilt	Union Steel Mfg. Co.	Brazil
1921-22	Coats Steamer	Coats Steamers Inc.	Indianapolis
1921-22	Lafayette	Lafayette Motors Co.	Indianapolis
1921-25	Frontenac	Frontenac Motor Co.	Indianapolis
1922	Alena Steam	Alena Steam Products Co.	Indianapolis
1922	Anahuac	Frontenac Motor Co.	Indianapolis
1922	McCurdy	Hercules Corp.	Evansville
1922-28	Durant	Durant Motors, Inc.	Muncie
1923	Star	Durant Motors, Inc.	Muncie
1923	Strattan	Strattan Motors Corp.	Indianapolis
1923	Streamline	Streamline Motor Car Co.	Indianapolis
1923-24	Elgin	Elgin Motors Inc.	Indianapolis
1923-24	Princeton	Durant Motors, Inc.	Muncie
1923-26	Premier Taxicab	Premier Motor Car Co.	Indianapolis
1924	Cross	Harry E. Cross	Indianapolis
1924	Red Ball-Taxi	Red Ball Transit Co.	Frankfort
1924-27	H.C.S. Cab	H.C.S. Cab Mfg. Co.	Indianapolis
1925	DaVinci	James Scripps-Booth	Indianapolis
1925-27	Martel	Elkhart Motor Co.	Elkhart
1925-27	Royal Martel	Elkhart Motor Co.	Elkhart
1926-28	Saf-T-Cab	Auburn Automobile Co.	Auburn
1927-28	New York Six	Automotive Corp. of America	Richmond
1927-30	Erskine	Studebaker Corp.	South Bend
1928	Automotive Syndicate	Automotive Syndicate	Indianapolis
1929	Cummins	Cummins Engine Co.	Columbus
1929-30	Blackhawk	Stutz Motor Car Co.	Indianapolis
1929-30	Roosevelt	Marmon Motor Car Co.	Indianapolis
1929-32	Cord	Cord Corp.	Auburn

1929-36	Auburn	Auburn Automobile Co.	Connersville
1930	Lever	Lever Motors Corp.	Elkhart
1930	Paragon Cab	Elcar Motor Co.	Elkhart
1930-38	Pak-Age-Car	Stutz Motor Co.	Indianapolis
1931	Mercer	Elcar Motor Co.	Elkhart
1931-35	El-Fay	Elkhart Motor Co.	Elkhart
1932-33	Rockne	Studebaker Corp.	South Bend
1932-34	Allied	Allied Cab Mfg. Co.	Elkhart
1933	Prosperity	Allied Cab Mfg. Co.	Elkhart
1935	Super Allied	Allied Cab Mfg. Co.	Elkhart
1935	Auburn-Cummins	Auburn Automobile Co.	Auburn
1935-56	Plymouth	Chrysler Corp.	Evansville
1936-37	Cord	Cord Corp.	Connersville
1938-41	Pak-Age-Car	Auburn Central Co.	Connersville
1939-42	Crosley	Crosley Motors Inc.	Richmond
1940-41	Packard Darrin	Packard Motor Car Co.	Connersville
1946-52	Crosley	Crosley Motors Inc.	Marion
1950-51	Muntz Jet	Muntz Car Co.	Evansville
1951	Farm O Road	Crosley Motors Inc.	Marion
1954-58	Packard	Studebaker-Packard Corp.	South Bend
1956	Glascar	Robert Tucker	Richmond
1961-80	Scout	International Harvester Co.	Fort Wayne
1962-63	Avanti	Studebaker Corp.	South Bend
1965-85	Avanti II	Avanti Motor Corp.	South Bend
1966	Duesenberg II	Duesenberg Corp.	Indianapolis
1974	Elcar Electric	Elcar Corp.	Elkhart
1985-present	HMMWV	AM General	Mishawaka
1988-present	Chevrolet Silverado	GM Truck Group	Fort Wayne
1988-present	GMC Sierra	GM Truck Group	Fort Wayne
1989-present	Subaru Legacy	Subaru Isuzu Automotive, Inc.	Lafayette
1989-present	Isuzu Trooper	Subaru Isuzu Automotive, Inc.	Lafayette
1990-present	Isuzu Rodeo	Subaru Isuzu Automotive, Inc.	Lafayette
1992-present	Hummer	AM General	Mishawaka
1994-present	Honda Passport	Subaru Isuzu Automotive, Inc.	Lafayette
1994	Hunter	Riley & Scott, Inc.	Indianapolis
1994	Prowler Prototype	Riley & Scott, Inc.	Indianapolis
1998-present	Isuzu Amigo	Subaru Isuzu Automotive, Inc.	Lafayette
1998-present	Toyota Tundra	Toyota Motor Manufacturing Indiana	Princeton
1999-present	Subaru Outback	Subaru Isuzu Automotive, Inc.	Lafayette
2000-present	Toyota Sequoia	Toyota Motor Manufacturing Indiana	Princeton
2001-present	Isuzu Axiom	Subaru Isuzu Automotive, Inc.	Lafayette
2002	Hummer H2	AM General	Mishawaka
2003	Toyota Sienna	Toyota Motor Manufacturing Indiana	Princeton

Indiana Cars Listed by City

City	Name	Manufacturer	Dates
Albany	Albany	Albany Automobile Co.	1907-08
Albany	Cory	The Cory Automobile Co.	1907
Albany	Coyote	Union Automobile Co. of Albany	1909
Albany	Craven	Craven Sectional Tire Co.	1905
Alexandria	Fowler	Fowler Manufacturing Co.	1910
Anderson	Anderson	Anderson Carriage Mfg. Co.	1907-10
Anderson	Anderson Steam	Anderson Steam Carriage Co.	1901-02
Anderson	Buckeye	J.W. Lambert-Buckeye Mfg. Co.	1895
Anderson	Caesar	Alonzo R. Marsh	1914
Anderson	Clark Special	J.D. Clark Auto Co.	1908
Anderson	Dart	Dart Mfg. Co.	1910
Anderson	De Tamble	De Tamble Motor Co.	1908-13
Anderson	Dolly Madison	Madison Motor Co.	1915
Anderson	Erie	Erie Cycle & Motor Carriage Co.	1899-1902
Anderson	Excellent Six	Rider-Lewis Motor Car Co.	1908-11
Anderson	Flandermobile	Flandermobile Co.	1901
Anderson	Lambert	Buckeye Mfg. Co.	1906-17
Anderson	Laurel	Laurel Motors Corp.	1917-20
Anderson	Madison	Madison Motors Corp.	1915-19
Anderson	Nyberg	Nyberg Automobile Works	1911-13
Anderson	Real Cyclecar	Real Cyclecar Co.	1914
Anderson	Rider-Lewis	Rider-Lewis Motor Car Co.	1908-11
Anderson	Shimer	Shimer & Co.	1901
Anderson	Union	Buckeye Mfg. Co.	1905
Attica	Attica	Attica Automobile Co.	1909
Auburn	Auburn	Auburn Automobile Co.	1900-36
Auburn	Auburn-Cummins	Auburn Automobile Co.	1935
Auburn	Auburn Motor Chassis	Auburn Motor Chassis Co.	1912-15
Auburn	Cord	Cord Corp.	1929-32
Auburn	De Soto	Zimmerman Mfg. Co.	1913-14
Auburn	Handy Wagon	Auburn Motor Chassis Co.	1912-15
Auburn	Imp	W. H. McIntyre Co.	1913-14
Auburn	Kiblinger	W. H. Kiblinger Co.	1907-08
Auburn	King	King Motor Vehicle Co.	1908
Auburn	McIntyre	W. H. McIntyre Co.	1909-15
Auburn	McIntyre Special	W. H. McIntyre Co.	1911-15
Auburn	Model	Model Gas Engine Works	1903-06
Auburn	Saf-T-Cab	Auburn Automobile Co.	1926-28
Auburn	Union	Union Automobile Co.	1916
Auburn	Zimmerman	Zimmerman Mfg. Co.	1908-15
Bedford	Anderson Highwheeler	Anderson Machine Co.	1906
Bedford	M.C.M	The M.C.M. Motor Co.	1914
Bedford	Postal	Postal Automobile & Engineering Co	1906-08
Bluffton	Kindall	A. J. Kindall	1903
Bourbon	Anghein	M. J. Anghein	1899

Brazil	Brazil	Brazil Motors Co.	1917
Brazil	Richter	H. Richter	1902
Brazil	Vanderbilt	Union Steel Mfg. Co.	1921
Bristol	Upton	Upton Automobile Co.	1914
Brook	Ade	Brook Motor Car Co.	1909
Brook	Brook	Brook Motor Car Co.	1909
Brook	Parkison	Parkison Gear Co.	1909
Butler	Butler High Wheel	Butler Co.	1908
Columbia City	Harper	Harper Buggy Co.	1907-08
Columbus	Cummins	Cummins Engine Co.	1929
Columbus	Octoauto	Reeves Pulley Co.	1911-12
Columbus	Ogden	Dore Ogden	1902
Columbus	Reeves	Reeves Pulley Co.	1896-1910
Columbus	Sextoauto	Reeves Pulley Co.	1912
Connersville	Ansted	Lexington Motor Car Co.	1921, 1926
Connersville	Auburn	Auburn Automobile Co.	1929-36
Connersville	Central	Central Manufacturing Co.	1905
Connersville	Connersville	Connersville Motor Vehicle Co.	1906
Connersville	Connersville	Connersville Buggy Co.	1914
Connersville	Cord	Cord Corp.	1936-37
Connersville	Empire	Empire Motor Car Co.	1912-15
Connersville	Howard	Lexington-Howard Co.	1913-14
Connersville	Lexington	Lexington Motor Co.	1910-27
Connersville	McFarlan	McFarlan Motor Car Co.	1910-28
Connersville	Pak-Age-Car	Auburn Central Co.	1938-41
Connersville	Packard Darrin	Packard Motor Car Co.	1940-41
Connersville	Van Auken Electric	Connersville Buggy Co.	1913
Converse	Real Light Car	Real Light Car Co.	1914-15
Covington	Geiger	Ray Geiger	1919
Crawfordsville	Dovetail	Dovetail Carriage Co.	1900
Decatur	Decatur	Decatur Motor Car Co.	1908-11
Decatur	Kirsch	Peter Kirsch	1905-16
East Chicago	Champion	Famous Manufacturing Co.	1909
East Chicago	Famous	Famous Manufacturing Co.	1908
Elkhart	Allied	Allied Cab Mfg. Co.	1932-34
Elkhart	Birch	Crow-Elkhart Motor Car Co.	1916-23
Elkhart	Black Crow	Crow Motor Car Co.	1909-11
Elkhart	Bush	Crow-Elkhart Motor Car Co.	1916-25
Elkhart	Crow	Crow Motor Car Co.	1911
Elkhart	Crow-Elkhart	Crow-Elkhart Motor Car Co.	1911-23
Elkhart	Elcar	Elkhart Motor Co.	1916-31
Elkhart	Elcar Electric	Elcar Corp.	1974
Elkhart	El-Fay	Elkhart Motor Co.	1931-35
Elkhart	Elmer	Elmer Auto Corp.	1911
Elkhart	Federal	Industrial Automobile Co.	1909
Elkhart	Frazier-Elkhart	O. Z. Frazier	1915
Elkhart	Huffman	Huffman Bros. Motor Co.	1920-25
Elkhart	Industrial	Industrial Automobile Co.	1909
Elkhart	Komet	Elkhart Motor Car Co.	1911
Elkhart	Lever	Lever Motors Corp.	1930
Elkhart	Lohr	Elmer Auto Corp.	1911
Elkhart	Martel	Elkhart Motor Co.	1925-27
Elkhart	Menges	Sterling-Hudson Whip Co.	1907
Elkhart	Mercer	Elcar Motor Co.	1931
Elkhart	Morriss-London	Century Motors Co.	1919-25
Elkhart	Niagara Four	Crow Motor Car Co.	1915-16

Elkhart	Paragon Cab	Elcar Motor Co.	1930
Elkhart	Pratt	Pratt Motor Car Co.	1911-15
Elkhart	Pratt-Elkhart	Elkhart Carriage & Harness Mfg. Co	1909-11
Elkhart	Prosperity	Allied Cab Mfg. Co.	1933
Elkhart	Royal	Royal Motor Co.	1913
Elkhart	Royal Martel	Elkhart Motor Co.	1925-27
Elkhart	St. Joe	St. Joe Motor Car Co.	1908
Elkhart	Shoemaker	Shoemaker Automobile Co.	1907-08
Elkhart	Signor	A. J. Signor	1901
Elkhart	Soudan	Soudan Mfg. Co.	1900-01
Elkhart	Sterling	Elkhart Motor Car Co.	1909-11
Elkhart	Super Allied	Allied Cab Mfg. Co.	1935
Elkhart	Sun	Sun Motor Car Co.	1916-17
Elwood	Bailey-Klapp	Elwood Iron Works	1915
Elwood	Elwood	Elwood Iron Works	1915
Evansville	Benninghof	Benninghof-Nolan Co.	1904
Evansville	Evansville	Evansville Automobile Co.	1907-09
Evansville	Fellwock	Fellwock Automobile Mfg. Co.	1907-08
Evansville	Hercules Electric	Hercules Corp.	1919
Evansville	McCurdy	Hercules Corp.	1922
Evansville	Muntz Jet	Muntz Car Co.	1950-51
Evansville	Plymouth	Chrysler Corp.	1935-56
Evansville	Sears Motor Buggy	Hercules Buggy Co.	1908-09
Evansville	Simplicity	Evansville Automobile Co.	1907-11
Evansville	Single-Center	Single-Center Buggy Co.	1906-08
Evansville	Traveler	Traveler Automobile Co.	1910-11
Evansville	Windsor	Windsor Automobile Co.	1906
Evansville	Worth	Worth Motor Car Mfg. Co.	1906-07
Evansville	Zentmobile	Schuyler W. Zent	1903
Fairmount	Carey	Carey Motor Car Co.	1905
Fort Wayne	Chevrolet Silverado	GM Truck Group	1988-present
Fort Wayne	Columbia	Columbia Machine Works	1902
Fort Wayne	De Kalb	De Kalb Mfg. Co.	1915
Fort Wayne	Eclipse	Eclipse Buggy Co.	1902
Fort Wayne	Economy	Economy Motor Buggy Co.	1908-09
Fort Wayne	Fort Wayne	Fort Wayne Automobile Co.	1903
Fort Wayne	Fort Wayne-Commercial	Fort Wayne Automobile Mfg. Co.	1911-13
Fort Wayne	GMC Sierra	GM Truck Group	1988-present
Fort Wayne	Ideal-Commercial	Ideal Auto Co.	1910-14
Fort Wayne	L.C.S.	L.C.S. Motor Co.	1910
Fort Wayne	Motor Buggy	Motor Buggy Co.	1909
Fort Wayne	Roach & Albanus	Roach & Albanus	1899-1900
Fort Wayne	Scout	International Harvester Co.	1961-80
Fort Wayne	Slattery Electric	M.M.M. Slattery	1899
Fort Wayne	T.J.K. Special	T.J. Kehoe	1909
Fort Wayne	Yarlott	Yarlott Bros. Motor & Car Co.	1919-20
Frankfort	Bour-Davis	Shadburne Bros. Co.	1918
Frankfort	Frankfort	Frankfort Motor Co.	1917
Frankfort	Kernodle-McDaniel	Kernodle-McDaniel Mfg. Co.	1912
Frankfort	Red Ball-Taxi	Red Ball Transit Co.	1924
Frankfort	Shad-Wyck	Shadburne Bros Co.	1917-18
Franklin	Continental	Indian Motor & Mfg. Co.	1910-13
Franklin	Martindale & Millikan	Indian Motor & Mfg. Co.	1914
Franklin	Ultimotor	Frank Martindale	1915

Garrett	Cramer	Claude Cramer	1901
Garrett	Garrett	Garrett Machine Works	1909
Gary	Gary Six	Gary Automobile Mfg. Co.	1914
Geneva	Geneva	Geneva Auto Specialty & Repair	1914
Goshen	Goshen	Goshen Motor Werks	1905-07
Goshen	Keller	J.M. Keller	1901
Greencastle	Bell	Carl Bell	1901
Greensburg	Hamiltonian	Harry Hamilton	1909
Greensburg	Simplicity	Ira J. Hollensbee	1902
Greensburg	United	United Engineering Co.	1919-20
Hagerstown	Teetor-Hartley	Teetor-Hartley Motor Co.	1916
Hartford City	Crimmell & Hailman	Crimmell & Hailman	1903
Huntingburg	Huntingburg	Huntingburg Wagon Works	1902-03
Indianapolis	Alena Steam	Alena Steam Products Co.	1922
Indianapolis	American	American Motors Co.	1906-14
Indianapolis	American Scout	American Motors Co.	1912-13
Indianapolis	American Tourist	American Motors Co.	1907-12
Indianapolis	American Traveler	American Motors Co.	1909-13
Indianapolis	American Underslung	American Motors Co.	1906-14
Indianapolis	Anahuac	Frontenac Motor Co.	1922
Indianapolis	Atlas Motor Buggy	Atlas Engine Works	1909
Indianapolis	Automotive Syndicate	Automotive Syndicate	1928
Indianapolis	Best	Best Automobile Co.	1908-10
Indianapolis	Barth-Keith	Barth-Keith Motor Car Co.	1919
Indianapolis	Black	C.H. Black Mfg. Co.	1896-1900
Indianapolis	Blackhawk	Stutz Motor Car Co.	1929-30
Indianapolis	Brook	Spacke Machine & Tool Co.	1920-21
Indianapolis	Capital	Capital Auto Co.	1906
Indianapolis	Central	Central Motor Car Co.	1903
Indianapolis	Co-Auto	Co-Auto Motor Co.	1910
Indianapolis	Coats Steamer	Coats Steamers Inc.	1921-22
Indianapolis	Cole	Cole Motor Car Co.	1909-25
Indianapolis	Cole Solid Tire Auto.	Cole Carriage Co.	1908-09
Indianapolis	Colonial Six	Colonial Automobile Co.	1917
Indianapolis	Comet	Comet Cyclecar Co.	1914
Indianapolis	Comet Racer	Marion Motor Car Co.	1904
Indianapolis	Craig-Hunt	Craig-Hunt Motor Co.	1920
Indianapolis	Cross	Harry E. Cross	1924
Indianapolis	Cyclop	L. Porter Smith & Bros.	1910
Indianapolis	Cyclops	Cyclops Cyclecar Co.	1914
Indianapolis	DaVinci	James Scripps-Booth	1925
Indianapolis	De Freet	Thomas M. De Freet	1895
Indianapolis	Duesenberg	Duesenberg Motors Corp.	1920-37
Indianapolis	Duesenberg II	Duesenberg Corp.	1966
Indianapolis	Electro	Electro Lighting Co.	1911
Indianapolis	Electrobile	National Vehicle Co.	1901-06
Indianapolis	Elgin	Elgin Motors Inc.	1923-24
Indianapolis	Empire	Empire Motor Car Co.	1909-19
Indianapolis	Fauber	Cyclecar Engineering Co.	1914
Indianapolis	Ford	Ford Motor Co.	1914-32
Indianapolis	Frontenac	Frontenac Motor Co.	1921-25
Indianapolis	Gale Four	Garde Gale	1920
Indianapolis	H.C.S.	H.C.S. Motor Co.	1920-25
Indianapolis	H.C.S. Cab	H.C.S. Cab Mfg. Co.	1924-27
Indianapolis	Hassler	Hassler Motor Co.	1917

Indianapolis	Hassler Motor Buggy	Robert H. Hassler	1898
Indianapolis	Henderson	Henderson Motor Car Co.	1912-14
Indianapolis	Herff-Brooks	Herff-Brooks Corp.	1915-16
Indianapolis	Hoosier Scout	Warren Electric & Machine Co.	1914
Indianapolis	Hunter	Riley & Scott, Inc.	1994
Indianapolis	Hunter-Hammond	Hunter-Hammond Auto Co.	1912
Indianapolis	Ideal	Ideal Motor Co.	1911-12
Indianapolis	Indiana	Indiana Motor & Vehicle Co.	1901
Indianapolis	Indianapolis	C. H. Black Mfg. Co.	1897-00
Indianapolis	Lafayette	Lafayette Motors Co.	1921-22
Indianapolis	Lindsay	T.J. Lindsay Automobile Parts Co.	1902-03
Indianapolis	Liquid Air	Liquid Air Co.	1900
Indianapolis	Lyons-Knight	Lyons-Atlas Co.	1913-15
Indianapolis	Marathon	Herff-Brooks Corp.	1915-16
Indianapolis	Marion	Marion Motor Car Co.	1904-14
Indianapolis	Marmon	Nordyke & Marmon Co.	1902-33
Indianapolis	McGill	McGee Mfg. Co.	1917-28
Indianapolis	McLellen	McLellen Auto Shop	1912
Indianapolis	Merz	Merz Cyclecar Co.	1914
Indianapolis	Mohawk	Mohawk Cycle & Automobile Co.	1903-05
Indianapolis	Monroe	William Small Co.	1918-23
Indianapolis	National	National Motor Vehicle Co.	1904-24
Indianapolis	National Electric	National Automobile & Electric Co.	1900-04
Indianapolis	Nesom	Nesom Motors Co.	1912
Indianapolis	New Parry	Parry Auto Co.	1911-12
Indianapolis	Overland	Standard Wheel Works	1905-06
Indianapolis	Overland	Overland Auto Co.	1906-08
Indianapolis	Overland	Willys-Overland Co.	1908-11
Indianapolis	Pak-Age-Car	Stutz Motor Co.	1930-38
Indianapolis	Pan	Pan Motor Co.	1919-21
Indianapolis	Parry	Parry Auto Co.	1910
Indianapolis	Pathfinder	Motor Car Mfg. Co.	1912-17
Indianapolis	Peters	Spacke Machine & Tool Co.	1921
Indianapolis	Pope-Waverley	Pope Motor Car Co.	1904-08
Indianapolis	Premier	Premier Motor Mfg. Co.	1903-26
Indianapolis	Premier Taxicab	Premier Motor Car Co.	1923-26
Indianapolis	Prowler Prototype	Riley & Scott, Inc.	1994
Indianapolis	Rex	Rex Motor Car Co.	1908
Indianapolis	Roosevelt	Marmon Motor Car Co.	1929-30
Indianapolis	Schebler	Wheeler & Schebler Carburetor Co.	1908-09
Indianapolis	Sears Steam	Sears Bros.	1901
Indianapolis	Smart	Smart Auto & Mfg. Co.	1912
Indianapolis	Spacke	Spacke Machine & Tool Co.	1919
Indianapolis	Star	Star Motor Car Co.	1909-11
Indianapolis	Strattan	Strattan Motors Corp.	1923
Indianapolis	Streamline	Streamline Motor Car Co.	1923
Indianapolis	Stutz	Stutz Motor Car Co.	1912-35
Indianapolis	Tone	Tone Car Corp.	1913
Indianapolis	Tricolet	H. Pokorney & Richards Auto. & Gas	1904-06
Indianapolis	Turner	George Turner	1910
Indianapolis	Vaughn	Marion E. Vaughn	1912
Indianapolis	Vixen	Vixen Motor Co.	1912
Indianapolis	Waverley	Waverley Co.	1909-16
Indianapolis	Waverley Electric	Indiana Bicycle Co.	1898-1903

Indianapolis	Wizard	Wizard Motor Co.	1914
Kendallville	Kendallville	Kendallville Buggy Co.	1910
Kendallville	Rupp	Kendallville Buggy Co.	1910
Knightstown	Knightstown	Knightstown Buggy Co.	1900
Knightstown	Leader	Leader Mfg. Co.	1907-12
Kokomo	Apperson	Apperson Bros. Automobile Co.	1902-26
Kokomo	Goabout	Standard Mfg. Co.	1901-02
Kokomo	Haynes	Haynes Automobile Co.	1904-25
Kokomo	Haynes-Apperson	Haynes-Apperson Automobile Co.	1898-1904
Kokomo	Haynes Pioneer	Elwood Haynes	1893-94
Kokomo	Jack Rabbit	Apperson Bros. Automobile Co.	1911-13
Kokomo	Kokomo	Shortridge, Sellers & Irvin	1901
Lafayette	American Junior	American Motor Vehicle Co.	1916-20
Lafayette	Auto Red Bug	American Motor Vehicle Co.	1916-20
Lafayette	Diehnart	Diehnart & Smith	1901
Lafayette	Honda Passport	Subaru Isuzu Automotive, Inc.	1994-present
Lafayette	Isuzu Amigo	Subaru Isuzu Automotive, Inc.	1998-present
Lafayette	Isuzu Axiom	Subaru Isuzu Automotive, Inc.	2001-present
Lafayette	Isuzu Rodeo	Subaru Isuzu Automotive, Inc.	1990-present
Lafayette	Isuzu Trooper	Subaru Isuzu Automotive, Inc.	1989-present
Lafayette	Mills Electric	Mills Electric Co.	1917
Lafayette	Subaru Legacy	Subaru Isuzu Automotive, Inc.	1989-present
Lafayette	Subaru Outback	Subaru Isuzu Automotive, Inc.	1999-present
LaPorte	Great Western	Great Western Mfg. Co.	1902-05
LaPorte	LaPorte	LaPorte Carriage Co.	1895
LaPorte	Munson	Munson Co.	1896-1900
LaPorte	Rubber Bill	Rubber Bill Co.	1919
Lawrenceburg	Dearborn	J & M Motor Car Co.	1911
Lawrenceburg	James	J & M Motor Car Co.	1909-11
Liberty	Stanley	Stanley Motor Co.	1913
Ligonier	Mier	Mier Carriage & Buggy Co.	1908-09
Logansport	Bendix	Bendix Co.	1908-09
Logansport	ReVere	Revere Motor Car Corp.	1918-26
Logansport	Rutenber	Rutenber Mfg. Co.	1902
Logansport	Six & Vance	Don Six & Claire Vance	1914
Marion	Coppock	Coppock Motor Car Co.	1906-07
Marion	Crosley	Crosley Motors Inc.	1946-52
Marion	Custer	Custer Mfg. Co.	1909
Marion	Farm O Road	Crosley Motors Inc.	1951
Marion	Marion Flyer	Marion Automobile & Mfg. Co.	1910
Marion	Murillo	Murillo Mfg. Co.	1906
McCordsville	Columbia Electric	The Columbia Electric Co.	1905-06
McCordsville	Leader	Leader Mfg. Co.	1905-07
Mentone	Mollenhour	A.T. Mollenhour	1908
Michigan City	Eichstaedt	Roman Eichstaedt	1898-1902
Michigan City	Leist	Leist Automobile Mfg. Co.	1911
Mishawaka	American Simplex	Simplex Motor Car Co.	1906-10
Mishawaka	Amplex	Simplex Motor Car Co.	1910-13
Mishawaka	Gillette	Gillette Motor Co.	1916
Mishawaka	Hayn	R.B. Hayn	1901
Mishawaka	HMMWV	AM General	1985-present
Mishawaka	Hummer	AM General	1992-present
Mishawaka	Hummer H2	AM General	2002

Mishawaka	Kenworthy	Kenworthy Motors Corp.	1920-21
Monticello	Million	Robert J. Million	1896
Mooreland	Stanley	Stanley Automobile Co.	1907-08
Mooreland	Troy	Troy Mfg. Co.	1911
Mooresville	Fisher	Fisher Automobile Co.	1903
Muncie	Derrickson	Derrickson Mfg. Co.	1903
Muncie	Durant	Durant Motors, Inc.	1922-28
Muncie	Feeny	Feeny Mfg. Co.	1914
Muncie	Inter-State	Inter-State Automobile Co.	1909-19
Muncie	Muncie	Muncie Wheel & Jobbing Co.	1903
Muncie	Princeton	Durant Motors, Inc.	1923-24
Muncie	Rider-Lewis	Rider-Lewis Motor Car Co.	1908
Muncie	Sheridan	Sheridan Motor Car Co.	1920-21
Muncie	Star	Durant Motors, Inc.	1923
Muncie	Stratton	Stratton Carriage Co.	1909
Muncie	Warner	Muncie Wheel & Jobbing Co.	1903-06
New Albany	Hercules	Hercules Motor Car Co.	1914-15
New Albany	Jonz	American Automobile Mfg. Co.	1910-12
New Albany	Ohio Falls	Ohio Falls Motor Car Co.	1913-14
New Albany	Pilgrim	Ohio Falls Motor Car Co.	1913-14
New Albany	Walker Steamer	Earl C. Walker	1901
New Castle	Adrem	Adrem Motor Co.	1909
New Castle	Ideal	Ideal Automobile Mfg. Co.	1902
New Castle	Lawter	Safety Shredder Co.	1909
New Castle	Maxwell	Maxwell-Briscoe Motor Co.	1906-16
New Castle	Rose City	Rose City Auto Co.	1912
New Castle	Universal	Universal Motor Co.	1910
Noblesville	Beetle Flyer	Fodrea-Malott Mfg. Co.	1909
North Manchester	DeWitt	DeWitt Motor Vehicle Co.	1909-10
North Webster	Ruth	Ruth Automobile Co.	1907
Peru	Bryan Steamer	Bryan Boiler Co.	1918-23
Peru	Great Western	Great Western Automobile Co.	1909-14
Peru	Izzer	Great Western Automobile Co.	1911
Peru	Model	Model Automobile Co.	1906-09
Peru	Pullman Flyer	Model Automobile Co.	1907-08
Peru	Rayfield	Great Western Automobile Co.	1915
Peru	Star	Model Automobile Co.	1908
Pittsboro	Olson	C.J. Olson Buggy & Carriage Mfg.	1908
Princeton	Toyota Sequoia	Toyota Motor Manufacturing Indiana	2000-present
Princeton	Toyota Sienna	Toyota Motor Manufacturing Indiana	2003
Princeton	Toyota Tundra	Toyota Motor Manufacturing Indiana	1998-present
Richmond	Crosley	Crosley Motors Inc.	1939-42
Richmond	Davis	George W. Davis Motor Car Co.	1908-29
Richmond	E.I.M.	Eastern Indiana Motor Car Co.	1915
Richmond	Glascar	Robert Tucker	1956
Richmond	Laurel	Laurel Motor Car Co.	1916-17
Richmond	Lorraine	Lorraine Car Co.	1920-21
Richmond	New York Six	Automotive Corp. of America	1927-28
Richmond	Parrish	William N. Parrish & Son	1915
Richmond	Pilot	Pilot Motor Car Co.	1909-24
Richmond	Richmond	Wayne Works	1904-17
Richmond	Richmond Steam	Richmond Automobile Co.	1902-03
Richmond	Rodefeld	Rodefeld Co.	1909-17
Richmond	Sedgwick Steam	Isham H. Sedgwick	1901

Richmond	Seidel	Seidel Buggy Co.	1908-09
Richmond	Westcott	Westcott Motor Car Co.	1909-16
Ridgeville	Senator	Victor Automobile Co.	1907-10
Rushville	Rea	Rea Machine Co.	1901-02
Scottsburg	Wyman	W.A. Wyman	1901
Seymour	Siefker Steam	William Siefker	1880
Shelbyville	Clark	Clark Motor Car Co.	1910-12
South Bend	Avanti	Studebaker Corp.	1962-63
South Bend	Avanti II	Avanti Motor Corp.	1965-85
South Bend	Casady	W.S. Casady Mfg. Co.	1905
South Bend	Coliseum	Coliseum Machine & Garage Co.	1914
South Bend	Diamond	Diamond Automobile Co.	1910
South Bend	Erskine	Studebaker Corp.	1927-30
South Bend	Oliver	Oliver Trackless Car Co.	1905
South Bend	Otis	Otis Motor Car Co.	1912
South Bend	Packard	Studebaker-Packard Corp.	1954-58
South Bend	Perfection	Perfection Automobile Works	1907-08
South Bend	R.A.C.	Ricketts Automobile Co.	1910-11
South Bend	Raber-Lang	Raber-Lang Co.	1909
South Bend	Ricketts	Ricketts Automobile Co.	1909-11
South Bend	Rockne	Studebaker Corp.	1932-33
South Bend	South Bend	South Bend Motor Car Works	1913-16
South Bend	Studebaker	Studebaker Corp.	1904-63
South Bend	Studebaker Electric	Studebaker Bros. Mfg. Co.	1902-12
South Bend	Tincher	Tincher Motor Car Co.	1907-09
South Bend	Tritt	Tritt Electric Co.	1905
South Bend	Williams	W.S. Casady Mfg. Co.	1905
Tell City	Herrmann	Charles Herrmann	1905
Terre Haute	Overland	Standard Wheel Works	1903-05
Terre Haute	Terre Haute	Terre Haute Carriage & Buggy Co.	1899
Union City	Union	Union Automobile Co.	1902-04
Union City	Union City Six	Union City Carriage Mfg. Co.	1916
Van Buren	Losure	Zan Losure	1906
Vincennes	Dixie	Dixie Mfg. Co.	1916
Vincennes	McGowan	W.H. McGowan	1913
Vincennes	Vanell Steam	Frank Vanell	1895
Vincennes	Vincennes	Vincennes Motor Mfg. Co.	1910
Wabash	Champion	Champion Auto Equipment Co.	1916
Wabash	Standard Six	Standard Automobile Co. of America	1910-11
Washington	Brown	Brown Motor Co.	1910
Washington	Washington	Washington Motor Car Co.	1906
Woodburn	W.A.C.	Woodburn Auto Co.	1905-12
Woodburn	Woodburn	Woodburn Auto Co.	1905-12

Appendix 6

Indiana Auto Museums and Collections

Auburn
Auburn Cord Duesenberg Museum
1600 South Wayne Street
Auburn, IN 46706
Phone: 260-925-1444
Hours: daily, 9 a.m. to 5 p.m.

National Automotive and Truck Museum
of the United States
1000 Gordon M. Buehrig Place
Auburn, IN 46706
Phone: 260-925-9100
Hours: daily, 9 a.m. to 5 p.m.

Bedford
The Antique Auto and Race Car Museum
3348 West 16th Street
Bedford, IN 47421
Phone: 812-275-0556
Hours: Monday through
Saturday, noon to 8 p.m.,
April through December

Elkhart
The Recreational Vehicle and Motor
Home Hall of Fame
801 Benham Avenue
Elkhart, IN 46516
Phone: 219-293-2344
Hours: Monday through Friday,
9 a.m. to 4 p.m., weekends by appointment

Fort Wayne
Corvette Classics
6702 Pointe Inverness Way
S.W. corner I 69 & SR 14
Fort Wayne, IN 46804
Phone: 260-436-3444
Hours:
Monday through Friday, 10 a.m. to 6 p.m.;
Saturday, 10 a.m. to 5 p.m.;
Sunday, 12 noon to 5 p.m.

The Fort Wayne Firefighters Museum
226 West Washington Street
Fort Wayne, IN 46852
Phone: 260-426-0051
Hours:
Wednesday only, 10 a.m. to 8 p.m.

Frankfort
The Goodwin Collection
200 South Main Street
Frankfort, IN 46041
Phone: 765-654-5533
Hours: call for appointment

Hagerstown
Collectible Classics Car Museum
403 East Main Street
Hagerstown, IN 47346
Phone: 765-489-5598
Winter hours:
Thursday and Friday, 5 to 8 p.m.;
Saturday, 1 to 6 p.m.
Summer hours: Monday through
Saturday, 11 a.m. to 5 p.m.

Indianapolis
Indianapolis Motor Speedway,
Hall of Fame Museum
4790 West 16th Street
Indianapolis, IN 46222
Phone: 317-484-6747
Hours: daily, 9 a.m. to 5 p.m.,
closed Christmas

Royce Motors Museum
6565 Coffman Road
Indianapolis, IN 46268
Phone: 317-290-3583
Hours: Monday through Friday,
8 a.m. to 5 p.m. Occasional
Saturdays – call for appointment

The Youth Education and
Historical Center, sponsored
by the Indiana State Police
8500 East 21st Street
Indianapolis, IN 46219
Phone: 317-899-8293
Hours: Monday through Friday,
8 to 11 a.m. and 1 to 4 p.m.

Kokomo
The Elwood Haynes Museum
1915 South Webster Street
Kokomo, IN 46902
Phone: 765-456-7500
Hours: Tuesday through Saturday,
1 to 4 p.m., Sunday, 1 to 5 p.m.

City of Firsts Automotive Heritage Museum
1500 N. Reed Road
(corner of U.S. 31 and North Street)
Kokomo, IN 46902
Phone: 765-454-9999
Hours: daily, 10 a.m. to 6 p.m.

Knightstown
Trump's Texaco Museum
Corner of Brewer and
Washington Streets
Knightstown, IN 46148
Phone: 765-345-7135
Hours: call for appointment

Lafayette
The Red Crown Mini-Museum
Corner of 6th and South Streets
Lafayette, IN 47901
Phone: 765-742-0280
Hours: call for appointment

LaPorte
Door Prairie Museum
2405 Indiana Avenue
LaPorte, IN 46350
Phone: 219-326-1337
Hours: Tuesday through Saturday,
10 a.m. to 4:30 p.m.;
Sunday, noon to 4:30 p.m.;
April to December

Richmond
Wayne County Historical Museum
1150 North A Street
Richmond, IN 47374
Phone: 765-962-5756
Hours:
Tuesday through Friday, 9 a.m. to 4 p.m.;
Saturday and Sunday, 1 to 4 p.m.;
February 4 through December 20.

Seymour
Al's Heartbeat Cafe
1541 West Tipton (U.S. 50 W)
Seymour, IN 47274
Phone: 812-522-4574
Hours: Sunday through Thursday,
11 a.m. to 9 p.m.;
Friday and Saturday, 11 a.m. to 10 p.m.

South Bend
The Studebaker National Museum
525 South Main Street
South Bend, IN 46601
Phone: 219-235-9714
Hours: Monday through Saturday,
9 a.m. to 5 p.m.; Sunday, noon to 5 p.m.

Published by Dennis E. Horvath
www.IndianaCarsBook.com/icb/
icbhome.htm

©2002

Indiana Marque-Specific Clubs

Auburn Cord Duesenberg Club
Vincent & Barbara Pietracatella
536 McClean Avenue
Staten Island, NY 10305-3544

Avanti Owners Assoc.
International, Inc.
Sheldon Harrison
P.O. Box 570709
Dallas, TX 75357-0709
(800) 527-3452

National Chevrolet/GMC Truck Assoc.
8918 Menard
Morton Grove, IL 60053

Cole Motor Club of America
Leroy D. Cole
P.O. Box 183
Goodrich, MI 48438
(810) 636-7221

Crosley Automobile Club
Jim Friday
217 N. Gilbert
Iowa City, IA 52245
(319) 338-9132

Dodge Brothers Club,
including Graham Brothers
commercial vehicles
Barry Cogan
P.O. Box 292
Eastpointe, MI 48021-0292

Durant Automobile Club
Yates Milton
9331 NC Hwy. 210
Four Oaks, NC 27524
(919) 989-9780

Durant Motors Automobile Club
incl. Durant, Flint, Star,
Rugby & De Vaux
Lance Haynes
4672 Mt. Gaywas Dr.
San Diego, CA 92117
(858) 560-5737

Elgin Motorcar Owners Registry
Jay David Wolf
2226 E. Apache Ln.
Vincennes, IN 47591
(812) 882-8666

Graham Owners Club International
Terry E. Graham
401 Center St.
Huron, OH 44839
(419) 433-5609

The Hummer Club
15392 Cobalt St.
Sylmar, CA 91342
(818) 362-5891

Scout & International Truck
P.O. Box 313
New Palestine, IN 46165

Inter-State Motor Car Registry
Jay Arendt
13883 Tesson Ferry Rd.
St. Louis, MO 63128
(314) 849-3391

The Marmon Club
Duke Marston
3044 Gainsborough Dr.
Pasadena, CA 91107-5577
(626) 449-2325

Maxwell-Briscoe Registry
Vern Campbell
4491 St. Anthony Road
Temperance, MI 48182
(734) 854-3622

Plymouth Owners Club, Inc.
P.O. Box 416
Cavalier, ND 58220
(701) 549-3746

Scripps-Booth Register
Ken Kaufman
735 W. Lemon Ave.
Monrovia, CA 91016-2507
(626) 358-7327

The Studebaker Drivers Club, Inc.
P.O. Box 1743
Maple Grove, MN 55311
(763) 420-7829

The Stutz Club
William J. Greer
7400 Lantern Road
Indianapolis, IN 46256

Willys-Overland-Knight Registry, Inc.
Duane Perrin
1440 Woodacre Dr.
McLean, VA 22101-2535
(703) 533-0396

Primary information list:
"2002 Club List," Old Cars April 25, 2002: 31-62

Reading Resources

America's First Automobile, Indianapolis News, 27 December 1913

Bailey, L. Scott, *1891 Lambert: A New Claim for America's First Gasoline Automobile*, Antique Automobile, October 1960

Bailey, L. Scott, *The American Car Since 1775*, New York, NY, Automobile Quarterly, Inc., © 1971

Baker, David L., *Indianapolis-Marion County Automobile Industry 1890-1940*, Indianapolis, IN, Indianapolis Historic Preservation Commission, © 1990

Beatty, Michael, *Studebaker: Less that they Promised*, South Bend, IN, And Books, © 1984

Berndt, Thomas, *Standard Catalog of U.S. Military Vehicles 1940-1965*, Iola, WI, Krause Publications, © 1993

Betts, Charles L., *The Auburn Straight-eight*, Leatherhead, Surrey, England, Profile Publications Ltd., © 1966

Bloemker, Al, *500 Miles to Go: The history of the Indianapolis Speedway*, New York, NY, Coward-McCann, Inc., © 1961

Blommel, Henry, *Indiana's Little Detroit*, Connersville, IN, n.d.

Blommel, Henry, *Connersville: The "Little Detroit of Indiana"*, Antique Automobile, March-April 1969

Blommel, Henry, *Auburn and Cord in Connersville*, Cars & Parts, May 1986

Bonsall, Thomas E., *More Than They Promised: The Studebaker Story*, Stanford, CA, Stanford University Press, © 2000

Borgeson, Griffith, *Errett Lobban Cord: His Empire, His Motor Cars*, Princeton, NJ, Automobile Quarterly Publications, © 1984

Bradley, George, *Reeves and the Automobile*, Cleveland, OH, Reliance Electric Company, © 1967

Brown, Arch, *Great Cars of the 20th Century*, Lincolnwood, IL, Publications International Ltd., © 1998

Buehrig, Gordon M., *The year 1936 is viewed fifty years later*, Auburn, IN, for the ACD Club 1986, © 1986

Burger, Dan, *Auburn Automobile Company*, Antique Automobile, reprint

Butler, Don, *Auburn Cord Duesenberg*, Osceola, WI, Motorbooks International, © 1992

Calder, J. Kent, *Traces: 100 Years of Automotive History*, Indianapolis, IN, Indiana Historical Society, Spring 1994

Calvert, Judy Stedman, *First Overland Motor Car Built in Terre Haute*, The Terre Haute Journal, 4 January 1985

Carson, Richard B., *The Olympian Cars: The Great American Luxury Automobiles of the Twenties*, New York, NY, Alfred A. Knopf, © 1976

Cannon, William A., *Studebaker: The Complete Story*, Blue Ridge Summit, PA, TAB Books, © 1981

Critchlow, Donald T., *Studebaker: The Life and Death of an American Corporation*, Bloomington, IN, Indiana University Press, © 1996

Cronin, J.F., *Crosley Streamlining Car*, The Cincinnati Enquirer, 20 January 1946

Cummins, Lyle, *The Diesel Odyssey of Clessie Cummins*, Wilsonville, OR, Carnot Press, © 1998

Darrell, James D., *The Auburn Story: the classics come home*, The Auburn Evening Star: supplement for 17th ACD festival, © 1972

Dauphinais, Dean E., *Car Crazy: The Official Motor City High-Octane, Turbocharged, Chrome-Plated, Back Road Book of Car Culture*, Detroit, MI, Visible Ink Press, © 1996

Delancy, Howard R., *History of the Cole Motor Car Company*, Bloomington, IN, D.B.A. dissertation, Indiana University., © 1954

Doolittle, James R., *Romance of the Automobile Industry*, New York, NY, Klebold Press, © 1916

Editor, *Briggs Purchases Graham Brothers Factory Property*, Evansville, IN, Evansville Courier, © 4 August 1936

Editors, *The Louis Chevrolet Memorial: Indianapolis Motor Speedway*, Indianapolis, IN, The Louis Chevrolet Memorial Committee, © 1976

Elbert, J. L., *Duesenberg: the mightiest American motor car*, Arcadia, CA, Post Era Books, © 1951

Erskine, Albert Russel, *History of the Studebaker Corporation*, Chicago, IL, Poole Bros., © 1918

Fisher, Jerry M., *The Pacesetter: The Untold Story of Carl G. Fisher*, Fort Bragg, CA, Lost Coast Press, © 1998

Flink, James J., *America Adopts the Automobile, 1895 - 1910*, Cambridge, MA, M.I.T. Press, © 1970

Flink, James J., *The Car Culture*, Cambridge, MA, M.I.T. Press, © 1975

Flink, James J., *The Automobile Age*, Cambridge, MA, M.I.T. Press, © 1988

Forbes, Bernice Charles, *Automotive Giants of America*, New York, B.C. Forbes Publishing Co., © 1926

Foster, Mark S., *Castles in the Sand: The Life and Times of Carl Graham Fisher*, Gainesville, FL, University Press of Florida, © 2000

Gentry, Lorna, *Autos: Imagination, Invention & Industry*, Cincinnati, OH, Creative Company, © 1991

Georgano, Nick, *Art of the American Automobile: The Great Stylists and Their Work*, New York, NY, Smithmark Publishers, © 1995

Georgano, G. N., *The Complete Encyclopedia of Motor cars 1885 to the Present*, New York, NY, E. P. Dutton and Company Inc., © 1968

Glasscock, Carl Burgess, *Motor History of America*, Los Angeles, CA, Floyd Clymer Co., © 1946

Gray, Ralph D., *Alloys and Automobiles: the Life of Elwood Haynes*, Indianapolis, IN, Indiana Historical Society, © 1979

Gross, Robert, *Timeline: Crosley 1937-1952*, Special Interest Autos, April-May 2001

Gunnell, John A., *Standard Catalog of American Light Duty Trucks*, Iola, WI, Krause Publications, © 1987

Hall, Asa E., *The Studebaker Century*, Contocook, NH, Dragonwyck Publishing, Inc., © 1983

Hampton, Charles C., *The Automobile Industry in Elkhart*, monograph, © 1977

Hanley, George P. and Stacey P., *The Marmon Heritage*, Rochester, MI, Doyle Hyk Publishing Co., © 1985

Haynes, Elwood, *The Complete Motorist*, Kokomo, IN, The Haynes Automobile Co., © 1913 and Shearer Printing Inc., © 1977

Hokanson, Drake, *The Lincoln Highway: Main Street Across America*, Iowa City, IA, University of Iowa Press, © 1988 and © 1999

Hudson, William W., *Pioneers of the Electric Automobile Industry*, American Motorist, April 1913

Huffman, Wallace S., *Indiana Built Motor Vehicles*, Indianapolis, IN, Indiana Historical Society, © 1994

Huffman, Wallace S., *ReVere: America's Incomparable Car*, Horseless Carriage Gazette, January-February 1964

Huffman, Wallace S., *Service Motor Truck Company*, Hershey, PA, Antique Automobile Club of America, November-December 1970

Yearbook, Indianapolis, IN, Horseless Carriage Club, © 1950

Jordan, Ben, *Ben Jordan's Automotive Jargon for the Car Owner from the Shade Tree Mechanic's Automobile Dictionary with Lagniappe*, Denver, CO, Windmill Jouster Books, © 1995

Katzell, Raymond A., *The Splendid Stutz: The Cars, Companies, People and Races*, Indianapolis, IN, The Stutz Club, © 1996

Keller, Michael E., *The Graham Legacy: Graham-Paige to 1932*, Paducah, KY, Turner Publishing Company, ©1998

Kimes, Beverly Rae, *Standard Catalog of American Cars: 1805 - 1942*, Iola, WI, Krause Publications, © 1996

Kollins, Michael J., *A Guy Named Louie*, Detroit, MI, National Automotive History Collection, © 1998 Wheels Winter/Spring

Kowalke, Ron, *Standard Catalog of Independents: The Struggle to Survive Among Giants*, Iola, WI, Krause Publications, © 1999

Lemasters, Ron, *Inter-State Brought Muncie Into the Auto World in 1908*, The Muncie Star, 3 July 1976

Leich, Alexander, *Cars of Indiana*, Motor Trend, September and October 1965

The Complete Official Road Guide of the Lincoln Highway — Fifth edition, Detroit, MI, Lincoln Highway Association, © 1924, and The Patrice Press, Tucson, AZ, © 1993

Locke, William S., *Elcar and Pratt Automobiles: The Complete History*, Jefferson, NC, McFarland & Company, Inc., © 2000

Manifold, Orrin, *North Manchester's Automobile Factory*, North Manchester, IN, North Manchester Historical Society, May 1986

Marvin, Keith; Arnheim, Alvin J.; and Blommel, Henry H.; *What was the McFarlan?*, New York, NY, Alvin J. Arnheim, © 1967

Meyer, Marjorie Teetor, *One Man's Vision: The Life of Automotive Pioneer Ralph R. Teetor*, Indianapolis, IN, Guild Press of Indiana, © 1995

Peters, Sue, *First Locally Built Car — The Richmond*, Palladium-Item, 3 July 1988

Rickenbacker, Edward V., *Rickenbacker*, Englewood Cliffs, NJ, Prentice-Hall, Inc, © 1967

Schlereth, Thomas J., *U.S. 40: A Roadscape of the American Experience*, Indianapolis, IN, Indiana Historical Society, © 1985

Seeley, Walter, *The American Underslung: A Car For The Discriminating Few*, Hershey PA, Antique Automobile, vol. 36, no. 4, July-August 1972

Smith, John Martin, *A History of DeKalb County Indiana 1837-1987*, © 1987

Smith, John Martin, *Ride With Us In A Kiblinger Automobile*, Auburn Dekalb Vanguard, Auburn, IN, April 1971

Smith, John Martin, *McIntyre Motor Vehicles*, Auburn Dekalb Vanguard, Auburn, IN, April 1971

Smith, John Martin, *Imp America's First Compact Car*, Auburn Dekalb Vanguard, Auburn, IN, April 1971

Starkey, John H., *Hoosiers Put Big Rigs On Road*, Indianapolis, IN, Indianapolis Star, © 1974

Steinwedel, Louis W., *The Duesenberg: The Story of America's Premier Car*, New York, NY, Norton, © 1982

Stout, Wesley W., *Bullets By The Billion*, Detroit, MI, Chrysler Corporation, © 1946

Thompson, Frances, *Pilot: "The Car Ahead"*, Tri-State Trader, 18 October 1980

Trager, James, *The People's Chronology*, Henry Holt and Company, © 1992

Tyndall, Bill, *Teetor-Hartley co-authored small-town success*, Palladium-Item, 14 August 1994

Walters, H. Max, *The making of Connersville and Fayette County*, Baltimore, MD, Gateway Press, Inc., © 1988

Weinhardt, Carl J., *An Investigation of the rise and fall of the automobile industry in Indiana*, B.A. thesis, Boston, MA, Harvard University, © 1948

Weintraut, Linda, *Losing the Business: How Hoosier Automobile Manufacturers Failed Middle America*, M.A. thesis, Indianapolis, Indiana University, © 1989

Glossary

AAA — American Automobile Association

Berline — a limousine for which the driver's compartment is enclosed

Bustle trunk — one of the first adaptations of the trunk into streamlined body work, such as on the Cord Westchester Sedan

Cabriolet — a less formal version of the coupe and more rounded in appearance and always convertible

Caliper — a mechanical or hydraulic device that grips a rotating brake disc

Carburetor — a device in the engine for mixing vaporized fuel with air to get a combustible mixture

c.i.d. — cubic inch displacement of an engine.

Coupe — a closed, two-door car that is shorter than a sedan of the same model

Dos-a-dos — a body type carried over from the carriage trade

Drive line and drive train — transmitting components such as the transmission, driveshaft, and differential

Freewheel — an overriding clutch that automatically disengages the drive shaft when needed

Front-wheel drive — a drive system that propels the front wheels

g.p.m. — gallons per minute

GCW — gross combined weight

GVW — gross vehicle weight

h.p. — horsepower

Independent suspension — a system in which each wheel's suspension contains a spring and shock absorber assembly

Internal combustion engine — one in which combustion of the fuel takes place in a confined space. Today's automobiles are powered by reciprocating, spark-ignition, four-stroke cycle, internal combustion engines.

Landaulet — a vehicle that has a convertible top for the back seat, with the front seat either roofed or open

L-head — a flat cylinder head arrangement with in-block valves on one side of the cylinder bore

m.p.h. — miles per hour

Magneto — an electric ignition device

Monocoque — a light-weight body structure in which the support frame and the external skin form the total construction system

Phaeton — a touring car that is usually fast and sporty

Piston — a disk in the engine that exerts pressure on gas inside a cylinder

Piston rings — a metallic ring fitted tightly around a piston

Pneumatic — refers to an item that is operated by air or gas

Rear-wheel drive — a drive system that propels the rear wheels

Roadster — an open car, seating two to four, and appropriate for the owner to drive. Usually provided with a top, light in tone and weight

Runabout — a small, light-weight vehicle, usually with an open top

Sedan — an enclosed vehicle having two or four doors with two full-width seats

Stanhope — a light, one-seat carriage

T-head — a flat cylinder head arrangement with in-block valves on both sides of the cylinder bore

Tonneau — the rear compartment of a car

Touring car — a term usually used to describe a car seating six or seven

Transaxle — a drive train component that combines the transmission and the axle

Transmission — the enclosed unit of gears that transfers force between mechanisms

Trap — another body type carried over from the carriage trade

Worm-drive — the mechanism that uses a driving gear that usually has two shafts placed at right angles to each other

Index
(Appendixes not included in list)

Edward Herrmann .
19 · V · 06
Auburn Indiana
on the occasion
of my investment
as a Trustee of
the ACD Museum.
Gift of
Tim Durham .

Overland

McIntyre

"The Car of
Quality."

STUTZ

=HAYNES=

Studebaker